PRACTICE
AND THE
HUMAN SCIENCES

SUNY series in the Philosophy of the Social Sciences

Lenore Langsdorf, editor

PRACTICE AND THE HUMAN SCIENCES

The Case for a Judgment-Based Practice of Care

Donald E. Polkinghorne

STATE UNIVERSITY OF NEW YORK PRESS

Table 6.1 from: Epstein, S. (1991). Cognitive-experiential self-theory: An integrative theory of self. In R. C. Curtis (Ed.), *The relational self: Theoretical convergences in psychoanalysis and social psychology.* New York: Gilford. Used by permission.

I want to thank The James Irvine Foundation, which provided support for the writing of this book as part of a larger project, *Designing and Implementing a Diversity Scorecard to Improve Institutional Effectiveness for Underserved Minority Students.* The findings and opinions written here are solely mine and do not reflect the position or priorities of the foundation.

Published by
State University of New York Press, Albany

© 2004 State University of New York

For information, address State University of New York Press,
90 State Street, Suite 700, Albany, NY 12207

Production by Christine L. Hamel
Marketing by Jennifer Giovani

Library of Congress Cataloging-in-Publication Data

Polkinghorne, Donald, 1936–
   Practice and the human sciences : the case for a judgment-based practice of care / by
Donald E. Polkinghorne.
      p. cm. — (SUNY series in the philosophy of the social sciences)
   Includes bibliographical references and index.
   ISBN 0-7914-6199-8 (alk. paper) — ISBN 0-7914-6200-5 (pbk. : alk. paper)
      1. Human services—Philosophy. I. Title. II. Series.

HV31.P67 2004
361'.001—dc22

2004041705

10 9 8 7 6 5 4 3 2 1

For Judy, the love of my life,
whose support, patience, and care
were essential to the writing of this book.

CONTENTS

PREFACE

I AM A FACULTY MEMBER in a doctoral counseling psychology program. The primary purpose of the program is to prepare our students to become practitioners of psychotherapy. This preparation involves assisting students to gain a deeper and broader understanding of human existence. We want the students to be sensitive to and respectful of the individual differences of the people they will serve. Our courses provide the students with psychology's conceptual repertoire. The students are to develop a conceptual array through which they can notice and understand the nuances in client actions and statements and from which they can adjust their responses. They are introduced to a variety of therapeutic theories; however, they are expected to be open to learning from their clients and not to impose on them a predetermined theoretical position. Our program adheres to the Boulder science-practice model. But our view is that this is a balanced model in which research learns from practice and practice learns from research. Students receive research training in both quantitative and qualitative methods and in the philosophy of science. They are instructed about the strengths and weaknesses of the various kinds of research and the necessity to monitor the effect of their actions on their clients and their clients' actions on them. We teach that psychotherapy is a historical process during which both they and their clients undergo change.

In recent years, the expectations for the training of psychotherapists have changed. We are now expected to produce students who are technically proficient in administering at least four manualized treatments that are on the list of empirically supported (or validated) therapy sequences. It is implied that using a nonempirically supported therapy is unethical. The new 2002 American Psychological Association's Code of Ethics directs psychologists to tell their "patients" when they plan to use a "new" or "experimental" treatment for which generally recognized techniques and procedures have not been established; that is, if they are going to use an experimental therapy that does not have empirically demonstrated efficacy.

Along with other psychotherapists, I believed that this move to limit psychotherapy to empirically demonstrated technical sequences was mistaken. In speaking with friends and colleagues from other fields, I found that the pressure to adopt a technical approach for practitioners is not limited to psychotherapy. It is also occurring in practices such as education, nursing, social work, and occupational therapy. These are the practices that involve direct person-to-person interaction and require situated and timely actions and responses. Traditionally, these practices have relied on practitioner judgment in the situation as the best way to achieve the objectives of care for those they serve.

I believe there is a case to be made for a judgment-based approach and against the technological approach for the practices of care. The purpose of this book is to present this case. The move to technologize the practices of care is part of a more general expansion of technical thinking into the control and management of the human realm. The move overlooks the significance of the unique characteristics of the human realm and the value of the differences among the individual members of the human realm. In making the case for a judgment-based practice I have drawn on a wide variety of sources in the philosophy of social science, philosophy of technology, and cognitive science.

This book is addressed to graduate students preparing to be practitioners of care—teachers, nurses, counselors, psychotherapists, social workers, and others—and to their professors. Its purpose is to assemble the case for the necessity of practitioner judgment in the performance of practices of care.

1

Introduction

THE PURPOSE OF THIS BOOK is to make the case that effective practices of
care require that practitioner actions are decided by their situated and timely
judgments. The practices of care are those in which practitioner and person
served are engaged in a face-to-face interaction. The aim of these practices is
the betterment of the individuals served, and the means for achieving this aim
includes a caring relationship and skilled and knowledgeable actions. The
practices of care include, among others, teaching, nursing, social work, and
psychotherapy. While these practices address the whole life of an individual,
they aim at the betterment of specific life areas. The aim of the practice of
teaching is learning; the aim of the practice of therapy is well-being; the aim
of the practice of nursing is health; and the aim of the practice of social work
is social support.

In recent decades, the practitioners of care have been challenged to substitute a technologically guided approach for determining their practice in
place of their situationally informed judgments. I argue in this book that this
move to apply technically generated decisions to the practices of care is part
of a more general cultural shift toward a technified worldview. This shift
involves the transfer of techniques that have been successful in mastering and
transforming nature to the management of human beings. The technification
of the practices of care devalues the uniqueness of the human realm by treating its members as if they were simply another resource to be processed. Such
treatment, because of the evolved characteristics of the human realm, is not as
effective and efficient in achieving the aims of the practices of care. The thesis of this book is that, because of the unique features of human beings, the
technical model of practice has limited applicability for the practices of care;
thus, successful practice in situations where practitioners engage others in
direct fact-to-face interaction requires a practice model that emphasizes the

1

situated judgment of practitioners. The rest of this introductory chapter first introduces the current controversy over what model should govern the decision making of practitioners of care and then explores in general terms the notion of practice.

The main argument of the book is contained in chapters 2 through 7 and draws support for the thesis from current positions in the philosophy of social science. Chapter 2 describes the human propensity to secure control over nature and transform it so that it better serves human needs and desires. The chapter traces the development of this technological control to its current state of high technology and to its expansion in the last century from the mastery of nature to the management and organization of human activity. It closes with an outline of the model for making technical decisions, the technical-rational model. Chapter 3 explores the effect of this expansion on human practices. Foucault, Bourdieu, and Certeau provide descriptions of the manifestation of the technification of modern society through the operations of bureaucratic forms of administration grounded in technical-rational procedures. They investigate the consequences of technification on practice and depict the ways it constricts the range of human actions. Chapter 4 differentiates the realms in which practices are carried out and argues that the practice model used to operate in the physical realm is inappropriate for use in the human realm. Chapters 5 through 7 develop a model of situated decision making for judgment based practices of care. Chapter 5 explores the distinction made by Aristotle between two kinds of practice: the practices of production *(poiesis)* and the practices of the good *(praxis)*. Aristotle held that decisions regarding the practices of the good, which concern the human realm, require a different kind of nontechnical thinking *(phronesis)* than what is required for decisions regarding production *(techne)*. Chapter 6 further develops the judgment model of deliberation through the inspection of the ideas of an expanded notion of rationality presented by Epstein, Lakoff, Gendlin, and Damasio. Chapter 7 draws together the ideas of *phronesis* and expanded rationality with Gadamer's notion of reflective-understanding into a model for practitioner judgment.

The final chapter reexamines the confrontation between the technical and judgment models of the practices of care through a case study of one profession of care: psychotherapy.

THE TECHNICAL-JUDGMENT PRACTICE CONTROVERSY

There is a growing controversy over who and what should determine the helping actions carried out by the practitioners of care. The controversy is about whether the practices of care should be technically based or judgment based.

The technically based side holds that practice should consist of the application of scientifically validated knowledge; the judgment-based side advocates that practice should be comprised of actions informed by situated judgments of practitioners.

Technically based practice is held up as being reliable because it is based on scientifically validated techniques. Practitioners are asked to adhere to scripted sequences of techniques or laid-out programs that have been experimentally demonstrated to accomplish a specified goal. In a technically based approach to practices of care, if the goal is to teach reading to third graders, teachers are expected to follow a scripted reading program by implementing, in order, the activities set out in the script. Technically based practice holds that it is the program or technique that produces change, not the caregiver.

Judgment-based practice calls for the use of professional judgment about what to do to accomplish a specified goal. On the basis of a practitioner's self-knowledge, experience, and training, he or she is expected to make judgments about what actions will accomplish a goal with a specific person, in a specific situation, at a specific time. Judgment-based practice focuses on the practitioner as the factor that produces change. It argues that practitioners can take into account the needs of particular individuals and respond to situational differences.

In the dispute over whether practices of care should be technically or judgment based, the technical position has gained dominance in recent years. It is represented by slogans such as "culture of evidence," "evidence-based decision making," and "empirically supported programs." In the technically based position, these slogans are interpreted to refer to the exclusive use of programs or sets of techniques that have been previously determined by scientific research to produce desired results. A program receives the designation of "empirically supported" when its use with several trial groups has produced mean scores on an index that are higher than the mean scores of comparable control groups.

The technically based approach for the determination of practice was developed by businesses to manage their employees. It has since been adopted by government agencies, health care institutions, and professional organizations to determine the activities of practitioners of care. For example, the news release of the United States Department of Education says that "the use of research-proven strategies is one of the key principles of *No Child Left Behind* [legislation]" (United States Department of Education, 2002, August 7). It describes the development of a national clearinghouse "which will summarize evidence on the effectiveness of different programs, products, and strategies intended to enhance academic achievement" and provide an "educational interventions registry that identifies potentially replicable programs, products, and practices." The program calls for "transforming education into an evidence based field." Managed health care programs have adopted a similar approach to determining practices through their policies of limiting payments only to procedures that have been experimentally validated (Polkinghorne, 2001). Psychologists have advocated that psychotherapy training focus on preparing graduates to deliver manualized, empirically supported treatments and have suggested that it is unethical to use treatments that have not been empirically validated.

Judgment-based practice represents a more traditional approach to the practices of care and emphasizes individual differences and the uniqueness of personal histories. Its approach to the idea of the culture of evidence is that positive outcomes are to be valued over adherence to a set of predetermined techniques. Accountability should be focused on the outcomes produced in a particular situation, not on the prior selection of a validated program or procedure. Because of individual differences, it holds that better outcomes are produced by adjusting practitioner actions to the characteristics of specific situations and to the changes taking place in the individuals being served. Evidence of the effect of actions in a situation is used to judge what action should be undertaken next to move the work toward a positive outcome. Judgment-based practice also recognizes that the effect of actions varies as a result of the particular personal characteristics of the practitioner undertaking it. Thus, a culture of evidence should attend to the actual outcomes produced in particular situations rather than to predictions of which programs might bring about positive outcomes.

Neither technically based nor judgment-based practice is adequate in and of itself. Experimentation with and evaluation of programs and techniques provide a knowledge base of the kinds of technical procedures found to be generally helpful in various settings. However, the simple implementation of a program or application of techniques because it has empirical support is not sufficient to accomplish the goals of caregivers. Determining whether an empirically supported program is appropriate for a particular group or if its protocols are appropriate for an individual requires practitioner judgment. Also, meeting the needs of those cared for by practitioners often requires the invention of new activities as well as creative responses.

Discussions about whether the actions of practitioners of care should be technologically or judgment based have traditionally focused their attention only on the situations of caregiving in which the actions are undertaken. However, the practices of care are social practices, and discussions about them need to be approached from the broader perspective of social practices in contemporary society. Thus, the discussion needs to address issues such as the nature of practice in contemporary society, in what ways practical decisions are determined, and the relation of the social context to the practices of care. The technological-judgment controversy about practices of care cannot be isolated from the general views of practice in current society. The purpose of this book is to examine the controversy from this broader perspective and to argue for the necessity of judgment-based practices of care.

The philosophy of social science has traditionally concerned itself with methodological and epistemological questions (Hollis, 1996). It has differentiated the human realm from the physical realm and asked if methods for generating knowledge about human beings need to be different from those used by the sciences of nature. However, in recent decades the understanding of the methods of the natural sciences has undergone significant changes. Natural science is now viewed less as means to pure knowledge and more as a human practice (Bachelard, 1958; Kuhn, 1970). The sharp division between the means for developing knowledge about the physical realm and the human realm has become somewhat dulled. However, although a sharp distinction between the natural and human or social sciences need not be maintained in terms of their methods, it does need to be maintained in terms of the objects under inquiry (Caws, 2000).

A philosophy of social science inquiry about practice draws a significant distinction between practices aimed at transforming physical materials into useful objects and practices involving human interaction. A premise of this book is that this distinction has faded in contemporary society and that technically informed decision processes appropriate for determining practices concerned with physical objects have been applied to practices in the human realm. This expansion of decision processes developed for the control and transformation of the realm of nature to the control and management of human behavior is an aspect of the general *technification* of the social world.

UNDERSTANDING PRACTICE

The general definition of the term *practice* includes all the things that people do. Theories of practice concern not only the things that people do but also why they do them. Practices range from tying shoelaces to writing books. Some practices require careful deliberation, while others occur without conscious thought. Practice is sometimes differentiated from theory, doing something as opposed to thinking about something. However, the distinction is overdrawn. Action and thought (both conscious and nonconscious) are interactive. Practices are grounded in understandings people have about the world, and these understandings are, in turn, influenced by the effect of their practices on the world. Contemporary practice theory focuses on the point of interaction of people with the world and others. While traditional theories have attended to people's subjective experiences or the objective region of physical objects, practice theory attends to the area of engagement and interconnection between subjects and objects. When this is the focal point, humans do not show up as bounded monads but as embodied beings actively involved in the world. Practice theory should be distinguished from pragmatism. Pragmatism is a philosophy that emphasizes that statements about the world should be evaluated primarily in terms of their usefulness or effectiveness in accomplishing a task. It argues against the position that statements should be judged on the basis of their accuracy in representing an independent reality.

The idea of practice covers human activity aimed at accomplishing a variety of tasks. Carpenters are engaged in practice when they work with physical materials to build houses. Scientists are involved in practice when they design and undertake research. Babysitters are practicing when they are caring for children. While the single term *practice* covers all of these situations, practices that involve working with physical materials differ from practices that involve working with people. Even though some activities involve working with both materials and people, the distinction needs to be maintained. For example, a father helping his son build a tree house will relate to and treat the wood in a manner that is different from the way he relates to and treats his son. Not only are humans inherently different from things, but the methods and procedures that lead to effective work with materials do not bring about the same results when used with people.

In this book the term *practice* is used primarily to refer to engaged action or activity. However, 'practice' has taken on some auxiliary meanings in English, and in the interest of clarification, it is worthwhile to review them. 'Practice' is used to refer to activities in which people engage to increase a skill; for example, practicing the piano. The term is used with a similar meaning in reference to preparation for a performance; a baseball player takes batting practice before a game to loosen up and refresh his or her timing. 'Practice' has also taken on the evolved meaning of carrying on a profession or occupation, as in the practice of law or medicine. I sometimes use 'practice' with this meaning in referring to the practices of care. The term *practical,* which comes from the same root as 'practice,' refers to the doing of something; an idea is practical when it is something that can be carried out. 'Practical' is also used as an adjective to note that something is related to practice; knowing what to do to accomplish a goal is practical knowing.

'Practice' has become current in sociology and anthropology to refer to the mainly nonconscious activities engaged in by members of a society or culture. Of interest in these studies is the diverse ways activities are carried out in various cultures and historical periods. Several of these studies (by Foucault, Bourdieu, and Certeau) that have investigated the practices of contemporary Western society will be discussed in this book. Turner, in his book *The Social Theory of Practices* (1994) claims that current philosophers and social theorists are using the term *practice* for what their predecessors used the terms *traditions, tacit knowledge, worldview, paradigm, ideology, framework,* or *presuppositions.* Although these studies have served to correct the view that people's actions are always determined by conscious, reflective thought, I believe their emphasis on the social determination of what people do is sometimes too strong.

Practices are most often engaged in to bring about a result. For example, people exercise each morning in order to achieve or maintain good health. Thus, practice has a means-end or instrumental structure. Explanations of a practice have a primitive narrative structure in which the meaning of an activity is its contribution to achieving a goal (see Polkinghorne, 1988). The explanation for why students engaged in the practice of intense studying would consist in giving a reason for this practice; for example, they wanted to achieve a high grade on an examination.

Its means-end structure allows the inquiry into a practice to be divided into two questions: what goal is being sought, and what is being done to accomplish that goal? Practice goals can focus on achieving results meant to serve oneself, to serve other individuals, or to serve a group or community (such as one's family, organization, nation, or all humanity). In addition to seeking knowledge about the goals of a practice, inquiry about practice is concerned with what activities need to be undertaken to achieve those goals. *Know-how* is the understanding of what to do to accomplish a goal. The sources of one's know-how are multiple. One can come to know how to attain a goal from trial and error learning, in which successful actions are differentiated from unsuccessful ones. One can derive knowledge from the various avenues through which social and cultural understanding is passed on to individuals. Over time, individuals build up a fund of knowledge from these sources and can call on this fund to accomplish new tasks. Some of the fund of know-how remains available to conscious recall, and some of it recedes into the background of awareness, where it is hidden from reflection but still available to inform actions. Part of the knowledge in the background is embodied, such as how to stay upright on a bicycle or how to hold a cup without spilling the coffee in it.

Once knowledge about how to do things is developed, it can be shared with others. Thus it can become the possession of a whole society, spreading among its members through various modes of communication and social institutions. For example, experts hold public discussions on how to make money in the stock market or how to find a mate. Teachers instruct children on how to do arithmetic and how to read. Technical schools, as advertised on television, train students on how to repair computers and other electronic equipment. Often, over time, new and better ideas on how to do something are invented. Our culture has gone through a series of transitions in which the "old" ways of doing things have been replaced with "new" technically informed ways.

As we go about our daily lives, the informal practical knowledge we accumulate is usually sufficient for knowing how to accomplish ordinary tasks. If a strategy based on one source of knowledge proves unsuccessful, not much is lost; one can try an alternate plan based on a different source. However, when the goal has greater significance, such as performing an operation to correct a diseased heart, building a bridge, or teaching a child to read, it is essential that the practical knowledge used to guide actions is sound and that by acting upon it the surgeon, the bridge builder, and the teacher will accomplish their respective goals. In such situations, the reliability of the source of practical knowledge becomes an issue. For our contemporary technological society, the legitimized source of practical knowledge is science. Thus, when the task is significant, it is thought that one should rely on instructions that have been validated scientifically. The practitioner's experientially accumulated fund of knowledge is considered less trustworthy.

The next two chapters explore the development of the technological control of nature and the expansion of the technological view into the social realm. The technical model of decision making for the practices of care is an expression of this expansion.

2

Technology and Technification

PRACTICES ARE HUMAN INTERVENTIONS that make things in the world different from what they were before. Practices alter the status quo and produce change. Without humans and their interventions, change in the world would be limited to natural processes and animal activity. The appearance of human beings, with their capacities to design and implement actions, to use tools, and to communicate among themselves, marks the point at which changes of a different magnitude began to occur in the natural world. Practices are directed at changes in various realms—the physical, organic, human, and social. Humans reshape the physical realm into objects and devices to serve their purposes. They take natural materials and transform them into skyscrapers, airplanes, and automobiles. They domesticate animals to meet their needs for transportation, power, and comfort. However, not all practice activities involve moving, gathering, and reshaping physical materials; some are directed at bringing order to the human realm. Human beings engage in practices that fulfill personal needs and provide care for others, such as rearing children and caring for the sick. They also create social organizations for defense and cooperative endeavors.

It is the thesis of this book that practices aimed at accomplishing tasks in the physical realm require approaches that are different from practices aimed at effecting changes in the human realm. "We must differentiate between, on the one hand, action in the sense of using, applying, and producing artifacts, above all tools—what we can call instrumental action—and on the other hand, various kinds of social interactions, both strategic and communicative" (Krogh, 1998, p. 17). This chapter is about human propensity to gain control over nature and to reshape it to accommodate human needs and desires. It traces the enormous amplification of the power of humans to transform nature that came about as a result of the Enlightenment. Practices based on

9

the new science of that era were so successful in manipulating nature that they replaced practices based on tradition and authority, and the understanding of nature presented by the new science came to dominate the worldview of modern Western culture. In time, the new science method was applied to the management of human behavior and became the authoritative way of determining practice in the human realm.

TECHNE

In describing the life of the ancient Greeks, Nussbaum (2001a) wrote about their fragile relationship with nature. Threatening and undependable, it could abruptly bring catastrophe to humans through storms, droughts, and illnesses. Nature, not humans, controlled the world and could unpredictably inflict suffering, such as a famine, or grant rewards, such as an abundant harvest. The early Greeks believed that whether an individual or city received benefit or harm from nature was a matter of luck *(tuche)*. Nussbaum (2001b) wrote:

> The late fifth century in Athens, the time of Plato's youth, was a time of acute anxiety and of exuberant confidence in human power. If human power seemed more than ever exposed to *tuche* in all its forms, Athenians were more than ever gripped by the idea that progress might bring about the elimination of ungoverned contingency from social life. This hope found expression in an antithesis and a story: the contrast between *tuche,* luck, and *techne,* human art or science; and the accompanying frequently told story of human progress against contingency through the reception or discovery of *techne.* (p. 153–54)

Techne is the knowledge and skills needed to protect oneself from the suffering that nature can inflict. It includes the tools of counting and calculating, articulate speech and writing, and knowledge of medicine. *Techne* enabled people to hunt, to build houses, to farm, to tame and yoke animals, and to engage in shipbuilding and metalworking. Without the gift of *techne,* humans would be entirely at the mercy of nature. Without a plentiful harvest, they would starve; without shelter, they would suffer from exposure to the elements; and without weapons, they would be killed by predators. In Greek mythology, it was the kindness of the Titan Prometheus (named for foresight and planning) that saved humanity from nature. He gave mortals the gift of *techne,* and "with all these arts they preserved and improved their lives; human existence became safer, more predictable; there was a measure of control over contingency" (Nussbaum, 2001b, p. 155).

Human beings, as well as many other organisms, engage in activities or practices that serve to reshape and manipulate aspects of the physical realm to meet their needs. Birds build nests, and beavers build dams and lodges. Compared to the abilities of other organisms, the human capacity to transform and control nature is of a higher order. The idea that humans are to hold dominion over nature is fundamental to the Western tradition. In the Old Testament, after creating the rest of the physical realm, God created man and woman and assigned to them this task.

> Then God said, "let us make man in our image and likeness to rule the fish in the sea, the birds of heaven, the cattle, all wild animals on earth, and all reptiles that crawl upon the earth." So God created him; male and female he created them. God blessed them and said to them, "Be fruitful and increase, fill the earth and subdue it, rule over the fish in the sea, the birds of heaven, and every living thing that moves upon the earth. . . . So it was; and God saw all that he had made, and it was very good. Evening came, and morning came, a sixth day. (Genesis 1: 26–31, The New English Bible)

The propensity to subdue and control nature is a universal human characteristic. Moreover, it has been confirmed as a right and a duty in the Western religious tradition. The history of Western civilization chronicles the ascendancy of human control over nature. We have reached the point of dominance at which parts of the physical and organic realm depend on our protection for their survival. We have reconfigured the natural world into devices and machines that function as our servants. We seem to be approaching fulfillment of the dream of the Enlightenment philosophers, in which a heavenly city would be constructed by us on earth (Becker, 1932).

Techne, the Greek term for the collection of skills by which humans exercise control over nature, serves as the root for our English word *technology*. Technology can therefore be defined as the practical knowledge and skills used to alter and master nature. However, in contemporary English usage, 'technology' has taken on several different and sometimes confusing meanings. Its original meaning, the *logos* of *techne*—that is, the study of skills and practices of making things (Simpson, 2002 3285)—has faded. One current use of the term refers to a collection of the kind of knowledge and skills used in reshaping nature; for example, the technology of medieval Europe. Another current use delimits the meaning of 'technology' to the particular knowledge and skills that are based on modern science. Thus, we are said to be living in the age of technology. To exacerbate the lack of clarity, the term is sometimes used to refer to the work of transforming nature. For example, Sussman (1997) defines technology as the manifestation of the human inclination to gain control over and to reshape nature. He wrote: "Technology is the . . . conversion of the natural, the built, or the conceptual world, leading to the creation or refinement of socially useful methods, tools, or products. . . . The deployment of a tree branch for striking prey or for feeding fire are rudimentary forms of technology" (p. 18). A final use of the term is to refer to the things and devices produced by the application of the skills and knowledge. For example, we are surrounded by technology—computers, cell phones, and other technical instruments. I will use 'technology' in all these senses and hope that the context will make the meaning clear.

THE EFFECT OF *TECHNOLOGY* ON CULTURE

The knowledge and skills to control and reshape nature vary from culture to culture and from one historical period to another. Cultures are made up of various features—social and economic organization, understandings about the world, beliefs concerning what is good and worthwhile, rituals, language, and technology. Some scholars, called "technical determinists," hold that technology gives direction to the other features of a culture (see Ihde, 1990). This view is generally regarded as placing too much emphasis on technology and neglecting the instances when a culture's social organization or beliefs affect its willingness to accept internal technological changes and its resistance to the introduction of alternative technologies from external sources.

Cultures change at different rates, some seeming to remain stable for long periods of time. During these stable periods, a fit and balance has been established among various features of the culture. For example, a somewhat stable reciprocal balance was maintained in the culture of medieval Europe. The world was seen as the creation of a beneficent God; God was the source of knowledge in revelation, as interpreted by the church; the church was the hierarchical social organization with rulers anointed by God; and the technology of the times was consistent with this worldview. For example, the technology for healing the sick called for the practitioner of care to offer prayers of supplication asking for God's intervention and to counsel the sick person to engage in acts of contrition. When technical innovations such as the water wheel were invented, their creation was regarded as a service to God.

The desire to gain greater control over nature makes a culture receptive to developing or importing more effective technologies. At times, a change in technology is directed by another culture, as when one people establish dominance over another through military conquest. At other times, changes in technology occur as the result of selective borrowing from groups that interact with each other, as in trade. Cultural change in technology can also occur through internal developments, such as the generation of knowledge or new inventions. Changes in any culture's technology are complex and can have multiple sources. However, small changes in technology can reverberate through a culture and have a profound impact on the entire system. Drucker (1997), for example, described the social impact of the technology that made it possible to establish irrigation cities in 5000 B.C. This development "completely revolutionized human society and community" (p. 39). It led to the first established governments as distinct and permanent institutions, to the development of social classes, to the organization and institutionalization of knowledge, and to the recognition of the importance of individuals over tribes. Sharp (1952), in his often quoted article "Steel Axes for Stone Age Australians," analyzed the disruption of the Australian aboriginal society of the Yir Yoront by the indiscriminate introduction of the steel axe to nonadult males.

Once a technological innovation is developed in a culture, it becomes a possession of that culture and is passed on from generation to generation. New methods replace or augment old ones. Previously acquired cognitive or physical tools can be used to build other tools. A culture's technology provides a foundation on which increasingly effective and efficient technological methods can be constructed. This has led to the idea that an impetus to grow incessantly is inherent in technology. From this perspective, present Western technology is the outcome of sequential growth in Western knowledge about how to manage and transform nature.

A popular view of the rise of modern technology (described by Taylor, 1999) is that it is the triumph of scientific reasoning over emotional, mystical, and irrational beliefs. In this view, although human beings have an innate capacity for thinking logically and mathematically, cultures often prize nonrational modes of thought over scientific thought. When scientific thought becomes ascendant in a culture, technological procedures become more effective, and the culture gains greater control over nature. Thus, technological advances are seen as the inevitable development that occurs when rationalized science replaces cultural myths and superstitions. This explanation of technological change is believed to hold for all cultures. The rise of a modern technology will occur when any traditional culture adopts rationalized scientific practice.

When this view is used to describe the specific rise of technology in our culture, it portrays earlier periods of Western civilization as functioning to build the technological edifice we currently inhabit. Because our means of controlling nature are derived from rationalized science (as defined by Descartes and other Enlightenment philosophers), the history of technology is understood as the triumph of rationalized scientific practice over elements of nonscientific beliefs about how to do things. In this portrait, Western history began with a primitive mystical mentality, moved though a period of relatively high reason during the classical period, then took a step back in the medieval period, before scientific reason finally triumphed during the Enlightenment. Once it was resolved that technology should be ruled by scientific reason, success in efforts to control nature increased exponentially.

Those who maintain a triumph of scientific reason theory describe the move to modernity in terms of growing out of traditional beliefs and maturing into modern, scientifically informed practice. What has occurred in the change from the medieval religious culture to the modern scientific culture can be attributed to a natural expansion of human capacities for rational scientific thought. It is like the development of a child moving from primitive childish beliefs to adult rational thinking. This propensity to grow into a "realistic" view of the world is present in all cultures. The difference among cultures is simply the rate at which this growth occurs.

This popular view, which holds the advent of scientific reasoning as exclusively responsible for the rise of modern technology, neglects the continuity of technological developments across historical periods. The medieval period produced technical innovations in agriculture and animal husbandry. It invented the water wheel to extract power from nature. It imported from Asia inventions such as the stirrup and gun powder. Its technological developments in clock and lens making provided the instruments necessary for carrying out the precise observations necessary for the implementation of the Enlightenment's new science (Idhe, 1990). The popular view also overlooks the social conditions that supported and encouraged the developments of Enlightenment science. The Protestant reformation lessened the authority and power of the once unified religious order to control new beliefs. The appearance of nation-states and secular city-states provided uncensored settings in which the ideas of the new science could be worked out. Advances in travel and the invention of the printing press provided for the spread of the new ideas (Toulmin, 1990).

The appearance of a high technology in one culture has implications for other cultures. Because of the efficacy of a high technology's approach for producing knowledge to transform nature into goods and weapons, "sooner or later, all societies are forced to acquire this efficacy or be dominated by others (and, hence, have it imposed on them anyway)" (Taylor, 1999, pp. 159). In one view, as cultures become technologized, they will come to look alike. They will go through essentially the same changes that have occurred in the West. They will replace traditional ways of doing things with scientifically informed practices and will become industrialized and their populations will become urbanized. This view holds that the ultimate outcome is a unified, homogeneous, Western-looking, technologically driven modern world culture.

Of those who see technology as producing one world culture, some hold a positive view about the loss of the old ways, while others hold a negative view. Those who have a positive view see the advance of modern technology as progress made possible by scientific reason; those with a negative view are filled with nostalgia for days gone by. Positive advocates of modern culture have concluded that traditional claims about nature and theology were false.

Negative viewers believe that modern culture has abandoned traditional beliefs without finding anything of comparable strength to replace them. They hold that a modern technological culture is "characterized by the loss of the horizon; by a loss of roots; by the hubris that denies human limits . . . [and] places unlimited confidence in the powers of frail human reason; by a trivializing self-indulgence that has no stomach for the heroic dimension of life, and so on" (Taylor, 1999, p. 155).

Taylor did not believe that technological development must lead to one world culture. He provided another perspective on the development of new technologies in various cultures. He did hold that the technological advances made possible by modern science and the communications that result from these advances will filter through all contemporary cultures and be adapted by them. The consequences of scientific practices, such as a market-industrial economy and a bureaucratically organized state or their equivalent, are inevitable. Cultures that do not change with the times will lag far behind in meeting the needs of their members. However, he held that the manner in which the various cultures will adopt scientific practices will differ, resulting in multiple or "alternative modernities" (Taylor, 1999, p. 162). A successful transition to a modern technology "involves a people finding resources in their traditional culture which, modified and transposed, will enable them to take on the new practices" (p. 162). The traditions of a culture will leave their imprint on its emerged modern technological form. He held that this actually happened in the West and that our traditions accommodated the integration of the new science and technological practices into our present culture.

Cultures do not start over when they adopt modern views; there is continuity with the past. Furthermore, because modernization works its way into cultures at different points, the results can vary from culture to culture.

> The point of the alternative modernities thesis is that these adaptations [to modernity] don't have to and generally won't be identical across civilizations. Indeed, something is converging here, while other things diverge. It might be tempting to say that the institutions and practices converge, while the cultures find new forms of differentiation. But that can only be a first approximation. Because, in fact, the institutional forms will also frequently differ. (Taylor, 1999, p. 164)

Taylor suggested that rationalized technification need not overtake and define a culture totally. Instead of allowing rationalized technology to annul a culture's traditions, the culture can adapt rationalized technology to its values and beliefs. While Foucault (1969/1973) held that modern rationalization has become totally dominant in the West, Taylor had a different view. He believed that the modern Western world, in addition to its advanced strategies of control over nature, can and ought to retain its traditional values of care and concern for the individual.

TECHNOLOGY AND *TECHNICAL*-RATIONAL PRACTICE

People develop cognitive and physical tools to inform those practices aimed at altering and remaking nature. Technology puts these tools to use. Practices based on technical knowledge of the modern Western world are far more effective and efficient than practices based on the technologies of earlier periods in Western history and other contemporary cultures. The effectiveness of our technology is derived from its link to contemporary rationalized science (Reynolds & Cutcliffe, 1997). Comparing the science of the Middle Ages with our science, it is obvious that the latter has produced an understanding of nature that is more useful for controlling its operations. During the past several centuries, scientifically informed technical practice has been so successful in harnessing nature that the kinds of technology practiced in other cultures pale by comparison. We consider our approach to technology to be more advanced than those of other cultures, and we have come to use the term *technology* simply to refer to what we use to manage the physical world.

The New Science

Medieval technological development took place within a religious worldview, and its inventions for the most part resulted from trial and error. Its science was limited by the view of nature embodied in religious and theological beliefs. Our contemporary technology emerged from the new science of the Enlightenment, which altered the medieval view of nature by replacing theological and Aristotelian theories with naturalistic ones. In the campaign for greater control over nature, Bacon (1620/1994) held that the medieval theories were of little use. He complained that the theories of his day were inadequate for making products of use to humankind. He wrote:

> The sciences are in an unhappy state, and have made no great progress; and . . . a path must be opened to man's understanding entirely different from that known to men before us, and other means of assistance provided so that the mind can exercise its rightful authority over the nature of things. (p. 7)

Accounting for the unhappy state of science of his day, Bacon held that insufficient attention had been paid to careful observation, and too much credit had been given to tradition and authority. He felt it was his task to offer a new and more accurate method for understanding nature. The knowledge developed by the new method would lead the way to a more effective technology.

To eliminate errors in thinking, Bacon proposed that claims about the operations of nature should be limited to those that were the result of a type of experimental science based on controlled, empirical observations. The observations were to be factual and free of prior interpretative or theoretical notions. Only after the hard data of factual observations had been collected would a theory be developed to explain these data. Theoretical statements about the operations of nature would be generated inductively from observed facts. For example, by observing the color of geese, one could conclude inductively that all geese are white. Once such a theory was generated, further observations could be made to test it. Because theories developed in this way predicted what future observations would be, they could be disproved by contradictory observations, and amendments would be required to account for the disconfirming observations. The key to Bacon's reform of science was to reject all forms of knowing about nature except those derived from observation and inductive reason.

Descartes advanced Bacon's call for a science based on experimentally controlled observation by proposing that the kind of reason used to produce geometric truths would yield a truthful and certain description of nature. When people employed this kind of reason, they necessarily would reach the same conclusion. The use of geometric reason lifts one above personal biases and overcomes the idols of the mind. When one's observations focus solely on the length and position of natural objects and are related by scientifically rational thought, nature is perceived as being ordered and stable. Its order matches the order of calculative thought and can be described mathematically. Nature does not behave randomly, and scientifically reasoned thought reveals its consistencies. The ability to describe the order of nature accurately led to the development of more powerful and successful technological means of control than had been possible before. Descartes (1637/1955) wrote:

> For they [the new understandings of nature] caused me to see that it is possible to attain knowledge which is very useful in life, and that instead of that speculative philosophy that is taught in the Schools, we may find a practical philosophy by means of which, . . . we can . . . employ them in all those uses to which they are adapted and thus render ourselves the masters and possessors of nature. (p. 119)

The recognition of geometric reason as the only legitimate way to think about nature set the Western world on a new technological trajectory. Although the new science of Bacon and Descartes has undergone significant revisions over the past four centuries, its basic principles of mathematically related controlled observations to produce theories of order have been retained. Application of these principles is held to produce knowledge that is unbiased, objective, predictive, and certain. The new science of the Enlightenment has evolved into a hypothetical-deductive method, in which a relationship between or among variables is proposed, data are collected by extracting scores on the variables, and an analysis is made to determine whether the mathematical relationships among the scores support the proposed relationship. Thus, Descartes' certainty of relationships has given way to the probability or likelihood of relationships.

The early Kuhnian (1970) view challenges the notion that social factors do not influence knowledge development. It contends that research groups have investments in their models of nature and that these models define the problems and variables they investigate. The mechanical model of nature that informed Descartes' philosophy has been replaced by the more complex idea of electronic and magnetic interactions. Furthermore, new theories of nonlinear or chaotic relationships have raised questions about the adequacy of traditional mathematics to describe all the interactions in nature. In the main, however, these challenges have not altered the way contemporary science is practiced.

Changes that were significant for the understanding of practice in the human realm occurred in the mid and late nineteenth century. Before then, human beings were held to be separate from nature. Although their bodies were included as part of the physical realm, their souls were considered supernatural. Knowledge from the new science led to the creation of a technology for controlling nature, but it was not considered applicable to human beings. This idea has largely been abandoned in contemporary science. The mental activity of human beings and their social products are now perceived as part of nature, and as such, they can be explained and predicted with the same cognitive tools used elsewhere in the natural realm. Following this line of thought, it stands to reason that human behavior is also susceptible to technological control. The new science, however, is limited to knowledge about means for changing the natural and social worlds; knowing what ends should be pursued cannot be determined through scientific inquiry.

As the new science has evolved, the knowledge it provides about the world has become more sophisticated and more abundant. Technological innovations produced by applying knowledge derived from the new science have stimulated its evolution, and vice versa. For example, the invention of the electron microscope (built from previous technological knowledge) provided direct visualization of cells and molecules and thereby enabled the further construction of knowledge about the growth and function of these micro parts of nature. Science is now so embodied in technology that they can be seen as parts of a single system. Having become inextricably intertwined, they are producing a spiraling output of knowledge and technological devices.

Deductive Reasoning

Reasoning is a process through which one can gain knowledge about something without examining it directly. This knowledge is attained by drawing a logical inference from what is known. Humans use thought to draw conclusions from known facts in various ways. In *Thinking and Reasoning* (1994) Garnham and Oakhill describe four types of thinking: inductive, abductive (conditional), statistical, and practical. As an example of how they differ, in inductive thinking, one infers a general statement from examination of known facts; but in abductive thinking, one infers from "if P is, then Q will be" and knowing that "P is," that "Q is." These kinds of thinking do not produce guaranteed results. However, there is one kind of thinking, deduction, in which conclusions necessarily follow from known premises. Because deduction produces certain results, it has been held to constitute the highest form of reasoning and to be the only kind of thinking that deserves to be called "rational" (Toulmin, 2001). It is used to test the validity of scientific theories and, by extension, to determine practical actions in technical-rational decision making.

Modern science is the result of the use of deductive reasoning to uncover patterns and consistencies among controlled observations. Bacon had proposed that science use inductive reasoning to conclude what were the properties of a class of objects. For example, induction from a number of careful observations of swans leads to the conclusion that all swans are white. However, inductive reasoning is flawed in producing certain conclusions. The next swan one observes could be black. It was Descartes' application of deductive reasoning to observations that produced logically certain conclusions and led to the development of modern science.

Deduction is a type of inference in which a conclusion is derived from one or more statements (premises). The conclusion is implicit in the premises. If the premises are correct, the conclusion is necessarily correct. Mathematical calculations are one type of deductive reasoning—for example, if there are three balls in a container, and a person adds four more, he or she concludes without having to check that there are now seven balls in the container. Aristotle's theoretical syllogism is another type—for example, all X are Y; all Y are Z; therefore, all X are Z. Traditionally, deduction was held to proceed from the "general to the specific" or from the "universal to the particular"; however, more current views of deduction include inferences that produce a logical conclusion as a consequence of any chain of statements.

The process of deduction will always draw correct conclusions from the premises given. However, the truth of the conclusions depends on the truth of the premises. As an example, premise one, the motion of the planets is perfect; premise two, the circular motion is the only perfect motion; deductive conclusion, the motion of the planets is circular. The error of the conclusion comes from the incorrect premises, not from the deductive process. To ensure that the premises were correct, Aristotle and Plato held that they should be limited to intuitively known truths, such as the axioms of geometry. Given the certainty of these premises, one could be assured that the theorems deduced from them would be true.

Western advances in knowledge about the world did not depend on the discovery of deductive reasoning, which was already known in ancient Greece. They resulted from the application of deductive reasoning to validate premises or statements about the world. It was understood that conclusions drawn from deductive reasoning held true in the nonphysical realm of mathematical and geometric truths and in the realm of Plato's forms. However, Descartes proposed that they also held true in the realm of nature. One could reason in theory that if a pipe three feet long were attached to a pipe four feet long, the result would be a pipe seven feet long. When one actually attached real pipes, it provided physical proof that the operations of nature matched calculations using deductive reasoning. This discovery led to the development of the new science, which applied it in a type of hypothetical deduction to explore nature.

The success of modern science can be attributed in large measure to the development of the hypothetical-deductive method for determining the correctness of a major premise. This method calls for proposing or hypothesizing a major premise (water freezes at 0° C), identifying an object as the minor premise (in this case, water), and then drawing a deductive conclusion (this water freezes at 0° C). By observing whether the conclusion actually holds, one can determine if the premise is true. If the deduced conclusion is not observed, the premise is adjusted until the conclusion deduced from it matches what is observed. The hypothetical-deductive method gave science a new tool for correcting premises about the operations of nature. Even so, it has not been accepted universally for science without criticism. Popper (1959), for example, argued that the hypothetical-deductive method cannot actually determine the truth of a premise; in his view, it is limited to demonstrating that a premise is false when the expected observation does not occur. Moreover, Kuhn (1970) noted that in practice the production of new premises does not always adhere to the method. Even so, the premises or knowledge statements were sufficient for the technological transformation of nature.

The match of the operations of nature and the process of deductive reasoning makes it possible to use deduction not only for validating knowledge statements but also for determining which practical action will produce the desired result. The use of deduction for practical decisions moves backward from a desired result to a general premise, then forward to a conclusion about what should be done. For example, I want to bend this piece of metal (desired result); metal of this kind becomes pliable at 400° F (general premise); therefore, I should heat this piece of metal to 400° F (conclusion about what to do). In practical deductive reasoning, the general premise has priority over the particular.

Descartes' view was that ordinary nondeductive thinking involved the interaction of the soul and the body and, thus, was susceptible to errors resulting from personal desires and needs. However, the special human capacity to engage in deductive reasoning is located in a special part of the soul that can be shielded from the distorting influences of the body. To engage in pure deductive reasoning, a person can be trained to disengage him- or herself from bodily desires and emotions so that deduction is free to operate without hindrance from personal and social biases. Since the mind-body separation in the West, deductive reasoning has been regarded as a purely mental activity, independent of the individual's cultural background or the situation in which it is employed. It is thought to be uniform in all individuals so that everyone who reasons deductively will employ the same mental operations, and anyone who starts from the same premises will come to the same conclusion. Deductive reasoning gives humans access to and knowledge of the realm of forms and mathematical truths that order and structure the observed world. This realm is unchanging and independent of human existence. For example, if all A is B, and all B is C, then all A is C holds whether humans exist or not. The truths of geometric proofs and mathematical calculations are not human constructions; rather, human deductive reasoning only provides access to these truths. It is the capacity of humans to employ deductive processes that is one of the characteristics that differentiates humans from other animals.

Scientific procedures were first applied to the study of the mind in the last decades of the nineteenth century. Wundt (1874/1904) proposed that the new science of the mind (psychology) use physical stimuli such as a bright light to evoke changes in subjects' consciousness. Subjects would then report their experiences through a kind of inner observation brought about by the stimuli. Brentano (1874/1995) put forward a view of the science of the mind as the study of the mind's activity through a type of reflection. However, with the mounting trend for scientists to focus on observable behavior, the science of the mind was dropped from the scientific agenda. Only in the later decades of the twentieth century was the study of mental processes renewed. This new depiction of the mind (cognitivism) serves as the contemporary backdrop for the technical-rational approach to decision making.

Hobbes, a contemporary of Descartes, proposed a secular interpretation of deductive reasoning in which he rejected the soul-body dualism and held that reasoning is a bodily process. "When a man *reasons,* he does nothing else but conceive a sum total from addition of parcels, for REASON . . . is nothing but reckoning" (Hobbes, 1651/1958, p. 45). According to Hobbes, thought does not have special access to a realm of forms and mathematical truths. His view would eventually prevail to gain acceptance in recent decades by the new sciences of the mind. Hobbes's mechanical calculator metaphor of mental operations has been replaced by electronic computer metaphor. Deduction is now conceived of as the activity of neural switches in the brain. The brain is (or is like) computer hardware that has been programmed to produce outputs from the input of information. However, as Hobbes proposed, thinking is understood to be a process of calculation. Like a computer, the brain is not aware of the meaning of the information on which it acts; it simply operates on arbitrary integers and alphabetic strings according to the way it has been programmed. As computer technology has advanced, the early simplified models of the brain's hardware and its programs have been replaced with more complex versions. They now include distributed processing, artificial neural networks, and other sophisticated forms of connectionism. Nevertheless, the idea that the brain/mind is a kind of computer persists. Reasoning is conceived of as a set of electrical processes that produce conclusions from inputs of information (Dupuy, 1994/2000). The argument appears to be that because computers can produce conclusions from information that are similar to the conclusions produced by human beings, human brains must be computerlike.

Deductive reasoning is not limited to human beings. The deductive processes carried out by human brains can be programmed to operate on other platforms, and they can operate independently of the platform on which they are implemented. Whether reasoning is done by a brain in a particular human body or a computer, given the same input and the same program, the processes and the results will be the same. Thus, deductive reasoning is a kind of "analysis wholly separated from the biological or neurological, on the one hand, and the sociological or cultural, on the other" (Gardner, 1985, p. 6). In this model, the mind is held to be a passive input-output device that processes information, and deduction is the logical manipulation of arbitrary symbols. Deductive reasoning is a process that derives conclusions based on the form of statements rather than their specific content. Figuring out what to do in a situation using technical-rational operations is a calculative procedure that can be performed by computers as well as human beings. When programmed correctly, computers can produce practical choices more efficiently and with fewer errors than reasoning humans. Moreover, they can deal with more complex information and provide answers more quickly than their human counterparts.

While it is recognized that humans often employ nondeductive reasoning in making choices, in technological societies deductive and calculative reasoning is held up as the standard for judging the adequacy of human thinking. In contemporary cognitivism, in which the mind itself is viewed as a calculating instrument, mistakes in thinking are generally regarded as the result of errors in the inputting of information, not in the deductive reasoning operation. The deductive process would produce errors only if the brain hardware were to malfunction or the programming contains errors. In their studies of human judgment, Kahneman and Tversky (for example 1982; 1972) found that people do not often reach the same conclusions in their thinking as are reached by deductive or statistical reasoning. The assumption is that the correct answers are those produced by deductive processes, not those produced by ordinary human judgments. As a result of this, the cumulative thrust of studies on human and clinical judgment is that, in comparison to statistical predictions, human beings are poor and even irrational decision makers. People were found to give wrong answers to presented probability problems. Tversky and Kahneman (1974) proposed that human thinking departs from the norms of deductive and probabilistic logic because people use shortcuts or heuristics, such as representativeness, availability, and anchoring and adjustment. It should be noted that these studies of human problem solving were laboratory based and consisted of contrived problems, not actual ones in which people make judgments about how to respond to another person.

Some theorists (see Garnham & Oakhill, 1994) do not regard deductive reasoning as the standard by which human judgments should be measured. They hold that the boundaries around what constitutes rational thinking have been drawn too narrowly by the tradition. If, as Aristotle indicated, rationality concerns the appropriate means for achieving a particular end or goal (Healy, 1993), then judgment should be included within the bounds of an expanded notion of rationality. The notion that correct thinking must consist of deductive and mathematical calculation was based on the conventions of logic used in argument. Human beings use many strategies and heuristics in their thinking. Lakoff and Núñez (2000) claim that mathematical truths do not exist in a Platonic super realm but are human constructions and that deductive reasoning and statistical reasoning do not provide access to eternal truths. Rather, deductive and other kinds of reasoning are humanly constructed cognitive tools that can be put to use when they are needed. Effective problem-solving reasoning is not limited to deduction and calculation. Humans are inventive in their problem solving and use diverse ways of thinking in determining what to do.

Brown (1988) noted that the deductive model of rationality breaks down in four areas. One, rational choice is defended on its effectiveness in achieving a goal; but as Weber pointed out, rationality breaks down in the choosing of goals. Decisions about what goals are worth pursuing cannot be reached through rationality as it is traditionally conceived. Two, rationality is held to function as a means of deducing subtruths from axiomatic truths; but the axioms themselves cannot be established through deductive rationality. They have to be established intuitively or arbitrarily. Three, there are alternative rational methods for reaching conclusions; however, there is no rational way to choose among the alternative methods. Four, the rules of rational deduction can be misapplied, "so that even if we have an appropriate set of rules, we must still know how to apply these rules" (p. 71).

Obviously, deductive and statistical reasoning are useful cognitive tools for reaching conclusions about what to do. However, they provide correct conclusions only when certain requirements are met. An accurate general knowledge statement is needed to serve as a major premise. Moreover, it has to be about a stable situation so that it will hold true over time and across situations. If the general knowledge is in the form of a probability statement, the choices it will produce are more likely to be correct for actions concerning aggregates rather than individuals. Practitioner judgment is required to determine whether a deductive reasoning procedure is appropriate for making a practical choice. If the conditions for deductive reasoning are not met, it is advisable to use another type of thinking to decide what to do. Practitioners of care often find themselves in such situations.

Situations that involve working with physical materials are more likely to meet the conditions in which formal reasoning can be used to make practical choices. Thus, deductive and calculative reasoning are appropriate for use in the kind of deliberation used in producing objects and devices. Whether and under what conditions practitioner judgment is necessary for making the right decisions in the physical realm is beyond consideration in this book. In contrast, practical choices in situations calling for actions to bring about the human good require a kind of thought that can deal with complex and competing goals and take into account the timing and context of the action, as well as the unique and particular characteristics of the situation and person for whom the action is undertaken.

High Technology

The philosophers of the Enlightenment believed that their new science would bring about steady progress in the quest for control of nature, and this of course is exactly what has occurred. From water wheels to steam engines, from internal combustion to electrical power and nuclear energy, there has been a persistent gain in the amount of energy that is extracted from nature. Knowledge of electronics made possible the invention of integrated circuits on silicon chips, which brought about the computer revolution. Recent developments in knowledge about the genetic code have been used to alter the DNA of grain in order to produce strains that grow faster and are not as susceptible to destruction by insects. Genetic knowledge may also lead to the control of genetically based diseases. The advances of high technology have progressively distanced us from the threats of nature, allowed us to transform our environment, and provided us with immense power. Our technological development has advanced so far that it is called "high" technology to differentiate it from prior technical achievement.

Most of what we encounter in our daily lives—the houses we live in, the beds we sleep on, the foods we eat, the clothes we wear, the sidewalks we walk on, and the devices we use to communicate with one another—are products of our technology. Often the only things we encounter that are not produced technologically are other people and animals (and even animals may be the products of scientifically designed breeding). Our lives have become thoroughly technologized.

The world we have built with our technological knowledge serves our material needs well. We are protected from many of the harmful contingencies of nature. We live longer, and there are now cures for many diseases that were debilitating or fatal before the twentieth century. We are more comfortable and the opportunities for accomplishment much greater. We were born into this world and reared in it; it is where we carry out our existence. Although there may be times when we would like to escape from our technologically built world to find relief from the stresses of modern life, on reflection we accept and appreciate the manufactured world in which we live.

Paradoxically, the power and technical efficiency that have allowed us to transform nature in order to lead happier and safer lives have also become threats to our happiness and safety. A consequence of the advances provided by our technology is that we also have the power to harm and kill people with unprecedented efficiency. Even devices intended to benefit humanity can result in great harm, as was the case in the Chernobyl nuclear meltdown. Moreover, we have used our advanced technology to create devices specifically intended to cause great harm. We have built weapons used for the saturation bombings of cities; for the nuclear annihilation of Hiroshima and Nagasaki; and for the napalm devastation of Vietnam. As our technology continues to advance, we are now able to build smart bombs and produce arsenals of biological and chemical weapons.

Technification of Contemporary Culture

Technification occurs when the technological worldview comes to permeate all the sectors of a culture. It differs from the mere presence of technological devices and objects in a culture in that the worldview of that culture has been changed by technology. The new science's perception of the world as neutral, inanimate, and logically ordered has pushed aside prior religious representations, and humanity has been absorbed into a single lawful and predictable realm. The scientific method is now considered the only legitimate source of valued and validated knowledge. According to the technological worldview, reality consists of what can be known through the scientific method, and the scientific method is the only way of knowing what is real.

Although there are pockets within our culture that embrace alternative ways of knowing and a larger view of reality, the technological worldview has come to be accepted as common sense by almost everyone. It has taken root in our background understanding of the world and therefore no longer needs to be thought about but serves as a basis for thinking. It is what our schools and universities teach and what informs the practices of our institutions.

One of the attributes of technification is that when one is thinking correctly, it follows the formal rules of logic and calculation. Other thought processes are held to be nonrational or irrational. Determining consistencies in nature and human behavior requires the use of correct thinking, as well as choosing the right practical actions. Correct thinking also requires a disengaged and disinterested stance toward what is being considered. Another attribute of technification is that correct knowing follows the pattern of isolating features or variables of composite entities and looking for relationships among the isolated features. For example, one can isolate exercise (a feature) and health (a feature) out of people (composites) and calculate the relationship between them. Knowing the measure of one feature makes it possible to predict the measure of what the other feature will be. From generalizable truths, one can surmise what the result of various actions is likely to be. If the goal to increase one's health score, one's practice should involve an increase in exercise. The scientific "way of knowing has become inflated into all knowing; . . . one particular exercise of reasoning [has] become synonymous with reason itself; one form of mental activity [has] become co-extensive with intellectual activity itself" (Abbey, 2000, pp. 176–77).

Another attribute of technification is the extension of the technological view of knowledge generation and practical decision making into to all areas of society. In technification, the knowledge procedures that were useful for building a technological physical environment are applied to study of the human or social realm. The core of these procedures is that they bring into focus only those aspects that lend themselves to measurement. Items that are not measurable cannot be seen through the lens of technical scientific procedures. The export of the new science's way of knowing to the human realm is not a neutral act. Just as it transformed the culture's beliefs about nature, it will transform beliefs about human nature.

In a technified culture, nature is regarded as a cornucopia of resources out of which products can be made to satisfy human needs and desires. When human beings are viewed through the same technified lens, they also appear to be resources that can be made into products. For example, a child is seen as raw material that can be made into an adequate reader; people can be converted into consumers of a company's products or into voters for a particular candidate; and one's friends are regarded as sources of capital for business opportunities. Employees are viewed as capital expenditures, and their value is calculated in the same way as the value of materials.

Technification promotes efficiency and lowers the cost of products and services. In our market economy, management strategies that deliver more product for less cost are highly prized, and the application of technological thinking to production and worker organization often results in greater profits. Practitioners of care are often employed by institutions under pressure to demonstrate by outcome measures that they are cost effective. They are asked to increase the number of clients they serve, to produce higher scores on standardized tests, and to reduce hospital stays. These pressures have created a demand for technical research on practice to determine what techniques produce better outcomes and what management styles stimulate greater worker efforts. Interests such as these are pushing technification deeper into the fabric of our culture.

TECHNICAL-RATIONAL PRACTICE

In our technified society, the technical-rational approach to decision making about what to do and how to do it is held as normative. It is proposed as the only scientific way to make decisions and as the way in which practitioners governed by a technical model would make decisions. In technical-rational practice, decisions about what to do are determined by applying scientifically validated general propositions to particular goals. The technical-rational model is the dominant method of making practical decisions in contemporary Western society. Its authority is derived from its use of scientifically validated knowledge. The application of scientific knowledge to a particular problem involves determining what means will achieve the desired result. The kind of reasoning used for this task is called "means-end" reasoning, "instrumental reasoning" (by Weber), or "strategic reasoning" (by Certeau). Technical-rational practice is the selection of means for accomplishing a task from the body of scientific knowledge. This model of determining how to achieve a desired end is held to produce more effective and efficient means than those derived from tradition or personal anecdotal knowledge.

To infer the correct means from the body of scientific knowledge, technical-rational practice uses the reasoning operations of classical rationality. These operations are thought to produce conclusions that are necessarily true and that hold universally (Brown, 1988). The exemplar models of classical rationality are geometry and mathematics. The steps through which one proceeds to reach a classical rational conclusion correspond to a set of rules or algorithms. For example, the quotient between two numbers can be determined by applying the rules of long division. If the rules are followed correctly, the correct answer is necessarily produced. Conclusions about what to do that result from the application of classical reasoning are not opinions or vague ideas but certainties. Anyone given the same knowledge who goes through the steps will arrive at the same answer.

The inference about what means to use to accomplish an end consists of three steps: (a) establishing a major premise in the form of a general proposition or knowledge statement; (b) determining a minor premise in the form of a particular proposition or description of a situation; and (c) deriving the conclusion that necessarily follows, given the major and minor premises.

The major premise is a general statement in the form "Whenever A, do B to accomplish C." The following are examples of major premises: (a) Whenever a person's blood pressure is high, administer the drug Lotensin to bring about a lowering of the blood pressure; and (b) Whenever a person is innocent, he or she will float in water, so put the accused in water to find out whether the person is innocent. The truth of the conclusion of the inference requires that the major premise be true. In technical-rational practice, only scientifically validated statements, such as (a), are acceptable for major premises. Statements that have not passed the test of scientific validation, such as (b), are not acceptable. Situations for which no applicable validated major premise has been developed call for experimentation to develop valid major premises.

The minor premise is in the form of a particular statement. For example, John Jones has high blood pressure. The minor premise requires a diagnosis or identification of the problem in a particular situation. The truth of the conclusion also requires that the minor premise be true. If the particular problem is misdiagnosed or is not covered by the major premise, the conclusion will not be correct.

The conclusion about what one ought to do in a particular situation necessarily follows from the major and minor premises. Thus, one ought to give John Jones Lotensin in order to lower his blood pressure.

Although the logic of technical-deliberative decision making follows the major premise-minor premise-conclusion pathway, in practice one often begins with a desired goal and works backward to a major premise; for example, one could begin with wanting to lower John Jones's blood pressure. Then the fund of scientifically validated knowledge (for example, the "educational interventions registry") is searched to find a proposition that can serve as the major premise for bringing about the desired result. From the proper major premise, one can infer what to do to bring about the result.

For more complex determinations of what to do when there are multiple goals and limited possibilities for action, the technical-rational approach to practice requires that the calculative method be used. The calculative method can provide the answer as to which of several possible actions will produce the maximum account of a single value; for example, which actions will produce the most pleasure or most profit. The method resembles the calculations of utilitarianism's "greatest good for the greatest number." However, in place of the "greatest good," other values, such as profit, can be substituted; and in place of the universal "greatest number," an individual or group, such as shareholders, can be substituted. Thus, technical-rational calculation can be employed to determine which actions will yield "the greatest pleasure for me personally" or "the greatest profit for the shareholders."

The calculative approach to decision making is called "decision theory" (Garnham & Oakhill, 1994). Decision theory proposes that the ideal, rational method for decision making involves the clarification of one's objectives or preferences and the calculation of advantages and disadvantages of possible actions to accomplish the preferences. Usually, it is assumed that people will choose to take the most advantageous action. When all the pertinent information is available about the cost and effect of each possible action, given the same goal and the same available options, different people making a rational choice would choose the same option; that is, the principle of invariance should hold.

For example, Mary Smith, who holds an egoistic hedonism position, seeks to engage in activities that will yield her the most pleasure or the least displeasure. On a day in which the weather forecast indicates the possibility of rain, she must decide whether or not to take along an umbrella. The burden of carrying an umbrella around all day yields an amount of displeasure; however, not carrying an umbrella and getting rained on also yields an amount of displeasure. A rational calculative procedure will enable Mary to decide what to do—leave the umbrella at home or take it with her. The procedure calls for assigning a value to the amount of displeasure that would be yielded by each action. Mary notes that the amount of displeasure resulting from the burden of carrying an unneeded umbrella all day is 2 on a 10-point displeasure scale. Getting rained on when not carrying an umbrella will yield a 5 on a 10 displeasure scale. In addition to these two displeasure weights, Mary has to factor in the probability that it will rain. If the likelihood of rain is 20 percent, she will minimize her displeasure by not taking along the umbrella; but if it is 80 percent, it is to her advantage to take the umbrella.

Management Practices in the Physical Realm

Contemporary corporations use calculative reasoning to determine which actions will produce the maximum financial profits. Practices determined by technical-rational methods serve most companies well and have allowed them to determine how to produce the most efficient and effective products at the lowest cost to consumers and highest profit for stock holders. As it is possible to determine by calculation which decision will maximize a chosen value, the mathematics can be performed by computers. Given the value that is to be maximized and other relevant information, a computer simulation will determine which scenario of actions will produce the greatest amount of the value. The generated answer is necessarily true, and anyone who does the calculations will find the same answer. If there is debate about which action to take, it will center on the value aimed at and/or the assumptions on which the calculation is based and not on the method of reckoning itself. In this sense, the technical-rational way of deciding in which practice to engage is neutral or indifferent to which goal is chosen. It is a tool to be used for decision making after a value has been chosen.

A critique of the technical-rational method offered by Weber and others is that it cannot determine at which ends to aim. When personal or corporate profit is the single goal, the technical-rational method can produce decisions that appear to exclude important human values. An extreme example of the limits of calculative reasoning took place at the Ford Motor Company in the early 1970s. The end to be achieved was the largest profit. Some of Ford's Pinto automobiles had defective gas tanks, and several motorists were killed when their Pintos burst into flames in accidents. To simplify, Ford was confronted with two choices: recall all Pinto automobiles and repair their gas tanks or settle lawsuits that might come up when additional accidents occurred. Using technical rationality to calculate which choice would have the least impact on Ford's profits, the rational choice was not to recall the Pintos for repair but to settle the lawsuits on a case-by-case basis (see Sassower, 1997).

> The financial analysis that Ford conducted on the Pinto concluded that it was not cost-efficient to add an $11 per car cost in order to correct a flaw. Benefits [corporate costs] derived from spending this amount of money were estimated to be $49.5 million. This estimate assumed that each death, which could be avoided, would be worth $200,000, that each major burn injury that could be avoided would be worth $67,000 and that an average repair cost of $700 per car involved in a rear end accident would be avoided. It further assumed that there would be 2,100 burned vehicles, 180 serious burn injuries, and 180 burn deaths in making this calculation. When the unit cost was spread out over the number of cars and light trucks which would be affected by the design change, at a cost of $11 per vehicle, the cost was calculated to be $137 million, much greater than the $49.5 million benefit [corporate cost]. (Wills, Swanson, Satchi, & Thompson, June, 2002)

More recent examples of restricting technical-rational calculations to the goal of personal profit have occurred in corporations where executives determined that the use of faulty accounting practices would drive up company stock prices. The calculations had to take into account the probability that the stock manipulations would be discovered and that the discovery would affect employee retirement investments more than the profits for executives.

Technical rationality need not always be used for such Machiavellian purposes. When Oregon was confronted with the problem of not having enough money to provide health care for all its citizens who were covered by state insurance, a plan was calculated through technical rationality to inform decisions about who would receive the needed care. The plan involved giving a weight to the age of the patient and the cost of the care. When a choice had to be made between giving an expensive treatment to an elderly person or to a younger one, the rational choice was to give it to the latter.

The effectiveness of decisions made through the technical-rational method depends on the accuracy of the premises on which calculations are based. The generalized premises need to describe not only how something has responded in the past but also how it will respond at the time the proposed action will take place. That is, the premises have to be predictive. Stability over time is a property of the physical realm, and technical-rational decisions are most efficacious for making decisions that deal with the use of physical objects. Deciding which materials to use in building a bridge assumes that the strength of a type of material is consistent across all individual pieces of that material and that what was determined about it in the past will hold true in the future. The character of human beings is less consistent across individuals and over time (see chapter 4). Nevertheless, the technical-rational method is still being used by social institutions to make decisions about practices in dealing with people. In fact, it has become the dominant approach for organizing and controlling people in contemporary Western society (see chapter 3).

Management Practices in the Human Realm

The technical-rational approach to decision making has been used by managers and administrators of government and private organizations to calculate and control costs associated with the human realm. Most of these calculations are based on a knowledge claim that people's behavior is governed by the pursuit of pleasure and the avoidance of pain. Although this assumption lacks the scientific validation of claims about operations of the physical realm, it is widely used in determining which management practices in dealing with human factors in production will maximize profit.

The management goal is to get workers to perform for the least cost. The major premise used in figuring out what to do about managing workers is the hedonistic proposition that people do what they do to receive pleasurable sensations or to avoid painful sensations. Stich (1985) holds that the hedonist proposition is one of the primary beliefs of Western folk psychology. Applied to the work setting, the proposition implies that rest and relaxation are pleasurable, and toil and work are painful. People will exert themselves and put forth effort to work only under threat of some discomfort or because of the expectation of a significant reward. Because financial rewards can be cashed in for various pleasurable activities, money serves as an incentive for workers to perform tasks they would not be willing to perform otherwise.

In his *Scientific Management*, Taylor (1911) proposed that it was the responsibility of managers to install a wage-incentive system in which workers could maximize their income by doing exactly what management told them to do and doing it as rapidly as possible. Since Taylor wrote, his ideas have undergone considerable amendment and refinement. The most sophisticated contemporary model using the hedonistic proposition is the expectancy-value theory (Vroom, 1964). Expectancy-value theory holds that persons behave hedonistically when choosing which tasks to do and how much effort to give to the task. People act on the basis of what they believe will maximize their positive affect and minimize their negative affect. Lawler (1994) wrote that expectancy theory is based on four principles of human motivation: (a) among the outcomes available to them, people prefer some more than others; (b) people evaluate how much effort is necessary on their part to achieve the available outcomes (and whether their effort would be sufficient to achieve it at all); (c) people have notions about the likelihood that certain outcomes will follow from their behavior; and (d) in any situation, the actions people choose to take are determined by their preferences, evaluations, and notions in the first three principles.

> We see that although simple behaviorism is dead in the academic world, it lives a hardy life in the corporate human resources environment. There, it is assumed that implementation is best achieved when incentive structures are aligned with the strategic objectives of the organization. People must be rewarded for acting in accord with new goals of the organization and punished if they act otherwise. (Flores, 2000, p. 282)

The expectancy-value theory of management is based on the assumption that workers themselves use a technical-rational calculus to determine their behavior. That is to say, they engage in conscious and rational deliberations (similar to that used in the example given above of deciding whether to carry an umbrella) to calculate what they will do. Contemporary expectancy theory has expanded the notion of what people seek as rewards. Rather than simple physical pleasure, the calculations are thought to take into account other goals, such as higher intellectual pursuits, socially imparted desires, and personally chosen goals (for example, earning enough money to pay for a child's college education). The understanding of the calculus that people use has also become more sophisticated. Expectancy theory has developed a model that includes people's estimation of the amount of effort necessary to achieve different rewards, their comparison of the amount of reward that different behaviors will produce, and their expectation that effort expended will actually lead to achieving the reward.

Contemporary management theory seeks to align a reward system precisely with the particular tasks and performances needed from individual employees for the goals and aims of the organization to be fully achieved (Lawler, 1990). For example, pay can be linked to how much is accomplished and how well tasks are performed and not simply to the kind of task that is performed. Diamond (1999) has provided guidelines for use by educational institutions to devise a reward system that is linked to performances contributing to the accomplishment of the organization's goals and the fulfillment of its mission. A variety of techniques for fine-tuning an organization's pay system are offered in the contemporary management literature. For example, managers can use performance appraisals to determine the amount of increments. Wilson (1995), in his *Innovative Reward Systems for the Changing Workplace,* calls for: (a) replacement of inflexible job-based pay systems with ones that reinforce the special competencies and contributions of individuals and teams; (b) creation of team incentives, gainsharing, and project-oriented reward systems; and (c) the use of a wide range of alternatives to cash rewards, such as equity, stock appreciation rights, symbolic reinforcers, and time off. Jorgensen (1996), in her *Pay for Results,* describes compensation plans that include merit and bonus pay beyond the salary base to reward extraordinary productivity, pay linked to sales results, team incentives, and a system of noncash rewards, such as recognition, time off, educational opportunities, and extra health benefits.

Although the various management models are based on different premises of worker motivation, they have the same primary goal, which is to gain employee compliance with managerial authority. Corporate technical-rational calculations of practices that maximize profit must include strategies that will produce maximum worker output at minimum company expense. Unlike calculations about the cost-effective use of materials, calculations about the cost-effective use of human resources are less precise.

In addition to calculating how to maximize worker production for least cost, managers need to control what workers do to ensure that they perform their tasks in the most efficient way and with the least risk of error. For example, practitioners of care are often told to limit their activities to those that have been determined by organizations (such as school districts, hospitals, and clinics) to deliver the most care to the greatest number of students or patients for the least cost. Activity sheets, multiple report forms, controls over the amount of time allotted for each session, and other devices are meant to enforce conformity with institutional directives. Worker conformity to directives also limits the liability risk to institutions. By restricting caregiver activities to those that are empirically validated, institutions are not as vulnerable to large legal judgments as they are when caregivers make intuitive judgments about what is needed.

Summary

The purpose of the technical-rational method is to identify the most efficacious and efficient action or practice for achieving a chosen end. This method has two aspects that are highly prized in contemporary Western culture: (a) it draws on the knowledge generated by the practitioners of science, and (b) it incorporates rational processes in its decision making. Largely because it has been proven effective for determining how to produce goods and devices from physical materials, decisions about practice based on the technical-rational model are thought to carry more weight than decisions based on other kinds of knowledge, such as understanding, self-knowledge, and religious convictions. In our technified society, the technical-rational method is often aggressively presented as the only legitimate way to make practical decisions, and other methods of decision making are often dismissed as being irrational.

However, the technical-rational approach has several limitations. First, its conclusions are only as valid as the propositions of its major premises. These propositions are based on certain assumptions about the properties of nature and people. For example, it is assumed that attributes of materials and people are stable over time, that their changes are determinative and predictable, and that all items of the same kind will respond in the same way. Second, although the technical-rational method can be used to decide how something can be accomplished, it cannot determine what ought to be accomplished. Decisions made through this method should be governed by the goals and values of a society or person. Practical decisions about values require other approaches. Third, although the technical-rational method can produce decisions about the most effective way to accomplish a goal, there is no assurance that these decisions will be implemented. People do not always choose to do what calculations indicate would be the most efficient way to achieve a goal.

The technical-rational approach is put forth as a normative model for decision making, not as a means of describing how, in fact, groups and individuals make decisions. Although some theories, such as the expectancy-value theory of management and classical rational choice economic theory (Mandler, 1984), depict people as rational decision makers, human thought processes appear less rational than the technical-rational model demands (Tversky & Kahneman, 1974). Technical-rational decision making calls for a disinterested, impersonal, unbiased stance in the making of calculations for practice. Freud (1900/1965) argued that decisions are actually the result of unconscious wishes, not rational thought. And Nussbaum (2001c) noted that practical choices are emotionally informed. Theorists who hold that human action is the result of background understandings that largely operate out of awareness (see chapter 6) question the correctness of the premise that individuals determine their actions on the basis of conscious, deliberative reasoning. Even practitioners of science, who are considered to be among those most governed by rational thought, have been known to search for evidence that sustains their own views and theories and to explain away evidence that does not support their positions (Faust, 1984; Kuhn, 1970). Furthermore, some scholars contend that the classical notion of rationality on which technical rationality is based is too narrow and excludes other reasonable decision-making procedures (Brown, 1988; Toulmin, 2001).

The effect of the increasing technification of the social world is to transform the human realm so that it is more controllable and predictable. It has constructed large bureaucratic hierarchies as a means to bring discipline and order to human resources. The next section presents the warnings voiced by German sociologist Weber and German philosopher Heidegger about the advent of the expansion of technological values and understanding to the social realm. They were fearful that technification would override and replace the traditional values of care and concern with the drives for acquisition and personal power.

CRITIQUE OF THE TECHNIFIED CULTURE

A distinction needs to be made between those critiques of technology itself and those that criticize the technification or colonization of culture by technical reason. Critics of technology fall into three groups: one group is worried that technological machines and devices are eliminating jobs; another group wants to return to an earlier, less complicated time; and the third group is fearful that technology is out of control. The first group takes the Luddite position that technology has produced machines and robots that are replacing human workers. When automation causes people to lose their jobs and wages, they are unable to support their families. The second group is epitomized by the rural commune movement of the 1960s. The idea was to get closer to the earth by growing one's own food and working with one's hands. This group felt that human relationships would be deepened by sharing duties and living together. The third group, represented by Ellul (1964) and Winner (1977) hold that technology is no longer in service to humans; now humans are controlled by technology. Although Ellul and Winner wrote before the computer revolution, their concerns may have even greater relevance now that so many manufacturing, business, and defense decisions are being made by computers.

Most of the critics of technology do not advocate turning back the clock. They acknowledge the benefits technology has brought in health care, communication, and production. Their criticism is directed at the technification of culture, and particularly the imposition of its singular type of reasoning—instrumental rationality—on the human realm. The operations of instrumental rationality consist of calculations. It is used to determine which means will most effectively and efficiently achieve a particular goal or maximize a given value. While instrumental rationality may be useful for deciding how to accomplish a task efficiently and effectively, it cannot indicate which ends are worth pursuing. As this type of reasoning gains dominance in a society, efficiency and effectiveness come to be regarded as values in and of themselves. Instrumental rationality employs the same logic that governs the validity of knowledge statements generated by the exact sciences. It represents a transfer of this logic to the realm of practice. When applied to social organizations, it inevitably determines that bureaucracy provides the most effective structure for accomplishing institutional and governmental goals.

Efficiency in the human realm results from gaining control over human actions. When people obey the rules and regulations established for the achievement of an institution's goals, it is more likely these goals will be accomplished. Thus, rewards and penalties are needed to ensure compliance. Because the calculations of instrumental reason are aimed at achieving the greatest efficiency, other uniquely human values do not enter into the equation. The neglect or loss of human values is the central focus of the critique of technification and its accompanying attribute, instrumental reason.

Weber

The late nineteenth and early twentieth century was a time of increasing industrialization and growth of the market economy in Germany. Weber is recognized as the first critical commentator to write about the effect technical progress was having on society. The aspirations of Enlightenment involved the production and accumulation of wealth, which it was believed would make the emancipation of humanity possible. Its fulfillment was to be the result of the application of the knowledge developed by the new science. Weber noted that although greater social wealth was being accumulated, rather than bringing about the emancipation of people, it led to acquisitiveness and greed (Scaff, 2000). In their pursuit of private goals, profits, and predictability, people had lost human warmth and the regard for individuality (Sica, 2000). They lived in the "mighty cosmos of the modern economic order . . . the iron cage [in which] specialists without spirit, sensualists without heart, [are] caught in the delusion that [they] have achieved a level of development never before attained by mankind" (Weber, 1921/1958, p. 182).

In analyzing the effect of technology and industrialization on society, Weber identified four types of human action: instrumental (technical) rationality, value-rationality, affectual, and traditional based (Weber, 1968).

1. Actions of the instrumental rational type are intended to accomplish the actor's own objectives; for example, to accumulate wealth. Through instrumental reason (or technical-rational planning), the most efficient and effective means of accomplishing the objective is calculated. Instrumental rational calculations make use of knowledge about how people or objects in the physical world will respond. The ability to predict how things or people will respond to various actions is necessary for determining the means that will produce one's intended outcome.

2. Actions of the value-rational type are undertaken because they are in themselves an expression of some ethical, aesthetic, religious, or other form of value. They are done because they are the right thing to do, not because doing them is the way to achieve a predetermined end.

3. Actions of the affectual type rise out of emotions; for example, those done out of anger or love. These actions are expressions of an actor's specific affect or feeling and are not informed by the calculations of instrumental reason.

4. Actions of the traditional type are carried out because they have been ingrained in the actor. They are done because the individual knows that such actions are habitually taken in certain situations. They are not calculated to produce a particular result, nor are they performed because they are the good or worthwhile thing to do.

Weber held that the instrumental rational type of action was dominant in the Germany of his day. Actions of the value-rational type (i.e., the right thing to do) had become devalued. The traditional systems of beliefs that motivated value-rational actions had lost all influence in the secularized, decadent German society. Consequently, as there was no longer a code of ethics to direct people's actions, instrumental rationality was used to figure out how to achieve one's objectives, and efficiency, order, and control took on their own value as the means that worked best.

Actions of the instrumental rational type serve as means to an end, and calculating which actions to take requires formal and impersonal thought. The calculative process involves breaking down problems into means-ends chains and examining the costs versus the benefits of each option. While the new understanding of the world led to an unprecedented increase in both the production and distribution of goods and services, the removal of moral and spiritual values had left only the mechanical motions of neutral entities. The aim of life was reduced to accumulating personal wealth, and thought was limited to figuring out how to accomplish this. Weber said that when life is stripped of its religious and ethical meaning, all that is left is a passion for wealth and power. What matters becomes enclosed within a narrow circle of personal concerns.

Weber believed that a process he called *rationalization* had brought about the transformation of the old European society into the modern industrialized, capitalistic society. In rationalization, a society's institutions become increasingly governed by the use of formal rationality, which is not to be confused with Weber's instrumental means-end rationality. When institutions adopt the formal rational approach, they move from an operating system in which employees are permitted to make decision on the basis of personal whim or favoritism to one based on the application of general rules. In addition to establishing a set of rules, they also take on a hierarchically organized structure and hire full-time officials and staff members with specialized training. Thus, formal rationality results in a bureaucratically organized institution that can in and of itself serve as the means for efficient functioning and the accomplishment of goals. For example, it is an efficient and effective means for the economically powerful to establish control and discipline over those who are managed by these institutions (Elster, 2000).

Such organizations as economic, legal, and government systems use procedures based on formal rationality to calculate and predict the consequence of their decisions. Weber described the operations of a bureaucratic system ordered by formal rationality as follows:

> From a purely technical point of view, a bureaucracy is capable of attaining the highest degree of efficiency, and is in this sense formally the most rational known means of exercising authority over human beings. It is superior to any other form in precision, in stability, in the stringency of its discipline, and in its reliability. It thus makes possible a particularly high degree of calculability of results for the heads of the organization and for those acting in relation to it. It is finally superior both in intensive efficiency and in the scope of its operations and is formally capable of application to all kinds of administrative tasks. (1921/1968, p. 223)

Weber held that modern technified society does not embrace the Enlightenment value of individualization, in which every human being is seen as an individual and people adapt their responses to one another accordingly. Allowing for individual differences is clearly at odds with the bureaucratic goal of efficiency. To treat the individual as a type of technical problem that can be solved by the application of general rules may suit the values of bureaucratic rationalization, but it amounts to an absolute rejection of individualization (McGowan, 1991). Although bureaucracies may be efficient, they depersonalize those they serve and impose oppressive routines on those who work in them.

Weber held that the rationalization of society was unavoidable and progressive, and that instrumental reasoning would inevitably dominate human relationships and actions. As he saw it, the technical approach will eventually be applied to all aspects of life and technical rationality will stand alone as the only form of rational thought. His question was how the human desire to live a meaningful life can still be fulfilled within a rationalized society. Weber was pessimistic about the future, and almost a century after he made his predictions, Western culture has become far more technified than he could have imagined and technical-rational thought has indeed become dominant.

Heidegger

The philosophical question Heidegger sought to answer was "What is the essence of being?" His first major publication, *Being and Time* (1927/1962), explored the appearance of being in human existence. In it, he contends that in the everyday mode of human existence, things appear as equipment to be used to accomplish ordinary tasks. Heidegger examined the appearance of being in contemporary technified culture in a later series of essays. Ihde (1993), himself a leading scholar of technology, called Heidegger one of the most significant founders of the philosophy of technology.

Heidegger began his essay "The Question Concerning Technology" (1954/1977) by simply asking, "What is technology?" He said that the answer ordinarily given to this question is that technology is "a means and a human activity" (p. 5). In modern technology, humans make use of sophisticated scientific instruments and tools as the means of achieving results. Heidegger goes on to note that there are beneficial technologies and lethal ones. An example of beneficial technology is modern medicine, which saves human lives and alleviates suffering; an example of lethal technology is weaponry, which is used to destroy human life. The assumption is that technology itself is a neutral instrument; thus, the basic question about technology is how it is to be used. The larger question is how it can be controlled.

Heidegger noted that although it is "correct" to say that technology is "a means and a human activity," this is not the "true" answer. The correct response depicts technology as instrumental, as a means for accomplishing things; and while this definition pinpoints something pertinent about technology, it misses what is essential. To find the "true" answer, one needs to ask about the essence of technology. The essence of something is not the object itself, but the way it pursues its course; the way it remains the way it is through time. For example, the essence of "tree" is not itself a tree. It cannot be found by examining existing trees, but it is what pervades all trees. It is the "tree-ness" by which something appears as a tree. "The essence of technology is by no means anything technological" (p. 4).

One cannot come to understand the essence of technology simply by examining a single example, such as contemporary technology. Rather, it is necessary to examine technology as it appeared in other historical periods. Heidegger turned to the Greek technology *(techne)* as a way to discover the essence of technology. For the Greeks, techne was the knowledge that produced or brought forth *(poiesis)* out of nature the shelters and objects that protected people from the forces of nature. Heidegger noted that *techne* reveals nature in such a way that the people who possess it can craft or make *(poiesis)* artifacts and produce arts. Thus, through *techne* one sees nature as something to be used and controlled. Thus, the ordinary definition of technology as a means to accomplish things misses its essence: technology is a way in which things appear; it is a revelation.

What makes modern technology different from previous technologies is the manner in which it brings forth objects and food from nature. In pre-modern technology, craftsmen and farmers worked with nature, rather than taking from nature. For example, the sails of a windmill turned with the prevailing winds, "but the windmill does not unlock the energy from the air currents in order to store it" (p. 27). In contrast, modern technology challenges nature. It commandeers energy from nature and stores it for future use. Modern technology besieges, orders, manipulates, and ultimately controls nature. Both pre-modern and modern technologies regard nature as something to be used. Premodern technology approached nature as something to be worked with in order to produce things for human benefit. Modern technology, however, approaches nature aggressively, attacking it head on, depleting its resources and draining its energy.

While Heidegger held that what is essential to technology is the perception that nature is something to be used and controlled, he understood that the balance of power between humans and nature changed with the rise of modern science. In fact, he viewed modern science as a manifestation of the human will to control. It has revealed nature as an aggregate of brute objects that can be explained by mechanical laws, abstract properties, and causal relations. It has created a lens that abstracts from the fullness of the world only a coherence of forces and then maintains that reality consists only of these abstracted forces.

> Modern science's way of representing pursues and entraps nature as a calculable coherence of forces. . . . Because physics, indeed already as pure theory, sets nature up to exhibit itself as a coherence of forces calculable in advance,

it therefore orders its experiments precisely for the purpose of asking whether and how nature reports itself when set up that way. (Heidegger, 1954/1977, p. 21)

The modern world appears to be stripped of meanings, values, and purposes. All that remains is a fund of resources and raw materials that can be controlled and manipulated by humans to serve their own interests. When the world appears to be without meaning, technology becomes aggressive and takes whatever it wants from nature. The alignment of the human desire to control nature with the exact sciences produced by this desire has created modern technology. The essence of modern technology is its enframing of the natural world as nothing more than standing energy reserves and a source of raw materials. This enframing also treats people as resources or assets to be ordered, enhanced, and used efficiently. Enframing identifies aspects of things that can be stored as stock for later use and consumption, but covers over and conceals any other aspects. "The coming to presence of technology threatens revealing, threatens it with the possibility that all revealing will be consumed by ordering and that everything will present itself only in the unconcealedness of standing-reserve" (p. 27). The threat of modern technology is not from its potentially lethal machines and apparatus; rather, its threat is to drive out every other possibility of openness to being, and to deny entrance into a more original revealing where one can "experience the call of a more primal truth" (p. 28). "Human activity can never directly counter this danger. Human achievement alone can never banish it. But human reflection can ponder the fact that all saving power must be of a higher essence than what is endangered, though at the same time kindred to it" (pp. 33–34).

In 'The Question Concerning Technology,' Heidegger examined the "correct" definition of technology, which focused attention on how people use, master, and control it to achieve human purposes. However, the "correct" definition obscured not only the essence of technology but also concealed the fact that modern technology regards people themselves as standing reserves, and as those who stand over others as stock from which to draw energy. The disclosure of modern technology is not something individuals do, but it is the enframing or portrait of the world in which we in our time exist. It is the way in which modern technology shows or unconceals the world that "determines what human activity has become in the modern epoch" (Bernstein, 1992, p. 100).

Heidegger says that it is our destiny to exist at a time when technological enframing is the mode through which nature and people are revealed. Modern technology is a legitimate mode of disclosure and it is our destiny to experience the world as modern technology brings it forth into presence as a stockpile of resources. But when we understand that the essence of technology is a particular mode of unconcealing, we can be open to other unconcealings of the world. We are not fated to remain within the confines of what modern technology reveals.

> When we consider the essence of technology, then we experience Enframing as a destining of revealing. In this way we are already sojourning within the open space of destining, a destining that in no way confines us to a stultified compulsion to push on blindly with technology or, what comes to the same thing, to rebel helplessly against it and curse it as the work of the devil. Quite to the contrary, when we once open ourselves expressly to the essence of technology, we find ourselves unexpectedly taken into a freeing claim. (Heidegger, 1954/1977, pp. 25–26)

While the people of earlier historical periods have used nature for their own ends, modern technology unconceals or brings to presence the world as something to be set upon and drawn from. This is not only a way in which the world can be revealed, but it is the way that has currency and potency in this particular period in this particular culture. Having recognized that modern technological revealing is a historically conditioned approach, one gains a free relation to it. It loses its dominance over us and becomes a tool to be used or not used, depending on circumstances. Heidegger (1959/1966) described a free relationship as one in which:

> We let technical devices enter our daily life, and at the same time leave them outside, . . . as things which are nothing absolute but remain dependent upon something higher. I would call the comportment toward technology which expresses "yes" and at the same time "no," by an old word, *releasement toward things*. (p. 54)

Compared to other possibilities of revealing, technological enframing shows nature as antithetical to humans. It tends to cover over the essence of human existence, which is revealing as such. "Enframing [of modern technology] not only conceals a former way of revealing, bring-forth, but it conceals revealing itself and with it That wherein unconcealment, i.e., truth, comes to pass" (Heidegger, 1954/1977, p. 27). Heidegger's fear is that once we have gained complete technological control over ourselves and our natural environment, we will have lost our openness to the fullness of reality. We will no longer be human (Dasein), because we will have become so entrapped by technology that we will not realize that there are other, richer ways in which being can show itself.

Heidegger did not advocate abandoning technology altogether. "It would be foolish to attack technology blindly. . . . We depend on technological devices; they even challenge us to ever greater advances" (1959/1966a, p. 53). He believed that it is possible for people to keep their technological devices and still not be dominated by the technological way of understanding the world. "We can use technical devices as they ought to be used, and also let them alone as something which does not affect our inner and real core" (p. 54). "We can affirm the unavoidable use of technical devices, and also deny them the right to dominate us, and so to warp, confuse, and lay waste our nature" (p. 54).

Heidegger saw the essence of modern technology as limiting the way in which the world is brought forth and that it is our destiny to live in a time dominated by technology. This raises the question of how one should respond to modern technology, to the enframing of the nature and people as stockpiles of resources. According to Heidegger, only two activities are available to contemporary people—actions that cause an effect (technological or instrumental action) and thinking (meditative thought that accomplishes the relation to being). The highest form of human activity is meditative thinking. There is no way that we can eliminate the technological enframing. The very attempt to control it is a manifestation of its essence—the will to control. "The sole possibility that is left for us is to prepare a sort of readiness, through thinking and poetizing; . . . in the face of the god who is absent" (Heidegger, 1966/1976, p. 278).

> But for the time being—we do not know for how long—man finds himself in a perilous situation. Why? Just because a third world war might break out unexpectedly and bring about the complete annihilation of humanity and the destruction of the earth? No. In this dawning atomic age a far greater danger threatens—precisely when the danger of a third world war has been removed. A strange assertion! Strange indeed, but only as long as we do not meditate. . . . What great danger then might move upon us? There might go hand in hand with the greatest ingenuity in calculative planning and inventing indifference toward meditative thinking, total thoughtlessness. And then? Then man would have denied and thrown away his own special nature—that he is a meditative being. Therefore, the issue is the saving of man's essential nature. Therefore, the issue is keeping meditative thinking alive. (Heidegger, 1959/1966b, pp. 55–56)

Meanwhile, enframing, which is not in our control, produces death chambers and concentration camps as well as automated food industries. Heidegger maintained that in essence these are the same: Both are manifestations of technological enframing or the way technology presents the world. In a discussion of the lack of housing, rather than dealing with the plight and misery of those living on the street, Heidegger took the opportunity to comment on "our real homelessness." Real homelessness is the absence of being and our failure to ponder being's abode and to respond to its call. Bernstein attributed Heidegger's apparent indifference to everyday human suffering to his position that all we can do in the face of pain and suffering caused by our use of technology is to think meditatively. In Bernstein's opinion, the problem is with "Heidegger's own understanding of a type of meditative thinking that *anesthetizes* us to the frightful contingencies of human life and death" (Bernstein, 1992, p. 133). Obsessed with the concealment of being, Heidegger feared that the capacity to keep watch over the disclosure, which he considered the "real" dignity of humans, would be lost.

What is left out of Heidegger's analysis of technology is *phronesis* (see chapter 5). Turning to Aristotle in "The Question Concerning Technology" to introduce the Greek concept of *techne* as bring-forth (which he compared with modern technology's challenging-forth), Heidegger omitted the other way of thinking, *phronesis,* which Aristotle describes in the same section. *Phronesis* is another way of revealing that human beings are alike in some ways and different in others; individuals whose speech and deeds reveal their uniqueness (Arendt, 1958). *Phronesis* is concerned about actions in the human realm. It provides a way of determining what actions to undertake to affect the good for another. Gadamer has proposed that *phronesis* enables us to respond to the dominance of contemporary technology in our lives (1963/1975).

Heidegger's venture into National Socialism was premised on overcoming modern technology and returning to the past where there was a greater openness to being (Safranski, 1994/1998).

> Another way to understand the shortcomings of Heidegger's political vision involves his preference for *poiesis* over *praxis*, for creative bring-forth over engaged social practice. Like many thinkers who have called for radical cultural change, Heidegger saw the state in artistic terms, as a creative advent fashioned by heroic founders. Seeing the state as an "artwork" fits a sense of revolutionary politics, a fundamental recasting of the social order from the ground up. Such a political vision is much like Plato's *poiesis* stemming from the insight of a visionary, rather than a more Aristotelian *praxis* that works out an interactive, collaborative shaping of the social order in the midst of existing conditions. For all his interest in Aristotle's ethics, Heidegger never followed through on Aristotle's *praxis,* and was given over instead to a kind of political Platonism. (Hatab, 2000, p. 203)

Heidegger spoke of only two behavioral options available to those of us who live in a technological society. We can engage in instrumental technological behaviors that manipulate nature or people, or we can engage in contemplative thinking. Because our technologically informed behaviors are simply manifestations of the force of enframing, we are not personally responsible for their effects. These behaviors are not differentiated from the results they produce. Medical advances and concentration camps are merely expressions of the same enframing. Our only response can be contemplation. However, Heidegger's two kinds of behavior are not the only options available to human beings. Phronetic thinking enables us to view people as feeling and concerned beings rather than as resources for stockpiling. A phronetic perspective on being with others reveals their needs and pains and calls forth a human caring response. *Phronesis* unconceals the moral dimension of human existence and seeks to promote the good and avoid causing harm to others. Aristotle's concept of *phronesis* will be examined in greater detail in chapter 5.

Both Weber and Heidegger held that modern Western culture is dominated by means-end rationalization and technology. Technical-rational decision making is presented by the culture as the only effective way of determining which actions to take in order to solve practical problems in both the physical and human realms. They held that technology is a way of understanding the world in which people and objects are ordered into categories so as to be readily available for use as resources. Both Weber and Heidegger accepted the value and accomplishments of instrumental reasoning, but they were concerned about the possibility of its leading to a world without meaning and life without value. The inherent danger in technology is its overwhelming tendency to present its view of the reality as the only true view.

This chapter has explored the propensity of humans to control and transform nature so that it serves our needs. The knowledge of how to accomplish this transformation has greatly expanded since the Enlightenment and has been used to build the world in which we live. Beginning in the last century, the idea of the use of a similar technological process to control and manage people has been developed. Critiques (for example, Weber and Heidegger) have been offered about the expansion of technological thinking into the human realm; nevertheless, contemporary society has become saturated by technical-rational reasoning. In the next chapter, Bourdieu and Certeau examine the effect of this technification of culture on its members' everyday practices.

3

Practice and Culture

CAREGIVERS ARE NOW BEING ENCOURAGED to follow scripts and program outlines, with the objective of making their practices technically based rather than judgment based. The movement toward a technically based approach in practice is a manifestation of the human propensity to control nature and to transform it into an environment that meets our needs and satisfies our desires. The previous chapter traced the progress of the human campaign to gain control over nature during the past four centuries. This campaign escalated steadily as a result of knowledge generated by the new science and its application in technically based practices. In the twentieth century, technically based practice came to dominate all sectors of society. Businesses, governments, social organizations, educational institutions, and providers of health care have chosen to manage their practices according to the technical model. This technification of society has tended to negate the significance of individual lives and personal care.

Technification has a tendency to discard former ways of knowing and practicing. In a drive for complete dominance, it eradicates areas that are not technified. When alternative ways of thinking and problem solving are summarily dismissed as being inefficient, irrational, or not scientifically validated, a culture becomes one dimensional. The hope of the Enlightenment was that the new science would lead to greater human freedom and autonomy. Instead, in its technified form, it has placed limits and restrictions on human actions and practices.

This chapter presents the views of two French practice theorists—Bourdieu and Certeau—who address the effect of technification on everyday human practice and look for oases in our technified culture for personal expression. Traditional philosophy divided reality into two areas: human subjectivity and worldly objects. Human subjectivity concerned human

47

experiences, and worldly objects concerned physical reality. How these two classes were related was the philosophical problem, and the issue was how accurately the subjective experiences of human beings reflect the world as it actually is. For example, Kant held that subjective experiences are mental constructions and that we could not know the character of nature as it is itself. Studies were divided into those that inquired about the experiences of subjects (phenomenology) and those that inquired about the composition of the world (the natural sciences). The practice theorist inquires about a third area between these two—the area of interaction between humans and the world. They termed this new area "practice." Practice is understood to be the more basic area from which the ideas of an independent subject and an independent world are abstracted.

> Heidegger works to unravel the subject-object binary by arguing for the priority of an engaged being-in-the-world that precedes abstract reflection, in the sense that the self is already shaped by contexts of meaning (historical tradition, practical involvement, everyday concerns, social relations, moods, and language uses) before the world is subjected to objectification. Philosophy has tended to miss this prereflective dimension precisely because it is less manageable and shows itself to be radically finite, which undermines foundationalist guarantees. (Hatab, 2000, p. 2)

In his *Outline of a Theory of Practice* (1972/1977), Bourdieu proposed that practice is the third way to understand social action, which mediates between culture (objectivity) and person (subjectivity). Practice theory changes the focus from what actors believe are their reasons for doing something to what they are actually doing. In practice theory the boundary between the person and the environment is porous. For example, personal experiences such as hunger take on the marks of social context. Hunger is experienced one way in a situation where it is not appropriate to request food from one's hosts and in another way when the food one ordered in a restaurant has not been served in a reasonable period of time. The action that follows these situations is the result of a person-environment interaction (Holland, Lachicotte, Skinner, & Cain, 1998).

Two-term accounts have tended to stress the person as primary or the culture as dominant. When the person is primary, people are understood to have innate, species-specific properties (such as rationality or unconscious structures) that are the same for everyone. The cultural environment is only a thin veneer covering the universal properties of humans. For example, using Freud's tripartite structure of the mind as a universal human property, members of a culture that talk about the deity in their hearts are held to be using metaphorical language to talk about the superego. If the contemporary psychological understanding of child development is universal, then misguided childrearing practices in any culture will lead to pathologies. When people are regarded as primary, their species-given properties remain constant beneath diverse cultural forms in the same way that the human body remains the same beneath whatever clothes one wears. From the other perspective, culture shapes people. Concepts of 'emotion', 'child development', and 'mental disorders' are products of culture. Just as liquid conforms to the shape of a bottle, a person conforms to his or her culture (Holland et al., 1998).

Practice theory addresses both everyday and specialized practices. Everyday practices are activities that people ordinarily engage in as they go about in the world and interact with other people. (*Practice* and *activity* are used as synonyms in this chapter and are interchanged in the text only for stylistic reasons.) Specialized practices in the human realm are bounded by specific, agreed-upon goals or shared assumptions about their purpose and are most often conducted in specified locations. They include such practices as law, medicine, nursing, social work, teaching, and psychotherapy. Practice theory does not make an essential distinction between everyday and specialized practices. Both take place in interactions between person and environment, and their operations can be understood through a general theory of practice. The two categories of practice also meld in people's lives. Specialized practices in the human realm make extensive use of everyday practical knowledge. People drive to work, draw on past everyday experiences in making responses in their specialized settings, and integrate everyday and specialized practice in other ways.

Studies of why people do what they do have traditionally employed the two-term account—*person* and *culture*. However, these two-term studies in the human realm inevitably come to an impasse in their attempts to understand one term as a function of the other. In social science studies, actions are cataloged according to type, and correlations are calculated among them. Practices, however, cannot be understood through cataloging. Ordinary, everyday actions are less ordered and variable and do not conform to empirical generalizations or covering laws. Furthermore, they are situation and time sensitive and determined by a logic that is different than scientific calculation.

In practice theory, attention is shifted from person or culture to the interaction between them. Neither person nor culture determines the other, but practice takes place in their conjoining. Likewise, human action is not a product of either person or culture alone but of a dialectic occurring between them. Actions take place within the bounds of culture, and culture lives through the actions of its members. *Practice* is the third term situated between the two traditional terms, *person* and *culture*, that heretofore governed studies of why people do what they do.

Two-Term Explanations of Practice

Practice theory is a response to and critique of the two-term, subject-object approaches to the source that determines human practice. The practice theorists' representative of the subject approach was Sartre and his existential philosophy. Their representative of the object approach was Lévi-Strauss, who held that culture is determinate of practice.

The Subject as Author of Practice

The subject-as-author position holds that humans are the agents of their practices and consciously choose what they do. Therefore, they are responsible for their choices and are held accountable for them. The subject-as-author position is based on the idea of a universal human characteristic that is more basic than what is transmitted by culture. Its proponents contend that a fundamental and stable characteristic of human nature operates in human decision making regardless of the cultural setting in which a practice takes place. An exemplar of this position is Sartre, who held the existential notion that consciousness transcends culture, and people must choose their actions. That is to say, people are autonomous agents, free to choose what they wish to do and what they wish to become.

From Sartre's existentialist perspective, the source of choice about what to do is in the unfettered human subject. Even in the most dire and limited circumstances, humans retain the possibility of free choice. Sartre held that human beings determine who they are by the choices they make. There is no stable human essence except the necessity to choose among possibilities. Humans are not passive objects moved about by unconscious forces but conscious beings free to choose, no matter what the circumstances. Although a culture pressures its members to act in prescribed ways, people have an innate capacity to rise above the pressures of culture and become agents of their own actions. Sartre posited that individuals are transcendental subjects (Being-in-itself) located in a realm of consciousness beyond the realm of things and culture (Being-for-itself). He believed that our freedom to act is absolute (but see Klockars, 1998, who held that the idea of absolute freedom is tempered in Sartre's later writings.). In situations of imprisonment and torture, the area for possible action may be very small, but as long as individuals retain the lucidity of consciousness, they can still exercise their freedom by saying "no."

In the existential view of the responsible agent, people are understood to be autonomous decision makers with the capacity to stand outside the beliefs and assumptions of their culture and to choose independently what actions to take. Individuals are the agents of their practices and their lives. To be an agent is to assume authorship of your own actions and to accept the responsibility for what you do.

[Agency is] the realized capacity of people to act upon their world and not only know about or give personal or intersubjective significance to it. That capacity is the power of people to act purposively and reflectively, in more or less complex interrelationship with one another, to reiterate and remake the world in which they live, in circumstances where they may consider different courses of action possible and desirable, though not necessarily from the same point of view. (Inden, 1990, p. 23)

These ideas of agency and individual responsibility are embedded in the Western culture, its judicial system, and the judgments made about people's actions. Individuals are expected to exercise control over their lives. Being free to choose their actions, they are blamed for their bad acts and credited for their good ones. In this view, practices originate within the individuals and are carried out through bodily movements.

The practice theorists reject Sartre's idea of the undetermined consciousness of the individual. The existential position of free agency has lost currency in recent decades, having been overruled by social science objectivist explanations of human practice. The practice theorists oppose Sartre's position for concealing people's embeddedness in the world.

The Culture as Author of Practice

In the two-term, subject/person versus object/culture explanations of human action, one term dominates the other. In the subject-as-author position, culture gives superficial labels to deep-seated, universal human needs and then provides superficial rituals for meeting those needs. To put it another way, culture is a veneer covering a common human nature, and people from different cultures can relate to and understand one another by getting beneath it. This section discusses the alternative viewpoint in two-term explanations, in which the cultural object is held to control human behavior. This has become the prevailing perspective in the social sciences, overlapping to some extent the psychological theory that human behavior is controlled by objective reinforcements.

Well into the past century, the person-as-author position was dominant in the West. Through trade and exploration, Europeans had long been aware that other peoples of the world held different beliefs and did things in different ways. Their interest in these differences was heightened by the rise of colonization in the nineteenth century. First through letters from travelers published in newspapers and then through anthropological studies, the people in the West became increasingly aware of cultural differences. The general attitude in the Western sphere was that other cultures were primitive and less developed than their own, and it was the duty of the West to spread its higher culture throughout the world.

Within many of the social sciences, the view of other cultures as being less developed and therefore inferior gradually changed to growing recognition that they were merely different. The realization that understandings of the world and what and how people do things vary from culture to culture (and from one historical period to another) challenges the concept of a universal human nature. Wittgenstein (1969) noted that our understanding of the world is not a product of independent rational thought, but a cultural inheritance.

> But I did not get my picture of the world by satisfying myself of its correctness; nor do I have it because I am satisfied with its correctness. No: it is the inherited background against which I distinguish between true and false. (p. 15)

The notion that practices, even our own, are embedded in a particular culture weakens the claim that they were founded on "real" knowledge of the world, while the practices of others were based on error and superstition.

The scholarly study of other cultures was taken up as the focus of anthropology and required field visits to "primitive" sites. As field sites were used up, anthropologists extended the idea of culture to include our own culture and its institutions, such as schools, self-help groups, and courtship practices (Holland et al., 1998). Brown (1991), an anthropologist, provided a definition of culture that can serve for the following discussion.

> Culture consists of the conventional patterns of thought, activity, and artifact that are passed on from generation to generation in a manner that is generally assumed to involve learning rather than specific genetic programming. . . . [Culture] is thought of as attached to collectivities rather than isolated individuals. This de-emphasis of the individual stems not from an anthropological belief that individuals do not create culture, but from the observation that any given individual receives more culture than he or she creates. (p. 40)

In the position of culture as the author of practice, culture is held to have an independent, objective existence. It is a separate reality, consisting of sets of rules about how people should behave, plans of social organization, understandings of the world, and ideas about what is valuable. Every culture molds its members' consciousness in its own way to produce the kind of human subjectivity it requires. What the subject-as-author view held to be a universal human nature is only a local cultural construction. The view of culture as an independent object leaves little room for human agency. People's subjectivities are constructed by their cultures, and people's practices are simply enactments of culturally provided, scripted instructions. Because these scripts are internalized in childhood, members of a culture are not aware that they are playing roles. Cultures define and determine their members' experienced needs, and they provide their own network of concepts though which their members think.

A culture also provides a system for communication and interaction for its members. Its symbolic systems—the arts, science, religion, and language—shape the members' understanding of reality and establish and maintain social hierarchies. Culture mediates practices by connecting individuals and groups to institutional hierarchies. It builds up a fund of practices that its members absorb as embodied skills and pretheoretical action strategies.

It is difficult for members of one culture to understand the practices of another. People cannot simply step out of or rise above their culture's depiction of the world. Winch (1958) held that cultures were incommensurate and that the only way to understand the practices of another culture was to go inside it. The culture-as-object view tends to regard a culture's repertoire of practices as unified and static. Studies based on this position rely on categories postulated by scientific theory rather than local knowledge. Explanations based on the latter are generally disregarded.

In the 1950s and 1960s, Lévi-Strauss (1958/1963; 1962/1972) developed an analysis of the formal structure of culture. He contended that the existential view of Sartre was not only wrong but diametrically opposed to the correct view, which is that subjectivity is an illusion. "To promote private preoccupations to the rank of philosophical problems is dangerous and may end in a kind of shop-girl philosophy" (Lévi-Strauss, 1955/1961, p. 62). Lévi-Strauss also called the idea of an individual subject "the spoilt brat of philosophy" (Sarup, 1993, p. 1). As he saw it, the goal of the human sciences should not be to constitute the human subject but to dissolve it. His search was for the objective structures of culture.

Lévi-Strauss was intrigued with the structural method used by de Saussere (1907–1911/1966) and Jakobson and Halle (1956) in their studies of language, which they approached as an object that existed independently of any speaker. Language has a grammatical structure and a system of signs that produced the speech uttered by individual subjects. Rather than examining the extensive variability of spoken language, de Saussere and Jakobson and Halle believed a scholar should look beneath this buzzing surface manifestation to where the stable and objective rules and signs of language are to be found. Lévi-Strauss held that examining culture with the structural approach developed to investigate language would raise the human studies to the level of a science. Because he considered all of human culture to be an extension of language, he could ask:

Whether the different aspects of social life (including even art and religion) cannot be only studied by the methods of, and with the help of concepts similar to those employed in linguistics, but also whether they do not constitute phenomena whose inmost nature is the same as language? (quoted in Hawkes, 1977, p. 33)

Lévi-Strauss believed not only that there are independent cultural structures but that all cultural structures share a common characteristic: the binary oppositional form. That is to say, they have all been built out of oppositions; for example, cooked versus raw. He came to the conclusion that the binary opposites in culture are reflections of the binary nature of language and the binary nature of the human mind.

Lévi-Strauss described his linguistically derived binary architecture of cultural structures in *Structural Anthropology* (1958/1963). The linguistic theories of Saussure and Jakobson held that the words and sounds of language were organized as binary oppositions. The binary opposition of words appears in dichotomies such as *light* versus *dark, male* versus *female, human* versus *animal, horizontal* versus *vertical,* and so on. The binary opposition of sounds can be found, for example, in voiced versus unvoiced consonants. Saussure's structural analysis of language made a distinction between words (signifiers) and the things in the "real" world that they signify. These "real" things can be divided into physical objects and cultural practices. The notion that "real" physical objects and language are structured in the same way is questionable, but the idea of the social realm or culture having a linguistic structure is more plausible. Lévi-Strauss proposed that the realities of the social world are constituted through language and therefore have the same architecture as language. Because he believed that binary opposition is the fundamental structure of every part of language (the phonological, sentence, and semantic structures) and that all languages have the same fundamental structure, he also believed that the structures of the social world in all cultures have the same binary structure. Underneath the diverse cultural structures of kinship, myth, and ritual, a common binary ordering operates.

Another of Lévi-Strauss's binary concepts came from his perception that the mind operates through on and off switches. Developing this idea in *The Savage Mind* (1962/1972), he posited that language has its binary oppositional structure because this is the structure of the human mind. Lévi-Strauss began with the notion that having a language is what differentiates human beings from animals. In his later theory, the binary architecture of language and cultural structures do not determine the organization of the mind, but the mind determines the organization of language and cultural structures.

Lévi-Strauss assumed that the deep binary architecture of language and mind is invariant; therefore, it is applicable to all ages and cultures. In its invariance, it has the universality and stability of the kinds of knowledge developed in the natural sciences. To illustrate, just as the structure of the heart is the same in every human being, so the binary linguistic and mental structure is present in all of us and in our cultural structures. And as an individual person does not determine the structure of his or her heart, Lévi-Strauss's theories bypass individual agents of practice. Individuals are simply the vehicles through which the binary ordered cultural structures produce their practices.

Lévi-Strauss's structuralist ideas and Sartre's existentialism have been criticized by the theorists of practice as well as others. Leach (1974) observed that the linguistic model borrowed from Jakobson is outmoded. "Present day [1974] theoreticians in the field of structural linguistics have come to recognize that . . . speech utterances must depend on mechanisms of much greater complexity than is suggested by the digital computer model which underlies the Jakobson-Lévi-Strauss theories" (p. 126). Seung (1982) held that Lévi-Strauss overlooked or even suppressed cultural differences in his attempt to prove the universal binary character of all myths and cultures. The universals that Lévi-Strauss claimed to have found now appear to be local, functionally determined attributes of particular individuals or cultural groups. No matter how contradictory the evidence might be, Lévi-Strauss always managed to force it into the predetermined theory he had devised. As Leach wrote, "His [Lévi-Strauss'] writings display increasing tendency to assert *as dogma* that his discoveries relate to facts which are *universal* characteristics of the unconscious process of human thought" (p. 131).

PRACTICE THEORY

In the past several decades, there has been a "critical disruption" (Holland et al., 1998, 23) or "retheorization" (Ortner, 1999, p. 6) in the study of culture. The traditional view of culture as a homogeneous object, without development, as bounded, and without internal power conflicts, has been rejected. Geertz's (1955) description of the questions raised against the traditional understanding of culture provides the context for the development of practice theory.

> Questions rained down, and continue to rain down, on the very idea of a cultural scheme. Questions about the coherence of life-ways, the degree to which they form connected wholes. Questions about their homogeneity, the degree to which everyone in a tribe, a community, or even a family (to say nothing of a nation or civilization) shares similar beliefs, practices, habits, feelings. Questions about the discreteness, the possibility of specifying where one culture . . . leaves off and the next . . . begins. Questions about continuity and change, objectivity and proof, determinism and relativism,

uniqueness and generalization, description and explanation, consensus and conflict, otherness and commensurability—and about the sheer possibility of anyone, insider or outsider, grasping so vast a thing as an entire way of life. . . . Anthropologists, or anyway the sort that studies cultures, proceeds amid charges of irrelevance, bias, illusion, and impracticability. (p. 43)

Feminist scholars have also noted that many anthropological descriptions were impositions that accorded privilege to one group over another. "Feminists, then, provide yet another basis for suspecting descriptions of seemingly holistic, coherent, integrated cultures" (Holland et al., 1998, p. 25).

Practice theorists offer a corrective response to the way culture has traditionally been viewed. They propose that cultures are not unities but composites of various groups with conflicting interests. Members of a culture are not all alike; they exhibit individual differences. Cultures are not static; they undergo change. There is latitude within a culture that allows for improvisation and creativity in determining practices.

Practice theorists hold that culture determines people's actions and practices to varying degrees. However, their view of culture is quite different from the traditional one, and their works contain reactions against and corrections of the concept of a unified culture. Certeau (1980/1988) wrote that the traditional view of culture is equivalent to looking down on a New York City street from the top of the World Trade Center (written prior to 9/11). From this height, one cannot see the details of urban life. Such an elevated vantage point puts the viewer at a distance; "to be a solar Eye, looking down like a god. . . . The fiction of knowledge is related to this lust to be a viewpoint and nothing more" (p. 92). What is seen from on high is an optical artifact, "a projection that is a way of keeping aloof" (pp. 91–92).

Ordinary practitioners live at ground level, and their practice takes place amidst the tumult and noise of human society. "The networks of these moving, intersecting writings [practices] compose a manifold story that has neither author nor spectator, shaped out of fragments of trajectories and alterations of spaces" (p. 93). "Within this ensemble, I shall try to locate the practices that are foreign to the 'geometrical' or 'geographical' space of visual, panoptic, or theoretical constructions" (p. 93).

Practice theorists position themselves within the world of practice. Rather than looking for the universal and unchanging properties of human beings or cultures, they adjust their lens to bring the diverse ways people do things into sharper focus. From on high, one can discern a separation between person and culture. For a clear view of practice, one must be close to it. Only then can one see diverse activities, specialized as well as ordinary, being carried out by heterogeneous groups of people with common interests, rather than homogeneous crowds operating from a single internalized cultural logic.

One sees conflicts between groups and notes that they possess different levels of power. One sees that individuals belong to multiple groups, and as they move in and out of them, they adapt their actions accordingly.

Practice theorists are interested in what is being done. Generally speaking, they are not looking for eternal verities outside of the activities and practices they investigate or for the essence of humanity or of culture. They recognize, perhaps begrudgingly, that they themselves are not looking down from above. As they are engaged in their own practice, their field of vision is limited by their locality. Although they understand that human subjectivity and practice are limited by a variety of culturally internalized controls, they are committed to the value of human freedom. They realize, however, that the notion of absolute freedom is untenable because actions can only take place within a social context. They differ on how much freedom is possible in human practice.

The ideas of two scholars of practice, Bourdieu and Certeau, will be discussed in the following section. Their use of the term *practice* refers to ordinary, everyday activities in which people engage. Previous investigations of human activity have often disregarded or overlooked these practices and the special situational logic that informs them. To shed light on these everyday practices, practice theorists employ a descriptive form of inquiry that differs from the disciplined measurement required by the exact sciences.

Bourdieu

Bourdieu, a French sociologist, is one of the foremost investigators of practice. He is interested in the everyday or ordinary practical activity of people. His investigations were aimed at describing how people do what they do by a "systematic exploration of the 'unthought categories of thought which delimit the thinkable and predetermine the thought'" (Bourdieu & Wacquant, 1992, p. 40). Bourdieu proposed his view as a move beyond the two opposing theoretical approaches to practice—the subjectivist approach and the objectivist approach. As an alternative to these approaches, he offered a relational approach. This is a mode of thinking that "identifies the real not with substances, but with relationships" (Bourdieu, 1984, p. 22). Relational thinking is not simply a middle road between subjectivism and objectivism, but the way to a new area of understanding that sheds light on human practices.

Bourdieu's break with subjective forms of understanding practice resulted from his belief that all human action is situated within determining structures that are not readily available to everyday consciousness (Swartz, 1997). He identifies three forms of subjectivist knowledge: Sartre's existentialism, rational actor theory, and the micro-approaches of social action. In Sartre's voluntarism and rational actor theory, actor decisions are abstracted from their social context. The micro-approaches, such as ethnomethodology, symbolic interactionism, and phenomenology, which build on actor accounts of their actions, fail to link face-to-face interaction and meaning systems to larger patterns of social arrangements. The only reality that subjectivism recognizes is that which is perceived through ordinary experience.

Objectivist forms of understanding, such as positivism, Lévi-Strauss's structuralism, and theoreticism, fail to note that practices constitute and generate social structures as well as being determined by them. Positivism often describes people's actions in the form of statistical regularities, which are constructed by the social scientist because they are seldom visible to the actors themselves. However, it is the action of individuals that is being described statistically, and it is the action of individuals that brings about changes in the described regularities. Bourdieu held that although actor perceptions are not enough in themselves, they need to be included in a comprehensive framework of explanation of practice. The structuralism of Lévi-Strauss reduces action to the mere execution of a nonhistorical, theoretical model. Although objective social structures exist, social action "both originates and develops in the *practical mastery* of those structures" (Swartz, 1997, p. 59). In theoreticism, a theoretical explanation is substituted for the mastery or intelligence practitioners employ in their actions. It is an "intellectualist fallacy" to conflate "the model of the reality [with] the reality of the model" (Bourdieu, 1972/1977). In the theoreticism mode of understanding, the formal properties of a theory are projected onto the informal world of everyday practices.

In place of the subjectivist and objectivist modes, Bourdieu proposed a relational mode for understanding practice. He opposes what he calls "substantialist" thinking, which "privileges substances over relationships" as "it treats the properties attached to agents—occupation, age, sex, qualifications—as *forces* independent of the relationship within 'which they act.'" (Bourdieu, 1984, p. 22). Substantialist thinking is present in positivism, phenomenology, and humanist/existentialist approaches, which tend to reify the attributes of individuals and groups by detaching them from their historical and social contexts. Like Lévi-Strauss, Bourdieu (1968) looked to structural linguistics as a model for relational thinking. There, words are not meaningful in and of themselves but draw their meaning from the relational contrast with other words. Relational thinking focuses on networks or bundles of relationships, such as a field or habitus. Understanding relationships cannot occur through linear thinking; it requires a kind of systemic thought. Relational thinking is not the same as the common practice in sociology of transforming the attributes of individuals or groups into variables. Substantialist thinking extracts the object of inquiry from the context of ordinary assumptions and perceptions, which forms the practical knowledge of social life and transforms it into an object of scientific knowledge (Bourdieu, Chambordedon, & Passeron, 1991).

Bourdieu assumed that relationships are basically competitive rather than cooperative and hierarchical rather than equalitarian. I think Bourdieu placed too much emphasis on a conflict view of practical actions, in which actors' primary motivations are to raise themselves above others and to dominate them. He also tends to overemphasize the fact that practitioner actions are unconscious rather than reflective and that practitioners misperceive why they do what they do.

Habitus. Bourdieu's personal stamp on practice theory is his concept of 'habitus'. Practices are the consequence of interaction between an individual's historically developed dispositions (habitus) and a specific field of contention. Bourdieu's use of habitus is different from the psychological notion of habit. In psychological theory, the term *habit* refers to a virtually automatic, mechanical, programmed response to a stimulus or situation. Habitus is a person's learned disposition to use similar strategies in the performance of actions across a variety of situations. Contrary to the psychological view that personality traits and dispositions are genetically determined, Bourdieu believed that one's habitus is not innate; rather, it is a consequence of socialization by family and friends. Habitus is Bourdieu's approach to overcoming the traditional individual-society, subject-object dualism that has been used to explain human action. While psychology has focused on looking at the individual human actor, sociology, political science, and economics have focused on structures beyond the individual. Bourdieu locates practice in the confluence of individual and structure that he conceptualizes as habitus.

Human actions flow from a person's habitus. They are not the consequences of following sets of socially embedded rules or norms that people simply enact. Instead, habitus depicts actions as the manifestation of people's strategies about how to achieve what they want. The idea of strategy recognizes the importance of agency in people's actions, but agency carried out within the limits of an internalized understanding of the possibilities and impossibilities inherent in a situation. Strategy also takes into account the timing of an action. Unlike rule-governed explanations, strategic actions are responsive to when an action is done. "To restore to practice its practical truth, we must therefore reintroduce time into the theoretical representation of a practice which, being temporally structured, is intrinsically defined by its *tempo*" (1972/1977, p. 8). The effectiveness of an action depends not merely on its being done but also on its being done at the right time. Thus, practices are timed actions that are deferred until the appropriate occasion. "To substitute *strategy* for the *rule*, is to reintroduce time, with its rhythm, its orientation, its irreversibility" (1972/1977, p. 9).

Most often, strategic action is not the result of conscious calculation, but an expression of the practical dispositions of one's habitus. Practical dispositions incorporate the ambiguities and uncertainties inherent in acting at a particular time and in a particular place. "Bourdieu employs the language 'practical knowledge' and 'sense of practice' to describe this fundamentally nonformalized, practical dimension of action. . . . Actors are not rule followers or norm obeyers, but strategic improvisers who respond dispositionally to the opportunities and constraints offered by various situations" (Swartz, 1997, p. 100).

One's habitus affects what one attends to in the world and others, as well as what one considers being reasonable or unreasonable. It is acted out in the cognitive, evaluative, and bodily dimensions of one's being. It is manifested in the way one speaks as well as in one's physical manners and style; for example, in posture and stride. It is expressed in our verbal and nonverbal communication and in our tastes, values, perceptions, and modes of reasoning. It is the master pattern that cuts across all of our activity. These master patterns, however, serve action through "a kind of practical generalization" (1980/1990, p. 94). They can be transferred by analogy to areas beyond those in which they were learned and adjusted to various situations in which one has to act. Bourdieu suggested that these master patterns of activity are like a person's handwriting, which embodies an individual style that is apparent in the various kinds of writing in which a person engages.

The habitus of each individual in the same group bears a close resemblance to those of the others. Because members of a group internalize much of the same learning and many of the same experiences, their "'personal style', the particular stamp marking all the products of the same habitus, . . . is never more than a *deviation* in relation to the *style* of a period or class so that it relates back to the common style not only by its conformity . . . but also by the difference which makes the whole 'manner'" (Bourdieu, 1972/1977, p. 86). Among people with similar backgrounds, a common tradition is transmitted to each individual, although sometimes this only occurs through language. The common tradition can become part of a person's habitus through tacit or embodied processes; an example is a child who imitates the batting stance of a baseball player, but adjusts the stance to fit his or her height and dexterity. Bourdieu's notion that the commonalities in people's actions are the result of common learning is his response to the idea that similar behavior among members of a group indicates that they are all following the same set of internalized social rules.

A person's habitus resists change. It always responds to present situations in terms of past experiences. Bourdieu considered the early formation of internal dispositions to be more significant than subsequent experiences in setting a person's habitus. Although people adapt to new situations, they still make use of defensive strategies that are consistent with their original dispositions. "There is an ongoing adaptation process as habitus encounters new situations, but this process tends to be slow, unconscious, and tends to elaborate rather than alter fundamentally the primary disposition" (Swartz, 1997, p. 107).

In the main, actions are expressions of one's habitus. However, Bourdieu understood that the habitus is not the only source of actions, and under certain circumstances it may be superceded, for example, in situations of crisis that disrupt the immediate adjustment of habitus to the field or by other principles such as rational and conscious computation (Bourdieu, 1987/1990). In situations where material interests are the foremost concern or there is eminent danger of violence, responses are formalized, and actions are not usually determined by the habitus of the individual. Even so, Bourdieu held that an individual's habitus can still influence his or her actions under such circumstances.

In summary, in Bourdieu's concept of habitus, a person's practice disposition to act in particular ways shapes his or her practice. One's habitus is formed by the internalization of external social structures and individual experience, particularly during early childhood. Just as one internalizes the rules of a language that normally operate out of awareness, so do they internalize the categories and ideas of their society. Like the nonconscious understanding of a language, the nonconscious understanding of the social world provides the structure that produces coherence to a person's practices. This nonconscious understanding forms the individual's responses to the solicitations of their social and physical environments. Command of a language enables a person to generate new sentences in response to varying situations; the structures of the habitus enable one to cope with constantly changing situations. Although social understandings are internalized in individuals, like language they transcend any particular person. The habitus has deep structures that function in a manner similar to Chomsky's deep structure, except that instead of being biologically invariant, the deep structures of the habitus are historically constituted, institutionally grounded, and therefore socially variable (Bourdieu, 1987/1990).

> [Habitus is] a system of durable, transposable dispositions, structured structures predisposed to function as structuring structures, that is, as principles which generate and organize practices and representations that can be objectively adapted to their outcomes without presupposing a conscious aiming at ends or an express mastery of the operation necessary in order to attain them. (1980/1990, p. 53)

Fields. The second major concept that Bourdieu used to explain practice is 'fields'. Fields are the spaces or social arenas in which actions take place. They include such areas as the field of law, the field of teaching, and the field of psychotherapy. They also include the professions of fashion design, publishing, writing, and other arenas of competitive action. Bourdieu (in Bourdieu & Wacquant, 1992) said, "We can, with caution, compare a field to a game although, unlike the latter, a field is not the product of a deliberate act of creation, and it follows rules or, better regularities, that are not explicit and codified."

The example Bourdieu used was a card game in which participants compete for stakes that can be won. The competition can become ferocious, but only because the players have come to believe in the worth of the game and its stakes. Players bring money or capital to invest or bet in the game in the hope that they will come away with a profit.

One of Bourdieu's intriguing ideas is to extend the concept of 'capital' from an exclusive reference to money to one that encompasses all forms of power. He distinguishes four different types of capital: (a) economic (money and property), (b) cultural (cultural goods and services, including educational credentials), (c) social (acquaintances and networks), and (d) symbolic (legitimization). Of the four, Bourdieu gave particular attention to the concept of 'cultural capital', which is embodied in a person's habitus. Cultural capital is *accumulated* through a socialization process that cultivates dispositions to appreciate and understand music, art, literature, and science, as well as various forms of popular culture. It is often manifested in the accumulation of cultural objects, such as recordings of music, works of art, a personal library, and a collection of scientific instruments. The investment of parents and others in sensitizing a child to cultural distinctions pays dividends in schools, which favor students with large accruals of cultural capital. Parents can convert their economic capital into cultural capital for their children in the form of educational credentials. The children can then convert these credentials back into economic capital by using them to achieve high-paying jobs.

Different fields or games place different values on different kinds of capital. For example, in the intellectual field, cultural capital is valued more than economic capital, while in the business field, the values are reversed. Dominant and subordinate positions within a field are determined by the unequal distribution of capital, not by the personal attributes of the participants. Fields impose a specific form of struggle on the players. What counts as winning a hand or moving up depends on the particular game. By entering a field, a player tacitly accepts the rules of the game. For example, in the academic game, the rules of tenure define winning in terms of the quantity of publications; in the lawyering game, the rules for partnership give value to billable hours. Fields have relative autonomy and are best understood when studied internally. External influences such as a changing market are retranslated into the internal logic of a field.

No matter what the field may be, the dispositions and strategies (habitus) of the actors will influence how they play the game. Bourdieu held that practice is motivated by the desire to maximize one's capital. In his approach, the study of practice focuses on how and under what conditions individuals and groups invest their capital to enhance their position in a particular field. What practices are carried out depends on the dispositions and strategies of our habitus and the rules of the game in which we are competing. Habitus is the disposition to act in certain ways, but actual actions take place in various fields. Thus, practice occurs when one's habitus interacts with the field in which one is engaged.

Practice. Practice is the result neither of rigid mechanical causation nor of an algorithm that allows for only one predetermined response to an environmental stimulus. Instead, practice has a certain plasticity stemming from the fuzziness, irregularity, and even incoherencies of its dispositional principles. "Practice has a logic which is not that of the logician" (1980/1990, p. 86), and there are certain principles of the logic of practice that elude theoretical apprehension. Practice is neither precise nor organized according to the principles of formal logic; therefore, the method for its study needs to be polymorphic, supple, and adaptable, rather than defined, calibrated, and rigid. *"Habitus is in cahoots with the fuzzy and the vague;* . . . it follows a *practical logic,* that of the fuzzy, of the more-or-less, which defines the ordinary relation to the world" (Bourdieu & Wacquant, 1992, p. 22).

Bourdieu's investigations of practice led him to the conclusion that much of everyday, ordinary human activity is nondeliberative and guided by our dispositions to act in certain ways in certain situations. In exploring the operations of the habitus, he found that practical reasoning is indeed practical rather than rational, prereflective rather than conscious, embodied as well as cognitive, durable though adaptive, reproductive though generative and inventive, and the product of particular social conditions though transposable to others (Bourdieu & Wacquant, 1992).

Some (see Collins, 1993) have perceived Bourdieu's view as being a kind of social determinism in that a person's habitus is an internalization of the worldview, social organization, values, and power relationships of his or her own culture, and that as such it established boundaries for personal action. Hoy (1999), however, detects hints of an emancipatory theme in Bourdieu's later writings. There Bourdieu refers to his investigations as a socioanalysis. He believed that, as in psychoanalysis, knowledge itself can dispel the myths that perpetuate domination (Bourdieu & Wacquant, 1992, p. 51).

> Habitus is not the fate that some people read into it. Being a product of history, it is an *open system of dispositions* that is constantly subjected to experiences, and therefore constantly affected by them in a way that either reinforces or modifies its structures. It is durable but not eternal. (Bourdieu & Wacquant, 1992, p. 133)

Bourdieu considered his writing as a form of critical resistance to our internalized habitus. If domination of one's imposed habitus is to be resisted, it must first be revealed. The habitus structures how a person understands the world, but it does not remove every vestige of freedom. By learning how the habitus tends to narrow the range of apparent possibilities, a person may be able to see other options and resist the compulsion to conform (Hoy, 1999).

Certeau

Certeau's *The Practice of Everyday Life* (1980/1988) was published the same year as Bourdieu's *The Logic of Practice* (1980/1990). Both argued that the use of scientific models that seek to understand culture by defining its elements through laws of identity, equivalence, and noncontradiction and then organizing these elements into a coherent category system are unable to account for the everyday practices of human actors. Using constructions based on what appears through the lens of scientific logic, these models are unable to account for actions that follow a practical logic based on timing and circumstance. They either overlook or disregard as noise the apparently unsystematic ordinary activities of daily life. Certeau commented that the exact sciences of nature have to refine their logic continually to account for the unpredictable and microscopic movements of nonhuman phenomena. Moreover, "the social sciences, whose object is still more 'subtle' and whose tools are much cruder, would have to defend their models (that is, their ambition to dominate and control) by exorcising" the unpredictable happenings by creating a stable reality behind what appears (de Certeau, 1980/1988, p. 59).

Both Certeau and Bourdieu held that differences in power between groups and individuals exist in the social world. Bourdieu focused on the strategies people and groups use to maximize and retain their power through the accumulation and exchange of kinds of capital. The manner in which they go about this is shaped by internalized dispositions (habitus) that reflect the class or group in which the individual was socialized. Arguing against Bourdieu's concept of habitus Certeau held that it is an "assumed reality" (1980/1988, p. 58) invented to account for flexibility within the principles and rules that sociologists use to explain behavior. By placing this flexibility in a theoretical structure (habitus) inscribed in a person's memory, Bourdieu sidesteps the task of analyzing the tactics people actually employ in their various actions. "The blanket Bourdieu's theory throws over tactics as if to put out their fire by certifying their amenability to socioeconomic rationality or as if to mourn their death by declaring them unconscious, should teach us something about their relationship to any theory" (p. 59).

Certeau's assessment of practical logic was more positive than Bourdieu's. Bourdieu wrote of the weakness of practical logic and its use of analogical reasoning in contrast to the exactness of scientific logic. Because the practitioner is required to make immediate responses with little information, he held that practice must make use of its own kind of analog logic. In situations of insecurity and misfortune, individuals are often reduced to seeking ways to maximize a purely "magic profit" (Bourdieu, 1980/1990, p. 264). Bourdieu also cautioned against the "demon of analogy" at work in practical logic, a demon that can "possess" those who make use of it (Ahearne, 1995, p. 151). Certeau, however, saw a worthwhile flexibility in practical logic's multiple forms.

While Bourdieu focused on how individuals and groups function to gain power and capital, Certeau's major theme in *The Practice of Everyday Life* (1980/1988) is the survival tactics that the weak or less powerful can employ in everyday life. In part, Certeau's work is a correction of Foucault's picture of a fully controlled modern society in *Discipline and Punish* (1975/1979). Foucault contended that since the Enlightenment, disciplinary procedures in the social world have grown to such an extent that no space remains for individual agency in our contemporary technologized society. The machinery of control manifests itself in dossiers, timetables, and grids (and now computer surveillance), providing a panoptic watchfulness that ensures everyone's proper behavior. These disciplining functions have become so internalized that people now monitor and discipline themselves, exercising self-control to ensure that they act appropriately. The docile and passive members of society have been molded into a total homogeneous controlled body. Certeau asks, "If it is true that the grid of 'discipline' is everywhere becoming clearer and more extensive, it is all the more urgent to discover how an entire society resists being reduced to it" (1980/1988, p. xiv).

Certeau held that Foucault's idea of a seamless web of social discipline is mistaken. Instead, he found openings in the social fabric that are not controlled by the society's disciplining operations. It is in these openings that Certeau's everyday practices are carried out, subverting and redirecting the dominating disciplinary practices of the institutions of control. Certeau identified an internal tension in contemporary technified society between the operators or managers and the objects operated on or the managed. The managers exercise power over the managed, directing them to carry out certain actions (Feenberg, 2000). Certeau used the terms *producer* and *consumer* euphemistically to refer to those who exercise power and those on whom the power is exercised. The thought and worldview of these two groups are quite different. The managers or producers think strategically, while the managed or consumers think tactically. Certeau is not interested in the individual agents of production or the individual agents of consumption but in the processes they use in their actions.

The concepts of 'strategy' and 'tactics' are the best known of Certeau's ideas. Bourdieu uses the term *strategy* to describe the habitus's adaptation to situations. For Certeau, 'strategy' refers to the kind of practice in which dominant institutions and groups exercise their power. Dominant groups include governments, manufacturers, academic institutions, third-party payers, professional organizations, and any other groups that exercise control over how things are to be done by those under their control. For example, managed health care organizations decide what activities practitioners of care are allowed to perform; academic institutions determine what counts as scholarly research; and professional organizations establish codes for proper behavior.

Dominant groups employ strategic thinking to establish a power base. "As in management, every 'strategic' rationalization seeks first of all to distinguish its 'own' place, that is, the place of its own power and will, from an environment" (de Certeau, 1980/1988, p. 36). Having established a boundary around the space in which it exercises control, a dominant group employs panoptic practices that "can transform foreign forces into objects that can be observed and measured, and thus [can] control and 'include' them within its scope of vision" (p. 36). Thus, strategies gain control by creating a protective zone in which the environment can be rendered predictable and therefore manageable. Operating within the zone, a dominant group has the advantage in relations with the targets or threats from outside the established boundaries (for example, customers or competitors and enemies). Certeau writes, "I call *strategy* the calculation (or manipulation) of power relationships that becomes possible as soon as a subject with will and power (a business, an army, a city, a scientific institution) can be isolated" (pp. 35–36). Strategies are the operations employed by groups or individuals in power to control knowledge, structure social life, and maintain order.

In addition to the strategic practices of dominance, Certeau looked for other practices that operate underneath the disciplining practices of social control. What he found was a form of practice that resists domination in which a nonstrategic type of reasoning—tactical reasoning—was used. Tactical practices, Certeau's practices of everyday life, are employed by those who are under the control of a dominant group. While Foucault pictured the controlled members of society as passive and submissive, Certeau observed them making use of openings in the social fabric to engage in everyday practices that subverted or redirected the rules of behavior established by the dominant institutions. Tactical practices exist as an indeterminate set of largely unremarkable activities. Certeau's aim was to bring attention to the operations of these everyday activities so that their logic could be delineated and articulated. "Tactics refers to the set of practices that strategies have not been able to domesticate" (Buchanan, 2000, p. 89). They offer daily proof of the limitations of strategic control and "constitute the irreducible mark of the human subject within the [social] order" (Ahearne, 1995, p. 159). Tactics make clever use of breaks in the boundaries of dominantly imposed order to open new symbolic and conceptual spaces.

Tactics are marginalized by the Western form of rationality; they "give us back what our culture has excluded from its discourse" (de Certeau, 1980/1988, p. 50). Tactics appear when one looks at what people make of "products" and how they use what is produced for them.

> For example, the analysis of the images broadcast by television (representation) and the time spent watching television (behavior) should be complemented by a study of what the cultural consumer "makes" or "does" during this time and with the images. . . . The "making" in question is a production, a *poiesis*—but a hidden one, because it is scattered over areas defined and occupied by systems of production. (de Certeau, 1980/1988, p. xii)

Marginal individuals and groups use tactics as a way of making do within the confines of rules imposed by dominant individuals and groups. However, marginality "today is no longer limited to minority groups, but is rather massive and pervasive. Tactics are the only way the dominated outsiders can express their own power. A tactic depends on timing and involves always being on the watch for opportunities that must be seized "on the wing" (p. xix).

In *The Practice of Everyday Life*, Certeau's purpose was simply to note that the tactics of everyday practices have a discernable form and a knowable logic; he did not set out to delineate and classify the logic of everyday practices. Unlike Bourdieu, Certeau does not locate the source of practical actions in an internalized, out-of-awareness logic; he only goes so far to say that cultural logic is like a menu of already-worked-out actions related to perceived needs from which subjects draw. He does suggest that this logic is related to the practical intelligence *(metis)* described in classical Greek texts. More details about the logic of practical knowing will be provided in a discussion of Aristotle's notion of *phronesis* in chapter 5.

Like Bourdieu, Certeau distinguished the logic of practical knowing from the logic of technical knowing. Practical knowing is responsive to particular persons, times, and situations. Technical knowing constructs category grids and then searches for stable relations between and among the grids. When viewed from the perspective of technical (strategic) knowing, practical (tactical) knowing appears less structured and less precise. Technical knowing offers assurance in advance that an action will necessarily (or with a degree of probability) bring about the intended result; practical knowing does not.

Bourdieu and Certeau both pictured the human realm as a hierarchically ordered sphere in which certain individuals and groups are in positions of power over others. Bourdieu believed that the strategic reasoning of the dominant position had infiltrated the social background of contemporary society.

As a result, the practices of individuals and groups are now governed by the desire to maximize their power and standing within their hierarchies. Individual choices of what activities in which to engage are determined by one's strategic dispositions to act in certain ways (maintained in one's habitus) and the rules of the particular games (fields) one plays. Focusing on gaps in the system of dominance, Certeau found places where people could engage in practices of personal expression. These practices are not intended to win the life games Bourdieu described; they simply provide an opportunity to exercise personal autonomy creatively. According to Certeau, these acts of resistance to dominance employ tactical thinking rather than the strategic thinking used by people and institutions in positions of power.

Certeau's analysis of the difference between the reasoning of those in power and those out of power will resonate with practitioners of care. When activity is thought about strategically, it is defined by the space it occupies on a mapped grid, some examples are the grids of insurance forms, employers' activity sheets, and diagnostic check-off boxes. From a strategic point of view, the worth of a practice is based on its having been scientifically determined to be effective and efficient for a category of situations. The function of strategic thinking is to simplify the understanding of activity so that it can be more easily managed and controlled.

Finding opportunities to exercise practitioner judgment may be difficult in contemporary society. Strategic thinking pervades the organizations in which practitioners of care work. The managers of these organizations are themselves under pressure to see that their institutions employ technologically determined practices. "[There are] powerful mechanisms of social life [that] press us in this direction" (Taylor, 1991, p. 7). Bureaucrats as well as managers and practitioners who recognize individual needs may be required to operate in accordance with rules and regulations that are contrary to their own views. Taylor, however, proposed that "our degrees of freedom are not [reduced to] zero," and there comes a point at which one must consider "whether instrumental reason ought to have a lesser role in our lives than it does" (p. 8).

Practitioners of care can apply their own tactical thinking to the strategically or technically constructed world in which they operate. When thought of tactically, activity appears as unique acts timed to respond to a particular situation. What has worked in similar situations before may not be what is called for at the present situation. In order for practitioners of care working within a dominant organization to perform activities they deem appropriate, they often must use tactical judgment to seize opportunities as they arise. Certeau would call for consumers of research to use the tactics of personal expression in making use of the knowledge that has been produced for them.

SUMMARY

The second and third chapters have traced the emergence of technical (strategic) rationality as the dominant form for determining practical actions in the human realm. Bourdieu and Certeau found little "wiggle room" within our strategically ordered society. For Bourdieu, this "wiggle room" was limited to the strategic moves we can make in the games we are playing; for Certeau there were a few places for tactical moves underneath the dominant order. However, I do not believe our culture is as tightly ordered as they do. Even within the strategically governed spaces, there can be room for personal judgments by practitioners. Certeau limited his investigation to identifying the existence of an alternative approach for thinking about practice. He did not examine the properties of this approach. The next chapter begins such an examination. As the first step in this examination, a case is presented for recognizing significant differences between practices carried out in the human realm from those carried out in the physical realm. The following chapters assemble the characteristics of the kind of decision making required for working productively in the human realm and for administering care to those in need. The chapters draw on Aristotle's notion of *phronesis*, an expanded view of rationality as an embodied process, and Gadamer's idea of reflective understanding.

4

The Realms of Practice

PRACTICE IS ACTIVITY directed toward accomplishing a goal. The practitioner is the subject who directs and engages in the activities aimed at the goal. Which activities will lead to successful accomplishment of the goal depends on the milieu in which the activities are carried out. When practice involves the manipulation and construction of physical objects, knowing how to perform a task requires knowing how physical entities respond to things that are done to them. For example, when the practical project is building a house, one should know about the properties of concrete, wood, roofing, and so on. With knowledge of these properties, one can calculate what and how much of a material is needed and where it should be placed in order to construct a house that will not collapse. When the milieu is organic, the practitioner must know the properties of growth and development that are part of the organic realm. For example, a veterinarian who is called upon in her practice to set a dog's broken leg needs to know the properties of bone growth and the responsiveness of dogs of its size to anesthesia. When the milieu of a practice is the human realm, one need understand not only the ways human beings generally respond to an intervention but also how a particular individual responds to a particular intervention. Thus, practical knowing requires that one take into account the diverse ways entities respond to a practitioner's activity.

Practice is future directed. It is intended to produce something new, to bring about a state that is different from what already exists. Even practices aimed at restoring a prior condition are still directed at making things different from what they are at present. Because of the future direction of practices, the form of practical knowledge is predictive or anticipatory. Practical knowledge about doing something is projective; that is, if you do these things (in this sequence), what you want to bring about will happen. The source of practical knowledge is past practices. The expectation is that what has worked before will work now if the situations are similar. Thus, deciding what to do in a new situation involves recalling a similar one about which the practitioner has practical knowledge. Practical knowledge can be codified into a set of formal rules, or it can be maintained in memory as a set of informal experiences. Codification results from an inductive or experimental process in which sequences that have worked in a particular type of situation in the past (determined under analog or field conditions) are expected to work in situations of the same type in the future. Informal notions are usually derived from one's own personal experiences or from experiences spoken or written about by others.

The usefulness of past experiences of either the formal or informal kind in determining present actions to bring about a future end depends upon how similar the past and present situations are. In the eighteenth century, Hume (1748) argued that there is no perceptual or logical reason to assume that the world will continue to operate in the future as it has in the past.

> Past *experience* can be allowed to give *direct* and *certain* information of those precise objects only, and that precise period of time, which fell under its cognizance: but why this experience should be extended to future times, and to other objects, which for aught we know, may be only in appearance similar: this is the main question of which I would insist. (p. 332)

Hume believed that because no rational argument can prove that the future will be like the past, science, as a rational enterprise, should be restricted to reporting past observations. He rejected Descartes' view that reason provides a firm and reliable foundation for knowledge, arguing instead that our beliefs about the world and religion are merely habitual associations. Nevertheless, while the efficacy of practical knowledge cannot be proved within the view of reason held by Hume, human beings do act on the expectation that what worked in the past will generally work in similar situations in the future. The idea of practice itself is about making changes, but it is clear that while some things change others remain the same. Because practical knowing is based on inferences, it is worthwhile to explore the variations of stability and change in the physical, organic, and human realms.

FORM AND FLUX

The issue of whether reality is primarily stability (form) or change (flux) has been discussed since the beginnings of Western philosophy. The question has been framed as whether the real consists of static and permanent forms and substances or of change and flux. Everyday experience consists of movement and transformations. People and animals move about, the weather changes, and the sun rises and sets. What used to be changes into what is now, and this will change into what will be. The debate is over what is most real, that which remains the same throughout time or that which changes.

Framing the question as a dichotomous choice between form or flux is misinformed and not true to our experience. We experience some things as remaining very stable over time and others as being quite changeable. Although astronomers picture the universe as having undergone a big bang and believe that it is moving outward from a once concentrated mass, the movements of the stars and planets appear stable over time. On the one hand, the practice of sending objects to other planets draws on an assumption that the motion of the planets will remain the same in the future as in the past. On the other hand, the practice of teaching children to read assumes that the way they learn in the seventh grade will not be the same as the way they learned in the first grade. Form and flux are not dichotomous categories; they compose a continuum between the unattainable abstractions of absolute stability and absolute change.

The degree of confidence in practical knowledge is based on assumptions about the relative stability or instability of the situation in which a practice will be carried out. As entities in the physical realm have relative stability over time, practical knowledge is usually sufficient for accomplishing current tasks in this realm. While entities in the organic realm have partial stability, not all of them respond to the same intervention in the same way. Even so, knowledge gained from past experience is likely to work in this realm. Entities in the human realm are the least stable and least like one another. Practical knowledge derived from experience with certain individuals or types of people is less generalizable to current situations in the human realm.

THE REALMS OF PRACTICE

As the organizational complexity of systems in nature increases, they may acquire novel and innovative properties that could not have been predicted on the basis of knowledge about the less complex systems (Miller, 1978). Because different systems have different properties, knowledge of the properties of one system cannot be assumed to hold for others. Husserl identified three primary regions: material nature, animate nature, and souls (or persons). He also stated that each primary region needs its own ontology: physics, somatology, and psychology (Dostal, 1993). Heidegger (1927/1962) held that physical entities have a kind of existence that is different from the kind of existence that human beings have. Physical objects are things and have categorical ontological characteristics, while humans are histories and have existentials as their ontological characteristics. In their dealings with the world, human beings interact differently with one another than they do with objects and tools. Merleau-Ponty (1942/1963) identified three realms, which he called the "physical order," the "vital order," and the "human order." In his book *Living Systems*, Miller (1978) proposed four supralevels of system organization—the "physical realm," the "organic realm," the "human realm," and the "social realm." Miller's four systems, as well as his nomenclature, are used in this chapter.

The Physical Realm

The form-flux debate originated as part of the first Western attempts to explain nature in rational rather than mythological terms. Pre-Socratic philosophers were the first Western thinkers to look for natural and rational explanations for changes and movements in the natural world. Rejecting mythological explanations of phenomena as being the acts of gods with humanlike passions and unpredictable intentions, these philosophers proposed various elements as the unchanging reality behind everyday experiences of change. Their importance for contemporary practice is not in the naive conclusions they reached but in the rational method they developed for uncovering the domain of stability.

Finding the Stable Order. The pre-Socratic philosophers held that a kind of cognitive process, which they termed "reason," was the tool by which stability could be found behind the tumult of everyday experiences. Anyone who uses this tool will necessarily arrive at the same conclusion. Reason is the tool by which diversity of opinion is overcome. Parmenides, born in 515 B.C., provides an example of the use of reason to prove that change is unreal. To combat the notion given by the senses that change is real, he presented the following rational argument. All thought must be about something. It is not possible to think about something that does not exist. Because it is impossible to think about nothing, one cannot hold that something no longer exists. As change requires that something that once existed no longer exists, change is impossible. Contemporary readers are not likely to be convinced by Parmenides' argument; nevertheless, his appeal to use reason as the tool for seeing order behind the flux of ordinary experience has been retained as an essential belief in the Western world.

   Plato (see Jones, 1969) advanced the use of reason as the vehicle to uncover order behind the flux of experience. While people experience movement and change through their senses and take it to be real, this is analogous to seeing shadows on a cave wall and taking them to have substance. Reason leads one to the conclusion that what is real is permanent; the real must exist in the form of stable ideas, rather than in the various imperfect copies that appear in experience. One encounters many different triangles through the senses, but reality lies in an unchanging form or structure through which the notion of triangularity is known.

Beginning with the Enlightenment philosophy in the seventeenth century, the notion of what was permanent was no longer held to be ideal forms or structures but rather the laws of nature. When the movements of nature were viewed properly, it could be seen that they were not random but regular and governed by unchanging mechanical laws. Bacon advanced an inductive form of rationality that could uncover these permanent laws (1620/1994). He found that through careful observation of particulars, one could inductively infer the regular patterns that governed nature. The rational method for uncovering permanent laws beneath the flux of particular experiences has evolved into the current hypothetical-deductive procedures. The process used to determine these laws is based on the assumption that reality consists of elemental particles and that stability is to be found in the relationships present among these separate particles. Although whole entities may appear unstable, stable relationships are revealed when their basic parts are abstracted. Though the specific procedures for determining the permanent order behind experiences have evolved over time, the aim of finding this order has been retained. If objects are governed by permanent laws, then one can be sure that they will respond to future actions as they have in the past. Thereby, practitioners can have certain knowledge that if they act in the specified ways, the results they are seeking will be achieved.

The knowledge for practice that flowed from the escalating discovery of stabilities throughout the physical realm has enabled practitioners (engineers) to transform the physical realm into our technological world of today. This kind of thinking has proved so successful that it has been extolled in contemporary Western society as the only source of valid practical knowledge. The thinking process it employs and the kind of knowledge it generates are deemed useful for practice not only in the physical realm but also in the organic and human realms (see chapter 2). In actuality, when practical knowledge processes are applied in these less stable realms there are limits to its usefulness.

Nevertheless, for practices that involve working with physical objects, when there is sufficient consistency across time, practical knowledge generated through these processes is sufficient to guide successful practice. In the physical realm, practices that have been validated in the past will work in the future. Validated practical knowledge may be lacking for some areas of practice in the physical realm. If this is the case, different actions can be tested under experimental conditions to determine which ones produce the desired result. It is assumed that actions found to work in experiments will produce the same results in practice.

Locating Areas of Flux. The new physics of the early decades of the twentieth century noted that there was disordered movement at the subatomic level of the physical realm. In recent decades, it has been noted that other phenomena, such as weather systems, do not exhibit an order that could be described by traditional mathematics. Among the new theories developed to explain these phenomena was the chaos theory described by Gleick (1987). Gleick observed that the order described by traditional science was derived from the mathematics of mechanical movement. In mechanics, causation is linear, as when one billiard ball transfers its energy to another ball by hitting it. The speed and direction of the second ball after the impact can be calculated by knowing the speed and direction (and friction coefficient) of the first ball. To explain the movements of weather systems, which are nonlinear, requires a more complex mathematics. In nonlinear systems, energy feeds back on itself (the billiard ball shot across the table collides with another ball, and that ball with another, and it collides with the original ball). In nonlinear systems, a different order appears in which very slight variations can be amplified, leading to seemingly unpredictable results. Chaos theory pictures a universe far more sensitive to small changes than is reflected in the traditional view. Proponents of chaos theory contend that those who hold the traditional view are incorrect in assuming that the universe can be studied in pieces.

> Where chaos begins, classical science stops. For as long as the world has had physicists inquiring into the laws of nature, it has suffered a special ignorance about disorder in the atmosphere, in the turbulent sea, in the fluctuations of wildlife populations in the oscillations of the heart and the brain. The irregular side of nature, the discontinuous and erratic side—these have been puzzles to science, or worse, monstrosities. (Gleick, 1987, p. 3)

What Prigogine and Stingers (1984) called "the new science" introduced time and change into the picture of nature. According to them, "Our vision of nature is undergoing a radical change toward the multiple, the temporal, and the complex" (p. xxvii). They also note that science is undergoing a transition from a static and deterministic view of nature to a new theory of dissipative structures based on principles of complexity, self-organization, and order emerging from conditions of nonequilibrium. The introduction of change and time into the view of nature brings about conditions of instability and disorder. Out of the instability, new and more complex forms of order are created.

> For a long time, a mechanistic world view dominated Western science. In this view the world appeared as a vast automaton. We now understand that we live in a pluralistic world. It is true there are phenomena that appear to us as deterministic and reversible, such as the motion of a frictionless pendulum or

the motion of the earth around the sun. Reversible processes do not know any privilege direction of *time*. But there are also irreversible processes that involve an arrow of time. (Prigogine & Stengers, 1984, p. xxvii)

The new science posits that regularities do not hold throughout the physical realm. Therefore, practice in chaotic areas cannot depend on a permanent view of natural laws for knowledge about what should be done to accomplish goals. For example, a decision about how to protect an endangered species cannot be made solely on the basis of what has worked in similar situations. Decisions about practice in these areas need to take into account the whole system in which the practice is to be carried out.

The factor of change that the new science introduces into the view of nature challenges the assumptions on which the search for stable order is based. In most cases, these assumptions have been adequate to guide practice in the physical realm, such as those dealing with nature. The new science notion of change over time has the greatest implications for practice in the organic and human realms. In these realms, modification over time reduces the possibility of knowing that what has worked before will work in the future.

The Organic Realm

Human beings are organic creatures, and in the organic realm there is the possibility of open-ended change. This means that practice in their realm requires additional processes for determining what to do. This section on the organic realm and the following one on the human realm present a view of human beings as temporally developing and changing entities.

Although the developmental changes that occur in the organic realm have some stability, they are not absolutely determinate. Not only are there variations among individuals of the same kind, but there are also variations resulting from the effect of the individual's interaction with the environment. Because knowledge in the organic realm is less certain, practitioners should not be overconfident about the results of their actions. They need to determine whether they have succeeded; if not, it may be necessary to try a different tack. Practice in the organic realm involves an element of trial and error, in that practitioners discover corrective actions to replace those that are unsuccessful.

In the organic realm, individuals should be looked upon as systems in which parts interact and changes in one part affect the system as a whole. Systemic assumptions differ from those that view nature as consisting of separate particles. In the particulate view, entities are investigated by breaking them into analyzable parts and then looking for properties of the parts. Selected properties of people and other organisms are lifted out of the complex in which they are situated. When these properties are removed from their complex, the essential characteristics inherent in their relational participation in the whole system are lost. According to systems theory, a whole system is greater than the sum of its parts, and a whole system exhibits patterns and structures that arise spontaneously from interaction of its parts. In the systems view, the world is composed of interacting systems, and to understand something requires approaching it as a system interlocked with other systems. Higher order properties emerge when less complex systems develop into more complex systems (von Bertalanffy, 1968).

Systems theory makes a fundamental distinction between closed and open systems. Each type of system reacts very differently to changes in its environment. A closed system—for example, a glass jar—does not need to interact with its environment to maintain itself. In contrast, open systems such as organisms and people must interact with their environments in order to maintain their existence. Their openness allows the exchange of information with other systems and the possibility of affecting other systems through their activity.

Open systems are dynamic and evolving; they are historical in that they cannot start over but must move on from where they are. Because of the inter-relatedness that exists among systems, changes that occur in them are often unique and unpredictable. Their processes are often unsteady and cannot be described with universal laws or generalizations. In systems thinking, the notions of uniqueness and individuality are necessary concerns.

Emergence. The idea of emerging systems has been described by Jantsch (1980), who proposed it as a general model of change throughout systems in the universe. He held that in the cosmic, biochemical, organic, human, and social spheres, processes of emergent systems create and tear down the structures that gave them temporary form and organization. Jantsch wrote:

> For more than 2000 years the main interest of Western physics has been devoted to the recognition of structure. From Democritus to our days the search was on for the ultimate building stones of matter, whether they were called atoms, subatomic particles . . . or quarks . . . the idea [proposed by Heisenberg] no longer corresponds to an atomistic view but represents a systemic view which focuses on the relations *between* components, not their individual properties, . . . which leads from a static view—the dissection of matter—to a dynamic one. To the spatial dimensions the time dimension is added. Instead of a timeless structure of matter, the processes of evolving matter moved to the foreground—or, to be even more precise, the evolving organization of matter. (p. 77)

In the theory of emerging systems, activity and process are held to be more basic than objects or things. In the traditional view, which focuses on the static properties of things, objects are held to consist of parts that can be disassembled and reassembled. Understanding a static system involves knowing how its basic elements are combined. Change or movement of a static system has to come from outside; there are no internal processes. In contrast, emergence theory focuses on the structure of processes; that is, the patterns of change. Processes do not interact as things do; they interpenetrate each other and affect changes in their given structural patterns. Processes exist primarily in the mode of becoming rather than being and appear as dynamic rather than static entities. The idea that process, not permanence, is the essential dimension of nature was adopted by the American pragmatist philosophers—Peirce, James, Dewey, and Mead. Browning (1965) has called them the "philosophers of process." In his later period, the American philosopher Whitehead (1929) also turned to process as his basic metaphysical principle. He wrote that "all things flow" and "the flux of things is one ultimate generalization around which we must weave our philosophical system" (chapter 10, part 2).

Self-organizing Systems. From a self-organizing perspective, systems are understood "as a set of coherent, evolving, interactive processes which temporarily manifest in globally stable structures" (Jantsch, 1980, p. 6). The idea of self-organizing systems was first developed from the study of living systems; however, it has become a general theory that is applied to all of nature. The characteristics of the general theory have been described as follows (see Nicolis & Prigogine, 1989):

1. Self-organizing systems are open to exchange of energy or information with their environments. Closed system theories hold that systems tend to wear down and to dissipate their unrecoverable energy. Whatever structure was held in place with this energy dissolves and the system comes to rest as useless entropy or chaos. Self-organizing systems have a dissipative structure in which "order and organization arise spontaneously out of disorder and chaos" (Prigogine & Stengers, 1984, p. xv). Instead of winding down into disorder, dissipative structures reconfigure themselves into new forms of organization that are adaptive to their changing environment.

2. Self-organizing systems undergo continuous change and, thus, are dynamic systems. They are connected to their environments and are in an uninterrupted interaction with them. They have the quality of *auto-poiesis;* that is, they can continuously renew themselves and regulate their interaction in such a way that the integrity of their structure is maintained.

3. Self-organizing systems cannot be understood in isolation because they are themselves contributing parts of larger systems that encompass them. In focusing on a particular self-organizing system, attention must be given to its local interactions, for each system has its own history and is located in a specific environment. Thus, its resiliency is uniquely played out, differing from how another system might maintain itself.

4. Self-organizing systems engage in a mutual exchange of information with the other parts of the larger system in which they are located. They are involved in feedback loops in which their activities affect other systems that in turn affect them in a non-linear way. In self-organizing systems, small-scale interactions can produce large-scale structural changes, a process described by chaos theory. The large-scale changes in turn modify the activity of its parts. The iterative changes through which self-organizing systems evolve require that understanding them needs a historical perspective that acknowledges their temporal development.

5. Self-organizing systems are emergent systems. Emergence calls attention to the unpredictability of higher-level dynamics from knowledge of its constituent, lower-level parts. Emergent phenomena include not only human characteristics such as mind, but also groups, societies, and cultures.

6. Self-organizing systems develop internal structures from information exchanged within themselves and with other systems. Information is a form of energy and it functions to organize matter into temporary forms and structures.

> The function of information is revealed in the word itself: in-*formation*. We haven't noticed information as structure because all around us are physical forms that we can see and touch and that beguile us into confusing the system's structure with its physical manifestation. Yet the real system, that which endures and evolves, is energy. Matter flows through it, assuming different forms as required. When the information changes (as when disturbances increase) a new structure materializes. (Wheatley, 1994, p. 104)

When nature is understood as constantly evolving and dynamic, information is its fundamental ingredient and the key source of its process for creating and altering structures. Information is not a thing or bit of something as it is sometimes pictured in information theory, nor is it a substance or the substance in which it is embedded. Its reality is in changing relationships that exist among substances. Although not a substance, it has the power to create order, prompt growth, and build and tear down structures. Information also has the capacity to generate and replicate itself.

In the organic realm, changes in physical structures are a consequence of changes in the information that organizes the physical material into forms. In this sense, information has life-giving properties. Thus, the understanding of living systems requires a focus on the evolving informational base that constructs and informs the living system. The human DNA information instructs how elements of the physical realm will be formed into the molecules, cells, and bodily structures that produce the kind of existence that can interact with and learn from its environment. Chopra (1989) described the relation that exists between information and matter in humans:

> At any point in the bodymind, two things come together—a bit of information and a bit of matter. Of the two, the information has a longer life span than the solid matter it is matched with. As the atoms of carbon, hydrogen, oxygen, and nitrogen swirl through our DNA, like birds of passage that alight only to migrate on, the bit of matter changes, yet there is always a structure waiting for the next atoms. In fact, DNA never budges so much as a thousandth of a millimeter in its precise structure, because the genomes—the bits of information in DNA—remember where everything goes, all 3 billion of them. This fact makes us realize that memory must be more permanent than matter. What is a cell then? It is a memory that has built some matter around itself, forming a specific pattern. Your body is just the place your memory calls home. (p. 87)

The type of information that affects changes in a self-organizing organism depends on the kind of emergent properties it possesses. Amoebas gather information from chemical stimuli they harvest from smaller organisms, while higher order organisms are able to glean information from sounds and other signs. Dogs can be trained to interpret different vocal sounds as commands for specific actions. Humans have a highly developed capacity to interpret linguistic sounds as denoting various meanings.

Biology and Practice. In the static view of nature, plant and animal species were considered to be permanent; then in the 1860s and 1870s, Darwin expounded his theory of evolution. The essential concept of Darwin's theory is that species are not fixed but change over time. In the time frame available to individual practitioners, there is not sufficient time for species to undergo significant evolutionary changes. Genetic theory, however, which provided an explanation for species change, noted that there was minor genetic variation among individuals within a species. At times these variations result in significant enough developmental and trait differences. This means that not all individuals of the same species respond in the same way to the same environmental situation. In addition to these innate differences, diversity in the environmental situations with which individuals of a species interact produces various learned ways of responding to these situations. Organisms are open to their environments and alter themselves by adjusting and adapting to the situations in which they find themselves. For example, one cannot predict what height an individual corn stalk in a field will reach by knowing the height reached by another stalk. Environmental conditions in a field vary—some plants receive more shade, some on a lower part of the field receive more water, and some receive more nutrients from the soil.

When individual organisms are examined, the organic realm appears to be governed by chance. However, when organisms are studied in groups or aggregates, behavior in the organic realm conforms to stable laws. What has worked with a group of organisms in the past can be expected to work with the same type of group in the future. When results are reported as central tendencies of aggregates rather than individual responses, practitioners can presume that similar central tendencies will result in the future if the same interventions are applied. In the physical realm, stability is found at the individual level, but in the organic realm, it is found at the group level. Thus, a practitioner who administers a program aimed at reducing bullying in a primary school in Boston can presume that the mean reduction in bullying achieved in Boston will also occur in a primary school in Los Angeles. However, to maintain the presumption of stability across organic groups, everything that is not included in the measurement of results must be essentially the same in both interventions. Keeping everything else the same is, of course, difficult to accomplish outside of laboratory settings.

The extent to which environmental differences affect changes in aggregate responses to practical interventions varies considerably. The response to an intervention by individual members of an aggregate also varies. A practitioner's decision to make use of knowledge about what has worked with other groups requires judgment about the similarity of circumstances and allowance for the degree of variation among group members. For example, in experimental trials, drug B was found to produce a mean wellness score of 6.5 among the group of individuals to whom it was administered. Drug C was found to produce a mean wellness score of 7.5. (The differences in the means of the groups would rarely occur as a result of sampling chance.) However, the scores of the members who took drug C ranged from 1.1 to 10.3. Those whose scores were below 3 became more ill while taking the drug, and those whose scores were above 7 were completely free of any symptoms. A practitioner's decision about whether to give the drug to a patient involves more than merely doing what has been shown to work, in the main, more effectively in group trials. Knowledge about past responses to an intervention is useful, but it does not provide practitioners with certain knowledge about what to do in a similar situation.

Practitioners involved in policy making are required to make judgments about the success of an intervention on the basis of means scores of aggregates. If giving a vaccine to eight year olds has been shown to result in fewer cases of measles in groups, then the practice should be undertaken. Although some individuals may become very ill from the vaccine, the overall group improvement can guide the practitioner. However, practitioners involved in assisting individuals need to temper the guidance from aggregate trials with knowledge of the particular history and situation of the individual. Because there is instability in the organic realm, practitioners cannot simply do what has worked in other situations in the past. They need to use a kind of judgment *(phronesis)* to determine the applicability of practical knowledge developed for situations that are stable across time.

The Human Realm

In Western culture, the human realm has been sharply differentiated from the natural realm. The religious tradition defined human beings as the center and purpose of the universe. A human was not primarily a mortal body but an immortal soul created by God that would survive death. Descartes proposed that there were two realms—the realm of physical objects and the realm of souls. The physical realm, which included human bodies and other organisms, had the properties of extension and location, but the realm of souls had the property of thought. With the theory of evolution and the secularization of Western culture, the notion of the brain governed by the laws of the physical realm supplanted the idea of the soul as the seat of thought. While the theory of emergence does not restore humans to their former status as the center of the universe, it acknowledges the unique place of *Homo sapiens* within the whole of reality.

The emerged properties of the human realm include the capacity for conceptual thought. Like other complex organisms, human beings learn by noticing that some experiences have common characteristics. However, the human capacity to conceptualize makes our learning far more complex, more intricate, and richer than that of other organisms. Humans also have the capacity for language, through which concepts can be linked logically and analogically in thought and through which they can be communicated to others. Internalized, culturally based networks enable us to organize our basic level concepts into higher order ones, such as using the concept 'furniture' to include the concepts of 'chair', 'table', and 'chest of drawers'. These conceptual networks provide us with another environment of meanings beyond the physical realm and the ability to defer responses to environmental stimuli. Humans can design abstract strategies for achieving goals by imaginatively anticipating the effect of a possible action. On the basis of these imagined outcomes, we can decide whether to carry it out or not. Humans can conceptualize ourselves as continuous beings, distinct from other persons, and as the authors of our own actions. We are responsive to changes in our environment, particularly the actions of other humans.

The primary attribute of human existence is its temporality and an awareness of the finiteness of one's life. A person's existence begins at a definite time in a definite place and continues through time until it ends in death. During their time of existence, humans are open to and engaged in the world. These engagements are cumulative. The emerged capacity for extensive memory along with the capacity to organize experiences under concepts enables humans to anticipate what will happen if they act in a certain way by remembering the results of similar actions in the past. For example, anyone who has been burned by touching a hot stove can imagine what will happen if he or she does it again.

The accumulation of experiences over time creates a fund to guide future actions. Involved in self-organization, people are continuously engaged in interaction with their environments—their cultures, physical objects, other persons, and themselves. They are not simply passive recipients of environmental stimuli (or information). Rather, they attend to and affect the world, which in turn affects and evokes changes in them. Apropos of this, two adages express the same truth metaphorically: The burnt child fears the fire and Once burned, twice shy. Thus, having learned from experience, a person responds to identical or similar situations differently at different times in his or her life.

Every human being is an evolving system that builds up a fund of experience over time, which, in turn, affects his or her future exchanges with the environment. Individuals gather unique sets of experiences even from similar environments. As part of the report on his genetic studies, Plomin (1990) noted that relatively small environmental influences account for significant differences among people. Siblings reared in the same family are as different from one another as they are from their playmates. Differences in the characteristics of siblings result in their unique responses to the same parental actions. Parents themselves change as they accumulate experience in child rearing and act differently in response to the same actions of different siblings. Thus, the shared environment of being brought up by the same parents accounts for few of the differences in siblings' performances.

Ricoeur (1992) locates personal identity in the dialectical interchange between what one has been and what one will be. He refers to the sedimented fund of what one has done as "idem" or the same self, and therein lies a person's character. What has been done is not changeable; it is stable. What one has been appears to posses a substantive identity, which endures as something that can be identified time and again as the same (idem). However, a human existence involves more than what one has been in the past. In the present, people project into the future through promises and commitments. They intend to engage in actions that lead to planned outcomes. They begin to take initiatives to make something happen. Ricoeur calls the future dimension of a person "ipseity." This is the aspect that aims at change and in its very doing will transform and alter what one has been. In these projected practices, one's identity is not substantive but in the process of becoming. It is out of a dialectic between these twofold identities that personal identity arises. A person is more than inflexible constancy; he or she becomes him- or herself through change.

Not only are people individuated by their unique histories and what they project for themselves, but they are also individuated by slight differences in genetic endowments that prompt them to respond in a different manner to the same events. Although everyone's genetic information is, in the main, the same—for example, the genetic information of an unrelated stranger varies only by approximately one-tenth of 1 percent (Ornstein, 1993)—the variation produces some genetically derived differences. For example, people differ in eye color, susceptibility to certain illnesses, and inclinations toward various physical characteristics (such as body type) and behavioral patterns (temperaments). Plomin's (1990) summary of studies of identical twins who were separated and brought up by adoptive parents suggests that "heritability of many behaviors are in the range of 30 percent (beliefs, schizophrenia), 40 per cent (specific cognitive abilities, personality, delinquency), and occasionally 50 percent (IQ)" (pp. 116–17).

Each person is different from every other person. Each is a unique and precious being who cannot be replaced by any other; not simply one among many, but someone special and valuable in and of him- or herself. Humans are not instances of a diagnostic type but individuals with personal histories in which concerns and needs are integrated into the whole of their beings. Every dyad of caregiver and person cared for constitutes a unique and special partnership with its own particular value. Although the caregiver may enter into many dyads, each holds its own distinct possibilities. Every person cared for is not a replacement for another, nor is the care given a simple replication of that which was given to another.

In human beings, the physical, organic, and human realms are not isolated from one another; they are integrated and interacting dimensions of one system. Like other physical objects, people will fall from heights at predictable rates. The gravitational field influences the form their bodies take (Feldenkrais, 1997), as well as the movements of their external limbs and the internal flow of bodily liquids. The organic aspects affect thought and emotions; for example, lesions in the brain can alter mental processes (Damasio, 1999; Merleau-Ponty, 1945/1962). Practitioner actions in the physical realm take place in the domain of physical energy and involve moving and manipulating objects; however, practitioner actions in the human realm most often take place in the unique domain of human meaning and consist of languaged interventions.

The emerged properties of humans make their responses to practice intervention even less stable than those of other organic entities. Much of human existence is taken up with everyday practices, and much of that time is given over to practices aimed at affecting other people. We say nice things and give presents with the purpose of making others happy; we do things and say things to make others think well of us; and we touch and hold our children to make them feel loved and safe. Some of us are engaged in specialized practices of care aimed at teaching, healing, or otherwise serving people in need. Because of the irregularity and lack of stable responses in the human realm, the application of practical knowledge to achieve one's purposes in this realm involves a level of personal judgment not often necessary for work in the physical or organic realm.

Human beings as human beings exist in an environment of meanings. They do not simply react to interpersonal, social, and physical events; rather, they respond to the meanings they attribute to them. Their bodily and spoken actions are based on the meanings they attribute to environmental events and to the intentions their responsive actions are meant to bring about. The capacity to use sounds and marks to stand for concepts allows humans to be moved by the spoken and written expressions of others. Furthermore, it makes it possible for them to be affected by cultural traditions and stories of people who have lived in the past, contemporaries whom they have not met, and imagined people created by novelists, playwrights, and screenwriters.

The responses of individuals to practitioner speech and bodily actions are not capricious and inexplicable, nor are they entirely predictable. As these responses result from interpretations of practitioner actions, practical knowledge in the human realm requires not only knowing what to do but also what the action means to the other. The sources through which people interpret practitioner actions are varied and complex. They include both socially provided and individually learned interpretations. For example, extending one's hand to another person is interpreted as a friendly greeting in our society. However, a child who has often been beaten by a parent might interpret an extended hand as an aggressive gesture. Often interpretations are attached to local situations. For example, wearing a Superman costume on the street and wearing one at a costume party elicit different responses. Statements about personal behavior made by a therapist in his or her office and the same statements by the therapist at a social gathering are understood differently.

Practice in the domain of meaning is much more complex than in the realm of physical objects. The permanency and stability of physical objects allow for transfer from previous practical knowledge about these objects to future actions involving them. Practice in the human realm presents the practitioner with a more difficult task. Individual human beings vary in their genetic traits and individual development. Their interpretations of practitioner actions vary according to what they have learned from their cultural and individual experiences. The temporal dimension of human existence, as is so with all self-governing systems, makes the simple transfer of what has worked in the past inadequate for determining what will work now with a particular individual.

In summary, our everyday practices are aimed at bringing about change to objects in the physical realm, entities in the organic realm, and people in the human realm. We can perceive that the things in each of these realms are different. Our experience of objects is not the same as our experience of people. People are actors, not inert objects. People initiate changes in an effort to accomplish goals. People are practitioners. Ricoeur (1984) wrote, "We have a pre-understanding of the world of action, its meaningful structures, its symbolic resources, and its temporal character" (p. 54). Actions are understood to be different from physical movement. They imply goals, not simply the anticipation of a foreseen or predicted result. Therefore, actions are motivated, and this distinguishes them from strictly physical movement in which one event leads to another. Our ordinary language distinguishes purposeful human actions from the movement of physical objects. We think and speak in two different, nonreducible, and logically incompatible conceptual schemes. One is used for talking about the physical realm and the other for talking about the human realm. The set of concepts we use to talk about people and their actions includes the ideas of agency, intention, motivation, and purpose. People view themselves as beings who have intentions and motives who act to achieve goals and who regulate their lives according to their values and social norms.

Practical action in the human realm requires working with others who are themselves actors with their own goals and intentions. It is an engagement that takes place between people within a common temporal space. Practice in the human realm cannot be regarded as simply the implementation of techniques or the administration of a program to passive entities who submit to the practitioner's efforts. Its goals are accomplished, not by doing something to people, but by assisting them to reach their own practical goals.

The Social Realm

Human beings are born into social groups that have been formed prior to their birth. An individual begins life as a member of various levels of social groups, extending from his or her family, their ethnic group and culture, to the neighborhood, city, state, and nation. Each of these groups has a style of engaging the world, as do the others into which new members are initiated. The overarching style is carried by a culture, while the narrower groups provide their own additions to and subtractions from the culture that serves as their host. A culture's style is multifaceted and includes a worldview—that is, a set of beliefs about the nature and operations of the world and the place of human beings within it. It maintains a set of practices or customary ways of doing things and has ways of organizing its members through institutions of governance and production. Cultures often divide their members into classes, such as the economic classes of proletariat and bourgeoisie or peasants and aristocracy. Some cultures maintain a unified worldview, while others tolerate multiple, conflicting styles; as an example of the latter, Western culture accommodates both religious and technical-scientific worldviews.

When Hegel (1807/1967) proposed that Being advances to the Absolute through a dialectical progression of cultural systems rather than through particular individuals, he acknowledged the formative power of the social realm. In the nineteenth century attention was given to the diversity of practices among cultures. Although the Enlightenment philosophers held that reason was a vehicle for overcoming the limitations of culturally imposed perspectives, this belief is understood by postmodern writers as merely the expression of what happens to be the current culture's worldview.

The operation of culture can be compared to the operation of language. Languages, with their grammars and vocabularies, exist prior to the individuals who learn them. New members are initiated into a language by imitating others who speak it. In infancy, a child begins to acquire knowledge of a spoken language—first of its sounds, then of its meanings. One does not first learn a set of rules for making well-formed sentences. The grammar of a language operates out of awareness, and speakers may not be able to describe the almost flawless grammar that informs their speech.

A culture's beliefs and practices are internalized by its members and function as the background from which they understand themselves, the world, and others, and from which they act. There are different views about the power of the social realm to control individuals. For example, it was Foucault's (1975/1979) understanding that the social realm controls the thoughts and practices of its members. He does hold, however, that knowing that one is under its control has a kind of liberating effect. Bourdieu (in Bourdieu & Wacquant, 1992) and Certeau (1980/1988) saw the social realm as setting limits within which people can make choices about their actions, but people mistakenly assume that the social realm allows more space for choices than it actually does. In contrast, Sartre (1943/1965) believed that people can overcome imposed social limitations and choose their actions freely.

The understandings and practices passed on by cultures vary over time and place. Members of different cultures see the world differently. People's internalized cultural views vary, as do the devices and artifacts they have created and among which they live. Our contemporary society has surrounded us with artifacts that are substantially different from those that surrounded our ancestors in the medieval period. The differentiated understandings from the groups in which people are reared tend to destabilize the transfer of practical knowledge from one group to another. This does not mean that what has worked with one group will not work with another but that deciding what will work in a situation requires practitioner judgment.

THE PRACTITIONER

Practice in the human realm involves two entities. The one to whom practice is directed is a person, and so is the entity who performs the practice. Whether the practice is carried out in the physical, organic, or human realm, the practitioner is him- or herself a person with the same characteristics as other members of the human race. Other organisms engage in a kind of practice, such as birds gathering items to build nests or a pack of wolves circling their prey; however, these practices are innately programmed and not the result of complex practical knowledge. Human practitioners have the same characteristics of individuation and cultural embedment as other members of the human race. Thus, when they engage in activities designed to accomplish a purpose, their actions will reflect their individuality and differ to some extent from the same activity carried out by another person.

The machines we invent to manufacture objects are designed to repeat the same actions consistently so that every item they produce will be identical to all the others. The aim of quality control is to eliminate all differences in the finished products. Mechanical production is based on the notion that the materials being processed by the machine react to particular actions in a stable way. If both the material and the actions remain the same, then so will the products. Beginning in the eighteenth century, production by machines replaced production by craftsmen as a more exact and efficient method for manufacturing goods. This was the cornerstone of the industrial revolution. The success of mechanical production has led to its adoption as the exemplar for all practice by our technologized society.

Although this exemplar works reasonably well for practice in the physical realm, it is less effective in the human realm. When applied to the latter, the model holds that if practitioners perform the same actions with the same type of persons, then the same results will be obtained. However, for this to be done the steps of the program must be scripted in minute detail and the practitioners trained not to deviate from the script. Judgment and improvisation are removed from the process and replaced by a formulaic series of actions. In the mechanical model of practice, the individual practitioner is much less important than the prescribed actions he or she performs. As on the assembly line, one practitioner can be replaced by another, because it is not the practitioner who is responsible for achieving an end, but the techniques or programs themselves.

A serious flaw in the mechanical model of practice is that it disregards the importance of practitioner judgment for accomplishing desired ends in the unstable and complex human realm. It also ignores a practitioner's reservoir of experience and ability to improvise. Both the practitioner and the person to whom his or her practice is directed are unique individuals. There is a dance-like flow to their interaction in which each movement of one partner is responded to by a movement of the other. Although their general movements have been outlined by a common culture, each partner responds in his or her own style. The accomplishment of goals in the human realm requires more flexibility and responsiveness to change than the mechanical model allows.

When a person wants to accomplish a task, the instructions derived from a culture-based fund of knowledge or from an individual's experiences will vary in usefulness. Practice takes place in current situations with particular arrangements. The fund of knowledge provides information about what has worked in the past, but sometimes the circumstances have changed to such an extent that what once worked is no longer effective. Some practical knowledge can be transferred readily to current situations, while some cannot. For example, a mechanic who learned at a training session how to repair the radiator of a 1985 Nissan like mine can use this knowledge to fix my radiator. Because my radiator is basically the same as the one he learned how to repair, his practical knowledge is readily transferable to the present situation. However, it would probably be of little use to him if he were attempting to repair an electrically powered car. Likewise, when dealing with people, practical knowledge of what has worked to effect changes in the past may not be useful in the present. Individuals are shaped by unique experiences, and their responses are based on their understanding of a situation. Because of this, an approach that has worked time and again in practice will not always achieve the desired results.

Accomplishing goals in the human realm depends on the motivation, imagination, and awareness of the practitioner. In this realm, practice involves a relationship between two persons. Although it may be useful to know what has worked in the mechanical model, the faithful application of a set of programmatic techniques is never enough. Goals are accomplished in the human realm by practitioners, not by programs or scripts. Highly motivated practitioners know that goals can be accomplished by various means, and they will not hesitate to try an unconventional approach if they feel a particular situation demands it.

The *Los Angeles Times* (Garrison, 2002, April 21) reported the story of a teacher in the Central Valley of California who worked indefatigably with farm workers' children to help them achieve admission to elite colleges. When Mrs. Mellor first moved to a middle school in the Valley, which had 51 percent Latino students, she found that no Latino students were in her advanced mathematics class. They had been told that their English was not good enough and also that the course was only for college-bound students. Deciding that she had to change this situation, Mrs. Mellor resolved to prepare the Latino students for higher education with the goal of having them admitted to the best colleges. She began by moving promising Latino students from her other classes into advanced mathematics. Garrison wrote:

> The anointed students were terrified. The middle-aged teacher with the fly-away hair and caged rat named Pepito allowed no lags in attention during class and piled on the homework. After reading that students test better if they are slightly uncomfortable physically, she threw open the classroom windows one winter morning before handing out exams. But the students were entranced by her talk about how the world would open up for them if they were willing to work hard. (p. 2)

Mrs. Mellor badgered her students to practice their writing and complete homework assignments. She worked with them on money-making projects so that they could attend workshops at UC Berkeley during the summers. Over the next decade, almost all of the farmworkers' children she worked with would attend college, nearly a hundred of them. Mrs. Mellor had returned to teaching when she was forty-seven and left the Valley school after teaching there for thirteen years. "But [since she left] the last few years have been rocky for Mellor's amazing college entrance machine. . . . Students no longer have her to bully and cajole them through the application process. Acceptances to elite colleges have fallen" (p. 2).

It was not Ms. Mellor's "machine" that made her work successful; it was her relationship with her students and her concern for their success. Much of what she did does not conform to approaches that are held to be effective in teaching children. Her actions and tactics cannot be packaged and replicated in other settings, nor are they included in any "best practices" collection for use by others. Nevertheless, given who she is and the situation in which she practiced teaching, Mrs. Mellor was immensely successful in accomplishing her goals.

Practitioners operate in three realms, each requiring its own processes for deciding what to do. Practice in the physical realm is aimed at making something out of available materials. Practice in the human realm is aimed at assisting others to accomplish their goals. We do not *make* children into readers or athletes; rather, we work with them so that they may become readers or athletes. To conflate these practices leads to treating people as if they were raw material for our intended products. The practitioner in the human realm needs to be governed by strong values and sound judgment. The people to whom our practices are directed are irreplaceable individuals of intrinsic worth, not mere replicas of a prototype. Practice with people always has an ethical dimension as well as a practical one.

THE HUMAN SCIENCES AND PRACTICAL KNOWING

Science is a specialized practice with the aim of generating knowledge about the world and its people. As a practice, this specialized field is historically and culturally situated (Kuhn, 1970). Methods and conceptual models change over time, but all scientific knowledge generated in different eras and in different ways pertains to the same world. As methods for generating knowledge about nature have improved continually, our contemporary understanding of the processes and structures of the physical realm is more accurate than ever before. In addition, the stability of the physical realm is such that scientists can build on the fund of knowledge that has been amassed over centuries.

Scientific practice aimed at producing knowledge about the human realm is only about a century and a half old. In the main, it resembles the physical sciences in that it seeks to discover the stable processes and structures that govern the human realm. Throughout the relatively brief history of the human sciences, there have been disagreements about the best way to determine stabilities in this realm or even if it is possible to do so. Most studies of the human realm have made use of inquiry processes adapted from those that were successful in locating stabilities in the physical realm.

Researchers who investigate the human realm practice in disciplines such as anthropology, psychology, sociology, education, economics, and linguistics. As a group, these disciplines make up what is termed the "human sciences" (Foucault, 1966/1971). They employ a common reasoning process to locate relationships and structures that hold across time and across people. This reasoning process is manifested in methods that use either mathematically based analyses or language-based analyses. The majority of current human science productions are in the form of probability statements about mathematical regularities that hold among isolated elements (variables) of human properties (for example, gender, age, socioeconomic status, and educational level). These regularities are empirical generalizations and need not be regarded as unchanging and universal stabilities that underlie human behavior. Some investigators (see discussion in Feenberg, 2000) hold that the complexity and historicity of human actions means that knowledge in this area should be limited to descriptions of specifically situated activities. That is to say, these descriptions should only be about local examples and should avoid general theoretical conclusions. However, in the main, human science investigators do not follow a pure localism of this sort but make use of the general theoretical ideas of social science, such as class, culture, and the state.

Knowledge produced by the human sciences consists of two basic types—structural and relational. Structural knowledge pertains to a consistent form or process that shapes various social and cultural configurations or developmental processes. For example, Erikson (1959) proposed that people move through a general pattern of stages in developing their identity; Piaget (1969) identified stages through which children develop cognitively; and Bourdieu (1980/1990) described the general features by which cultures operate in people's lives. Relational knowledge pertains to relationships that hold between and among human variables. For example, outcome studies render a probability statement between an intervention and a predicted outcome. The prototype for this kind of relational research involves the selection of two equal groups of people with relatively similar characteristics. One is used as a treatment group, which receives an intervention, and the other is used as a control group, which does not. After the intervention, the groups are measured on an outcome index to determine whether the intervention made a difference.

Basic research inquiries are conducted to generate knowledge without regard to its applicability to practice. Applied research is intended to produce knowledge that is useful for practice. The distinction between these types of research has lessened in recent years, in that the findings of basic research contain implications for practice and the findings of applied research serve to inform basic understandings of artifacts and entities. The findings of research on human beings are of most interest to practitioners who work in the human realm.

In general, when human science researchers examine individual people, the purpose is to gather a group of scores or observations that can be used inductively to generate a statement at the level of relations among kinds of things. Induction occurs through probability logic that determines population characteristics from samples or through thematic analysis. Knowledge of relations among kinds of things is intended to produce knowledge deductively about the individuals who make up the kind. For example, the statement that there is a significant probability relationship between people of the Asian American kind and people of the high level of school achievement kind implies that most often one can expect an Asian American to have a high level of school achievement.

At issue is the usefulness of the knowledge produced by the human sciences for practitioners in the human realm. As described above, practitioners in the human realm deal with individual people (whether singly or in groups). At the individual level, people vary in their responses to interventions, yet the knowledge produced by researchers comes in the form of statements about kinds of things, not statements about a particular individual. Because of this, practitioners themselves have to interpret human science knowledge in terms of its applicability to the particular situation in which they are engaged. Researcher-generated knowledge does not provide direct instruction that is certain to produce the desired results.

The direct application of human science findings by practitioners working with people is limited in three ways: (a) Findings are historically situated in that they have been obtained at a particular time with particular people. The actual observations on which the findings are based were about those people who actually participated in the study. The projection by probability logic that these findings apply to people with the same characteristics, but who were not participants in the study, is based on assumptions about the stability of the findings across all the members of a certain type and about the stability of the findings over time. (b) There are variations among the members of a type, and knowledge about what is generally so does not apply directly to the particular person that a practice is meant to assist. (c) As individuals are affected and changed by what they encounter, the impact of applications varies when they are used again with the same person (see Polkinghorne, 1999).

Although the findings about relationships among kinds of things are not directly applicable to practice in the human realm, they are indirectly applicable. They provide practitioners with a repertoire of actions and techniques that have brought about a preferred result in a previous application. The kinds of things identified in studies can serve as lenses to focus attention on aspects that a practitioner might overlook. They often provide suggestions for approaches that one might try initially in the attempt to accomplish an end. Knowledge of findings also increases the density of the background from which practitioners can draw in making judgments about what to do. However, the individualization and lack of stability of the human realm do not allow practitioners simply to do what the findings suggest. They need to monitor the effects of their actions and be ready to engage in situational improvisation, making adjustments in response to changes brought on by the previous action. Practical knowing is a process that is carried on in the action of practice. It draws on personal experiences and human science findings to interpret how people respond to the practitioner's actions. Practitioners learn in the midst of a situation what next action might move the practice toward its goal. The value of human science findings is not in instructing practitioners how they must proceed to reach the end they are seeking but in providing useful descriptions of what has worked in other situations and might work in the present one.

Practitioners of care are social actors who have been reared in a culture that values technical solutions. This chapter has argued that practices involving human-to-human interaction cannot readily be reduced to technical-rational approaches. Because of the unique, emerged characteristics of human beings, successful practice with them requires improvisation and ongoing adjustments informed by situated practitioner judgment. Such a practice was taught by Aristotle for use in human interactions. He spelled out the characteristics of this nontechnical practice and termed the kind of deliberation employed in it to determine actions "phronesis." The next chapter presents Aristotle's *phronesis* as a judgment model for practitioners of care.

5

Techne and *Phronesis*

THE SECOND AND THIRD CHAPTERS described the technification of contemporary culture through the application of formal reasoning and calculative thinking to the social realm. Technification employs a technical-rational model for making practice decisions, including decisions by practitioners of care. The technical-rational model requires a scientifically validated general knowledge statement about what to do to achieve a goal one wishes to accomplish. For example, if the goal is to increase a particular child's reading comprehension, validated knowledge about what practice generally leads to such an increase is needed. Then the practitioner should follow the instructions in the general knowledge statement. The previous two chapters noted that for those living in the late twentieth and early twenty-first centuries, the culture has been infiltrated by the technical-rational approach to making practical decisions. As a result, it appears only reasonable that decisions about what to do in practice should be made through the technical-rational process.

The last chapter identified four realms in which practices are carried out: the physical, the organic, human, and the social. It was argued that because of the inconsistencies and individual particularities, the technical-rational process does not produce the best decisions for practices in the human realm, particularly in the person-to-person interactions initiated by practitioners of care. The purpose of this chapter is to recover a model of practice for use in human interactions and to bring it into the foreground for practices of care. The model needs to include the full range of human knowing and embrace emotional and imaginative knowing as well as reflective thinking. The recovery of such a model requires looking outside our current historical period where correct thinking is held to be hindered by processes other than calculation. Aristotle is the philosopher who provides

97

this model. He made the distinction between the kind of deliberations that were appropriate for making things and those that were appropriate for acting in the human realm.

THE FUSION OF HORIZONS

Because there is not an overlap between our current assumptions about the world (our horizon) and those of writers of other historical periods and cultures, understanding their ideas involves interpretation. Thus, understanding Aristotle's practice model entails an engagement across cultures. Gadamer has offered a guide to reading authors from prior historical periods. Gadamer used the term *horizon* to denote the limits of the field of vision provided by one's cultural background. However, he did not believe that this horizon was permanent or static. It can be extended to encompass wisdom from other cultures and historical periods. Gadamer valued the wisdom of the preceding traditions of thought in the West. His position is at odds with those who held that these traditional wisdoms needed to be overcome. Heidegger, for example, believed that the destruction of traditions, not their re-appropriation, was essential to the exposure of Being. For Gadamer, interacting with and rehabilitating traditional wisdoms enables an individual to overcome the restrictions of his or her own acculturated background. Commenting on Gadamer, Habermas (1983) wrote:

> Gadamer promises to rehabilitate the substance of the philosophies of Plato and Hegel. He wants thereby to bridge (as he supposes) the false opposition between the metaphysical and the modern apprehension of the world. . . . This conception contrasts . . . with Heidegger's lordly destruction of Western thought, with the project that devalues the history of philosophy from Plato through Thomas to Descartes and Hegel as the drama of a mounting forgetfulness of being. (p. 190)

In Gadamer's view, background understandings are a repertoire of responses to particular situations, not a source of general knowledge about universal truths. Like others, Gadamer held that backgrounds vary historically and present the world and people differently. He also believed that the knowledge generated in earlier periods contains wisdom that is often overlooked or only partially understood by contemporary culture. Recovery of the wisdom of past traditions can help us overcome the limitations of our present technical understanding of the world.

Surviving texts are our only means of access to the wisdom of the past traditions. However, when we read these texts, it is from the perspective of our own background assumptions or prejudgments. Gadamer said that gaining understanding from texts written by those of another historical period requires an openness to be taught by them and a willingness to enter into dialogue with them. Diverse texts can broaden the provincial view provided by our own culture. Reading them is like a conversation in which each party learns from the other by listening and questioning, and at the end each comes away with a greater appreciation and understanding of the other's position than he or she had before. Gadamer said that through dialogue with a text from another historical period, one's prejudgments are transformed in a manner that closely resembles an educational process.

A greater appreciation of the judgment approach to practice can be gained by engaging in a dialogue with Aristotle's *Nicomachean Ethics*.

> I think Aristotle's conception of the human being, and of practical deliberation, is of great importance for contemporary ethical and political thought, and I believe that the depiction of the plurality of goods and of conflicts among them that we find in both the poets and Aristotle offers insights that are absent from much of contemporary social reasoning. (Nussbaum, 2001a, p. xv)

The following interpretation of Aristotle is taken primarily from Nussbaum (1990; 1994; 2001a; 2001b; 2001c), who provided a fuller understanding of Aristotle's texts by placing them in the cultural context of his time. Specifically, she clarified Aristotle's positions by noting how they differ from those of Plato and the classical Greek poets. Citations are given only when Nussbaum's writings are quoted directly.

TECHNE (SCIENCE) VERSUS TUCHE (LUCK)

Nussbaum (2001a) proposed that the early Greek experience could be understood as a contest between the power of nature and the intellectual power of people (see chapter 2). Arbitrary and unpredictable, nature operated beyond the control of human beings and was capable of causing pain and suffering through drought, storms at sea, and disease. Who would be struck down by nature was a matter of *tuche* (luck). To gain some control over the whims of nature, human beings were given the gift of intellect, through which they developed *techne* (knowledge) about how nature operates. Because of *techne*, people's vulnerability to the power of nature was reduced, and they were able to harness some of its aspects to meet their needs and satisfy their desires. "They did not want to look on the naked face of luck *(tuche)*, so they turned themselves over to science *(techne)*. As a result, they are released from their dependence on luck; but not from their dependence on science" (Hippocratic treatise, *On Science,* quoted by Nussbaum, 2001a, p. 89).

Techne is the application of human intelligence to an area of nature in order to gain some control over it. A person with *techne* about an area approaches it with foresight and understanding; he or she is not blindly dependent on chance but has the confidence that comes from intellectual resourcefulness. The Greeks used the term *techne* to refer to various kinds of knowledge, such as knowledge about making crafts (building houses, weaving, and shoemaking), and knowledge about creating arts (playing the flute, dancing, and writing poetry). 'Techne' was also used to refer to scientific knowledge about the operations of nature (medicine, mathematics, and meteorology).

There were various levels of *techne.* The highest and most complete form of knowledge about nature had four features: (a) it was about universal and unchanging properties, and having identified an instance as member of a universal property, one could predict its response; (b) it could be taught to others; (c) it was mathematical and precise, allowing for calculations; and (d) it included causal explanations of why things occurred. *Technai* (the plural of *techne*), which did not have all these features, were considered less complete.

Medicine, for example, was included among the *technai.* Its knowledge had a universal quality in that it was about categories or types of cases. By noting on the basis of past experiences that a case belongs to one of these groups, it was possible to predict what treatment would cure it. Because its knowledge was about general types, it could be taught to others, who could then apply it in their practice. Medical knowledge was not only about what would happen when a treatment was applied, but it also provided an explanation of why the treatment worked. However, it was deficient in the area of precision, for it did not include a metric for measuring treatment or illnesses.

Techne is, in general, the art of applying human intelligence to control nature. However, another area in which human beings lacked control was their personal choices. Whether their lives were happy or unhappy, whether they were blessed or cursed, it was all a matter of luck *(tuche).* Because people formed attachments to other people and objects that they could not control or that could be taken from them, their choices could lead to sorrow or anger; for example, a loved one might die or a favorite object be destroyed. In pursuing a plurality of values, people were sometimes obliged to make difficult choices. The tragic poets told of people having to choose between two actions, either of which would have dire consequences. There was also the matter of passions that could overcome human beings, causing them to ignore their own values and abandon the path they had chosen in life. With everything depending on *tuche,* it is not surprising that deliberations about what to do were unsystematic and confused.

This was the question: Could a *techne* or body of knowledge be developed that would give people control over their own lives in the way that the *technai* gave them control over nature? Could a science of living be formulated that would eliminate pain and suffering? As the science of medicine had made the healing of the body possible, could another science heal the diseases of the soul? People had sought guidance about how to live their lives in the teachings of magicians and in the popular religions. Plato claimed that his philosophy could provide a science of the soul that would cure diseases of thought, judgment, and desire and deliver people from the sufferings of their ordinary lives. Aristotle's philosophy also addressed people's concerns about living successfully; however, he held that this could not be reduced to a science. Instead, he offered a clarification and explication in which he used those who were held to be living flourishing lives as examples.

Both Plato and Aristotle offered philosophical instruction about their conflicting ideas for living a good and fulfilling life. The next section describes Plato's *techne* or science for living, and the one that follows presents Aristotle's view of the flourishing life. Aristotle opposed Plato's position. Contrasting their positions can lead to a clearer understanding of both philosophers' ideas.

PLATO'S SCIENCE OF LIVING

Plato proposed a *techne* that called for people to elevate their lives by focusing on scientific and mathematical reasoning. He theorized that engaging in this kind of reasoning produces a life that is free of pain, consistent, and directed at unchanging truths. It also provides stability because one's thought is directed toward eternal and universal ideas, which do not vary and are not affected by what human beings say or do. Such a life of reason offers freedom from the miseries brought about by choices based on the false beliefs and passions of everyday life. Plato held that this *techne* is scientific in that it has the characteristics of true knowledge or *episteme:* it is universal, precise, and explanatory.

Plato's program called for separating one's intellect as much as possible from the disturbing influences of the bodily senses and emotion. In an approach similar to contemporary cognitive therapy, he sought to correct the irrational and false beliefs that produce agony in people's lives. Plato believed that people who followed his teaching would be transformed and freed from the uncontrolled happenings that lead to pain and suffering. When applied to making practical choices, his *techne* emphasized three propositions: (a) there is a single life value that can be used to calculate which of the possible choices will yield the most of that value; (b) there are universal or general principles that can be organized in a system of rules and applied in new cases to determine the correct choice; and (c) correct choices are not made under the influence of emotion or imagination.

Plato held that significant progress in gaining control over one's life will occur only with his *techne,* in which practical choices are determined by the use of the rationality that involves counting, weighing, and measuring. Correct choice can be determined by measuring the amount of value that will result from various actions. One then chooses the action that produces the largest amount of value. For example, using pleasure as the value, if one action results in one hundred units of pleasure, and another results in fifty units, the correct action is the one that produces one hundred units. Actions are not valuable in and of themselves; they only serve as means to the valued consequences they produce. Correct choices are those that maximize the total amount of value. In his dialogue *Protagoras,* Plato had Socrates compare making decisions on the basis of what appears to be right at the moment to making decisions by using the *techne* of measurement. Socrates then asked Protagoras which approach is the right one:

> "Haven't we seen that the appearance leads us astray and throws us into confusion, so that in our actions and choices between great and small we are constantly accepting and rejecting the same things, whereas the metric art would have canceled the effect of the appearance, and by revealing the truth would have canceled the effect of the impression, and by revealing the true state of affairs would have caused the soul to live in peace and quiet and abide in the truth, thus saving our life?" Faced with these considerations, would people agree that our salvation would lie in the art of measurement? He [Protagoras] agreed that they would. (Plato, 356d–e)

The key to Plato's concept of a 'metric of choice' is the notion that there is a single value on which all choices can be measured. The single value must be intrinsically true and not relative to a specific context. One must give up the idea of multiple values and see everything in terms of the single true value. For example, if the value is money, acts of friendship must be measured on the basis of how much money will result from them. Personal attachments to people and things have to be transformed into calculations about the financial benefit that will be derived, and if another relationship offers a greater reward, it is to be chosen. Using a metric in deliberations of choice frees one from the temptation to choose immediate gain over long-term benefits. Contingency management can be employed to determine the total reward that the various choices will accrue. A metric of choice based on a single value eliminates the confusion and uncertainty that arise when a person is committed to conflicting multiple values. Detachment from individuals and things is difficult to effect because personal attachments are developed as a part of a normal childhood; for example, the attachment a child develops to his or her own parents. However, with sufficient training, one can come to see everything in terms of a single value and experience the comfort and simplicity provided by a deliberative system that brings certainty to choice.

Plato's scientific *techne* of practical action locates all possible actions within a finite set of general principles that can be used to govern and inform all actions. Every new situation is only an instance of a general case for which a set of rules about how to act has been developed. For example, if a particular child falls under the category of dyslexia, then certain activities are to be undertaken. The set of rules is applicable in all cases within the category; therefore, one would act no differently if the child with dyslexia were one's own. The use of rules generated from what has generally worked in similar cases simplifies and systematizes the choices to be made. One is trained to see characteristics in every new situation that relate to the categories for which rules have been devised. For example, in meeting with a new client, a therapist would look for characteristics that indicate the appropriate Diagnostic and Statistical Manual (DSM) diagnosis. Other characteristics of the client are subsidiary to those that are needed for diagnosis. Once the diagnosis has been made, the rules for what to do in such cases can guide the therapist's actions. The principle that the general precedes the particular removes the tension and responsibility of having to decide what to do in each new situation.

According to Plato, the emotions and imagination prevent people from making the sound judgments about choice that can be produced by metrics and rules. Human appetites are blind animal forces that drive actions toward the objects of desire without regard for the intellect's judgments of what is truly of value. When appetites are allowed to control one's choices, excessive indulgence results. Plato holds that the emotions are bodily pushes and pulls without cognitive value, which the intellect must control. Passions are self-centered and indulgent, and they can lure an individual away from the pursuit of what he or she knows is of real value. Through training, however, one can learn to resist bodily desires and passions. In the Platonic *techne*, the rational element of the soul alone should determine action. The intellect is necessary and sufficient for making correct choices.

The peace and calm that the scientific *techne* brings requires a transformation of life as it is ordinarily lived. When a person accepts its premises, love and fear depart from his or her life, as well as all the pain and uncertainty that accompany them. No decision is left without guidance; nothing is left to chance. Plato offers his techne as a life-saving tool that will remove the power of contingency and luck over one's life and bring intellectual purity and clarity to one's practical actions.

Aristotle's *Phronesis* and Practical Action

Like Plato, Aristotle, was concerned that people were confused about values and needed to determine which actions would result in a successful life. Also like Plato, he offered instruction that was intended to improve his students' life practices. However, Aristotle's understanding of what it means for human beings to live fully differed significantly from Plato's. Plato taught that the good life was one in which the intellect governs and overcomes the brutish desires of bodily appetites. From his perspective, a human being consists of an intellect and a body, but the intellect is the true self and the place in which the good person dwells. Aristotle disagreed with the idea that the good life involves rejection of the bodily dimension of our humanness. He held that we are embodied beings with passions and attachments, as well as social beings living among friends and in communities. The flourishing life involves the totality of our humanness, not a reduction of it.

Aristotle believed that having a good life required some external goods that were primarily determined by the luck of birth and were beyond an individual's control. For example, one needed good parents, good health, sufficient wealth, to live in a good city-state, not to be a slave or servant, and (probably) to be male. However, these in themselves are not sufficient for the good life. In a full life, one is blessed with external goods, and one engages in good actions. As people have a certain amount of control over their actions, the good life requires that we make worthwhile choices about what to do. We are not automatons whose actions are determined solely by physical laws, nor are we playing parts orchestrated by our culture. The good life is a practice that involves making wise decisions and following through with actions that will implement them. In his teaching, Aristotle explained the kind of activities that characterize a full life and how to choose such activities in one's own situation.

Aristotle's teachings about the good life came from his examination of people's ordinary beliefs and sayings about the best way to live. He held that access to knowledge about the good life, as well as knowledge about the world, comes from the human perspective. We do not have access to a point of view outside of the human realm from which to view the world. Aristotle argued against Plato's notion that the shared concepts and beliefs of human beings did not present things as they really are. Plato had sought to escape from the distortions and limitations of ordinary knowing by ascending through mathematical reason to a god's-eye point of view, from which the stable and eternal truths could be known as they really are. He thought that the earthly, human point of view could only produce knowledge that is relative to different contexts and languages.

Aristotle did not believe that the escape envisioned by Plato was possible. He was convinced that knowledge about the actions that characterize a flourishing life could only come from human experiences. Therefore, he set about collecting the various beliefs and understandings of the good life that were held by the Greeks and members of other "civilized" communities (Polansky, 2000). In his study, Aristotle was looking for descriptions among oral and written accounts of the good life. By sifting through the information he collected, he was able to summarize the activities people observed on the part of those who were considered to be living fulfilling lives. The next step was to clarify confused descriptions and resolve differences among contradictory ones. Then Aristotle produced a general description of what people held to be the properties and characteristics of a flourishing life. His intent was to make explicit and clarify the ideas contained across the gathered statements. From his findings, Aristotle concluded that the good life was composed of multiple dimensions and is so complex that its activities could not be contained within a single, simple idea. A flourishing life involves choosing good ends and good actions. Because the human realm is contingent and uncertain, choices about what ends to pursue may lead to disappointment instead of fulfillment. Also, all human activities involve an element of risk; there is no assurance that actions we choose will always produce the desired outcomes.

Aristotle concluded that the good life was a thoroughly human one, reflecting the intricacies and richness of human existence. He regarded life itself as being rich and valuable. Understanding that love and friendship are among the activities that make us vulnerable, he saw that they also give life its depth and fullness. However, reflecting some of the prejudices of his background, Aristotle held that the successful life was only possible for free men with leisure to contribute to the governance of the city-state. He did not exhibit the value of universal human dignity. Woman, slaves, foreigners, and the poor and lower classes were excluded from the successful life as he understood it. Furthermore, his notion of citizenship bound him morally to the people of Athens. He did not accept the obligation not to wage aggressive wars against other city-states. His idea of the state placed no inherent limits on government's power to interfere in areas of personal liberty, nor did it hold the government responsible for assisting the needy.

Nevertheless, Aristotle's view about the role of practical wisdom (phronesis) in living a full and flourishing life has resonated with many contemporary scholars. Dunne (1993) has written about the use of Aristotle's ideas by Newman, Collingwood, Arendt, Gadamer, and Habermas. His notion of *phronesis,* which appears in Lyotard (Gallagher, 1993), and Heidegger (Bernasconi, 1989) among others, provides an antidote to the dominance of technical-rational decision making in all areas of contemporary life. Aristotle's views are presented as descriptions of human experience that hold across cultures and history. They are based on the assumption that features and properties of humanness are grounded in our embodied nature. People are not merely lumps of clay that can be molded into any shape by culture; they have an unalterable core of shared characteristics that define them as human beings. The relevance of Aristotle's ideas for contemporary society depends on whether they speak to us about our own experience and understanding.

The Humanness of the Good Life

Aristotle's view of the good life was grounded in human experience, which placed it at odds with the science-of-life view expounded by Plato. Plato held that what people ordinarily perceived about the good life was not reality. Their perceptions were like shadows on the wall of a cave, which were cast there by the true light. Only by knowing the light itself could one know the true good. To know the light, people must elevate themselves above their ordinary existence in the world. The tool for accomplishing this elevation is scientific reasoning, through which one can overcome the limits of the body with its appetites and passions and replace the disappointments and pains of ordinary existence with the stability and purity of the realm of ideas. By focusing on the true light instead of the human realm, people come to know that the good life consists of a single idea. Deliberations about what to do can be calculated, and the different amounts of good each action would produce can be determined. When decisions are based on what will produce the greatest good, choices become clear, and appropriate actions follow. As this is the natural consequence of formal or scientific reasoning, any other course of action would be irrational. Plato's body of knowledge or *techne* about how to live the good life called for approaching life through the intellect alone. He believed this approach would provide pure and precise answers about what to do.

Aristotle argued against Plato's idea that ethical deliberation could be made into a calculative procedure. Aristotle held that the good life was a fully human life, not a life reduced to the intellect alone. It was to be found in the everyday existence of embodied human beings interacting with the world, others, and self. Aristotle addressed the question about the life choices and activities that characterize a good life in two manuscripts, the *Eudemian Ethics* (EE) and the *Nicomachean Ethics* (NE). The title *Nicomachean* refers to the name of either Aristotle's father or his son (Hutchinson, 1995). Consisting of unpolished collections of notes, these manuscripts have three books in common.

Deliberation about what activities to undertake for the good life required the use of a kind of reasoning called "practical wisdom" or *"phronesis."* Phronetic reasoning produces a perceptive understanding or insight about what is called for in a particular situation. People's actions take place in situations of complexity and conflict. For an action to be appropriate to the occasion, it cannot simply be deduced from general knowledge or codified into a metric. "That practical wisdom *[phronesis]* is not scientific knowledge is evident; for it is, as has been said, concerned with the ultimate particular fact" (NE 1142a, 23–24). (The quotations of Aristotle are from the Ross translation as reprinted in McKeon, 1947.)

Phronesis is closer to the *technai* of medicine and navigation than to Plato's formal *technai*. Medicine and navigation are nonmetric *technai* and attend to particular circumstances and appropriate timing.

> But this must be agreed upon beforehand, that the whole account of matters of conduct must be given in outline and not precisely, as we said at the very beginning that the accounts we demand must be in accordance with the subject-matter; matters concerned with conduct and questions of what is good for us have no fixity, any more than matters of health. The general account being of this nature, the account of particular cases is yet more lacking in exactness; for they do not fall under any art or precept but the agents themselves must in each case consider what is appropriate to the occasion, as happens also in the art of medicine and of navigation. (NE 1104a, 1–5)

When decisions are simplified into an intellectual calculus, instead of life becoming more flourishing, it becomes less full. Practical wisdom draws on all our human sensitivities, including our emotions. Eliminating any aspect of our humanness from the deliberative process produces less effective life choices, not more effective ones.

Aristotle looked to human beings for knowledge of the good life. His notions came from the experiences of people. He held that it is people themselves who know about human happiness and fulfillment. Thus, he did look to the divine realm or Plato's realm of forms for principles or laws for how to live the good life. From within the human realm, decisions about actions are not mere casuistry but complex determinations integrating multiple values with the particularity of situations. Because of this complexity, decisions about life choices require phronetic judgment rather than deductive calculation. Aristotle explored three characteristics of human choice that necessitate the use of phronetic reason in deliberations about human actions: (a) Human beings are committed to multiple values, and therefore multiple consequences must be considered in deliberation. (b) In the human realm, particular instances have priority over general rules, so in deliberation the unique and special requirements of each situation must be taken into account. (c) Emotions provide guidance to and motivation for action, so deliberation must include felt understanding.

Multiple Values. Human beings aim at the target of a flourishing life composed of values or excellences. Each of these values is separate, distinct, and worthy in its own right. Each is an end in itself, not simply a means to some higher value. It is possible to judge whether something is a true value of life by asking a simple question. If this value were missing from a person's life, would that life be incomplete even though it was sufficient in all other values? For example, if one were without friendship yet had everything else one could wish for, would his or her life be fulfilled? The good life consists of a plurality of valuable activities, each with its own characteristics. Aristotle held that rational adults are intuitively attached to multiple values and understand that courage, justice, generosity, friendship, and many other values are elements of the good life.

The plurality of life values means that conflict among these values is inevitable. Situations will arise in which difficult decisions must be made. For example, one can be faced with the dilemma of being loyal to a friend or reporting something he or she has done that might endanger the lives of others. Either choice will go against one of our life values. As we live in a world of happenings beyond our control, Aristotle knew that our commitment to multiple values would produce irreconcilable conflict and risk into the center of the ethical sphere. The stratagem to remove risk by adopting a single value, such as pleasure, against which alternatives can be measured lessens the richness and fullness of human existence. It displaces the emotion and feelings of guilt that result from having to choose among bad alternatives. While such a move can free a person from the uncertainty and complexity of practical actions, it does so at the cost of reducing life values into simple means. Such deliberation is turned into a technology for calculating the amount of pleasure or other single good that will result from carrying out a just or loyal act and then choosing the one that will produce more of the single value.

Priority of the Particular Judgments to Universals. To understand events in the human realm, it is necessary to take their particularity into account. Individuals differ in the way they respond to happenings of the same kind, and they differ in the way they respond at different times. Action in the human realm is imprecise, indeterminate, and indefinite. Simply following general rules of how one should act is not sufficient for making correct choices. Therefore, determining what is the just or caring thing to do requires a fine-tuned attention to the situation at hand.

General rules cannot take into account new and unanticipated aspects of situations. Aristotle uses medicine and navigation as examples of the need to respond to changing circumstances. Physicians and navigators who are trained only to follow general rules such as one would find in textbooks are not prepared to deal with unexpected occurrences in the flow of life. Because their knowledge is limited to generalizations about what has happened in past cases, it is insufficient to prepare them for everything that might happen in the present. Choosing the correct action is only part of the formula; resourcefulness also requires that one act at the proper time.

Practitioners need to attend to any new features that appear in situations in which they act professionally, and they also need to attend to contexts in which the situation is embedded. The meaning of a situation's features depends on their connection to one another. In complex situations, the application of a general rule on the basis of having identified an isolated feature is not likely to bring about the desired effect.

Every human being is unique. The structure of embodied life is that it is lived only once moving forward through time. Each person has his or her own history of actions and relationships. Our love and concern for another— a mate, a child, a relative, or a friend—is for an irreplaceable individual, not a set of properties that he or she happens to have. The quality of human love does not allow for the simple substitution of someone similar or a clone. Human relationships involve a shared history of interactions and memories. The loss of a loved one cannot be remedied by finding a replacement. Because the good life includes care and love for others, we are vulnerable to the pain that occurs when the relationship is severed or when someone we love dies.

In the human realm, individuals are unique, meanings are contextualized, and new and unexpected happenings occur; as a result, particulars have priority over general rules in practical deliberation. However, Aristotle held that general rules do have a limited usefulness in that people who have not yet developed practical wisdom can be guided by the wise judgments of others. General rules can also provide a starting point for identifying the salient features of a situation. When one is unable to deliberate in a timely manner or when judgment may be distorted by bias, it may be appropriate to apply rules. As Aristotle observed, "Rules are necessities because we are not always good judges; if we really were operating ethically as well as we should, we would not have the same need of them" (Nussbaum, 2001a, p. 304).

Emotions and Imagination. Aristotle regarded human beings as fully embodied entities and held that emotions have a place in decisions about how to live the good life and in the acts of people who lived flourishing lives. Full understanding of a situation includes how one feels about it as well as what one thinks about it. Unlike Plato, who held that the emotions were blind animal forces from which the intellect had to be shielded, Aristotle viewed the emotions as a form of rich intentional awareness. As they are both about and directed at people and situations, emotions illuminate their subject or object from the agent's point of view.

Emotions are important and necessary for good deliberation in that they serve as sources of information about right actions. Recognizing a situation and what is salient in it for determining action is a matter of both emotion and cognition. Aristotle does not sharply divide these two aspects of the soul. Frequently, it is an emotional response to a situation rather than detached intellectual thought that serves as a guide to appropriate action. Emotion can focus one's attention to reveal aspects of a situation that might otherwise remain hidden. For example, one often feels a friend's needs intuitively before becoming cognitively aware of them. Because we know and understand with our whole being, practical wisdom requires an emotional openness and responsiveness to comprehend situations fully. A wrong response is often prompted by an excess of intellectual consideration and a deficiency of emotion. "Without them [emotions] its approach to a new situation would be blind and obtuse. And even where a correct choice is reached in the absence of feeling and emotional response, Aristotle will insist that it is less virtuous than choice that is emotional" (Nussbaum, 1990, p. 79).

In addition to being involved in deliberations about how to respond, emotion is often part of an appropriate response. Although someone may "know" a friend has died, she has not truly understood the event unless her response includes feelings of pain and loss. A response based on intellect alone without the appropriate emotional element is not the action of a person who is living a full life.

Emotions are closely related to a person's beliefs and can be modified on the basis of what one believes about a situation. For example, believing that one has been harmed deliberately by another person will usually inspire anger. However, if one discovers that the harm was in fact caused by someone else, then the anger will be removed or shifted to the guilty party. Aristotle believed that it is possible for a person to cultivate virtuous emotions that direct anger appropriately.

> Fear and confidence and appetite and anger and pity and in general pleasure and pain may be felt too much and too little, and in both cases not well; but to feel them at the right times, with reference to the right objects, toward the right people, with the right motive, and in the right way, is what is intermediate and best, and this is characteristic of virtue. (NE 1106b 18–24)

The emotions also serve as motivating forces when they are properly directed. They become part of what constitutes excellence in character. However, because emotions are primarily formed during childhood in interactions with parents and other persons of care, the extent of their cultivation in adulthood is limited.

In addition to the cognitive function of emotions, Aristotle also held, in opposition to Plato, that *phantasia* or the imagination has a cognitive function. What Aristotle meant is that the imagination is capable of focusing on a concrete item, either present or absent, so as to perceive it *as* something; that is, to isolate and identify the salient element of a situation. It is the selective part of perception. Working together with memory, imagination can focus on remembered items that are absent as well as those in front of the individual. It can rearrange remembered items to create scenes not actually experienced. For Aristotle, these are not free-floating fantasies; his emphasis is on the imagination's selective and discriminatory functions.

Because imagination has the capacity to isolate the salient aspects of situations, it plays an important role in practical deliberation. Imagination locates items in the environment that correspond to an individual's interests or concerns. An imaginative view of a situation categorizes items according to whether they are to be pursued or avoided. Aristotle held that human beings and animals have an embodied ability to notice what is of interest in the environment. However, humans have a special capacity, deliberative imagination, which enables them to associate several imaginings or perceptions together without disregarding the concrete particulars. "Instead of ascending from the particular to general, deliberative imagination links particulars without dispensing with their particularity. It would involve, for example, the ability to recall past experience as one with, as relevant to, the case at hand, while still conceiving of both with rich and vivid concreteness" (Nussbaum, 1990, p. 78).

For Plato, the good life required overcoming and abandoning the human condition. It was through a type of intellect alone that one could ascend to the good. The portion of intellect Plato favored operated at the level of general and universal truth. From this level, one could deduce subsidiary truths in the manner that theorems can be deduced from the axioms of geometry. For ethical action, there was a single axiom, the good, from which one could deduce what was required in particular cases. Possible actions could be measured to determine which would produce the greatest good. Because truth resided in the general, the general precedes the particular. Having conceived of the good life as a life fully lived within the human condition, Aristotle rejected the three basic elements of Plato's ethics: (a) As humans experience the good life, it consists of multiple values, not a single value; (b) it takes place among the diverse and actual situations in which one is called on to act; (c) and its deliberations make use of embodied and imaginative knowing in tandem with the full range of cognition.

Phronesis

Phronesis is the excellence by which one deliberates well about what to do in the human realm. It is the process of reasoning used to make the appropriate practical choices that constitute a good life. Given Aristotle's view that in the good life there are multiple values, the particular has priority, and emotional and imaginative processes are involved in practical deliberation, the reasoning used in phronetic decision making is more complex than Plato's deductive thought. As it deals with contingent and changing situations, it does not produce answers that have the certainty of mathematical calculation. Aristotle sought to clarify phronetic reasoning by differentiating it from the reasoning used in other tasks.

Aristotle's Theoria, Techne, *and* Phronesis. Aristotle proposed that there were three major kinds of tasks in life and that to accomplish each kind properly required the use of its own type of reasoning. The life tasks were (a) *theoria* or developing theory about substances and properties, which requires the use of *episteme* or the kind of reasoning used in formal logic and mathematical calculation; (b) *techne* or the making of artifacts, which requires the use of *poiesis* or the reason used to put together materials to produce objects; and (c) *praxis* or acting for the good of the other or the state, which requires the use of *phronesis* or practical reasoning. (Here, Aristotle used *techne* to specify craft-making, and not as a general reference to a body of knowledge or as a reference to Plato's calculative *techne*.) The Greek terms are retained because the ideas they refer to are not the same as those of such current terms as *theory, technology, production, practical deliberation,* and *practice*.

Gadamer (1960/1975) used Aristotle's distinction between *episteme* and *phronesis* to support his contention that the human sciences require a kind of reasoning that is different from the one required by the natural sciences. Gadamer wrote that "the old Aristotelian distinction between practical and theoretical knowledge is operative here" (p. 21), that is, in the differences between the human and natural sciences.

> [This is] a distinction which cannot be reduced to that between the true and the probable. Practical knowledge, phronesis, is another kind of knowledge. Primarily, it means that it is directed towards the concrete situation. Thus, it must grasp the "circumstances" in their infinite variety. (p. 21)

Putnam (1978) also noted Aristotle's distinction between types of knowledge:

> I think that Aristotle was profoundly right in holding that ethics is concerned with how to live and with human happiness, and also profoundly right in holding that this sort of *knowledge* ('practical knowledge') is different from theoretical knowledge. A view of knowledge that acknowledges that the sphere of knowledge is wider than the sphere of sciences seems to me a cultural necessity if we are to arrive at a sane and human view of ourselves *or* of science. (p. 5)

Theoria. The *theoria* that Aristotle discussed is not the same as the contemporary notion of scientific theory. Contemporary theory produced through experimental methods is aimed at describing laws that govern or regularities that hold among natural objects, social phenomena, and human behaviors. The use of scientific theories to guide practice is central to contemporary technology. Aristotle also referred to theoretical knowledge as *scientific* knowledge; however, he was not using the term in the contemporary sense. Aristotle's *theoria* or science was knowledge about necessary and eternal first principles and first causes. These included mathematical entities, the heavenly bodies, and the divine first mover. Although this knowledge was furthest removed from sense experience, it was the highest form of intelligibility. Theoretical knowledge of the first principles was arrived at through a process of intuitive induction similar to the reasoning through which geometric axioms are known. From the principles one moved down to explain lower items through deductive, syllogistic reasoning in the way geometric theorems are deduced from axioms. Plato identified the theoretical knowledge as real knowing *(episteme)* to distinguish it from the mere opinions that made up lesser knowledge.

Aristotle said that the contemplative reasoning used for theoretical knowledge was not applicable in making practical choices. It dealt with a divine realm in which no change occurred, while practice deals with the realm of change.

> But if the argument be that man is the best of the animals, this makes no difference; for there are other things much more divine in the nature even than man, e.g., most conspicuously, the bodies of which the heavens are framed. From what has been said it is plain, then, that philosophic wisdom is scientific [theoretical] knowledge, combined with intuitive reason, of the things that are highest by nature. This is why we say Anaxagoras, Thales, and men like them have philosophic but not practical wisdom, when we see them ignorant of what is to their own advantage, and why we say that they know things that are remarkable, admirable, difficult, and divine, but useless; viz. because it is not human goods that they seek. (NE 1141a 36–1141b 8)

The capacity for theoretical reasoning is not part of the embodiment of human beings; it is something additional and appears as a nonpersonal, divine capacity residing in humans. "But such a life [of contemplation] would be too high for man; for it is not in so far as he is man that he will live so, but in so far as something divine is present within him; and by so much as this is superior to our composite nature is its activity superior to that which is the exercise of the other kind of virtue [the good life]" (NE 1171b 25–29).

Through theoretical reason, one becomes open to the divine and to the eternal order of the cosmos. From the relationship with this order, one's soul is transformed, and one experiences the serenity of the eternal. Aristotle's description of the theoretical intellect and its realm seems to capture the essential ideas of Plato's ethical ideal. In three chapters, six through eight, in book 10 of *Nicomachean Ethics,* there is a claim that the contemplative life is the good life. Nussbaum (2001a, pp. 373–77) contends that these three chapters may not be part of the original text as they are basically at odds with the rest of Aristotle's position in which the good life takes place within the fullness of one's existence and among others. They also contradict his view that there is not a superior contemplative good above the multiple values from which the full life is composed. Book 9 begins with a summary of text at the end of book 5. I will treat the claim that the contemplative life is the best life as external to Aristotle's primary argument that the good life is lived among the realm of the changing and contingent.

TABLE 5.1
Practice in the Realm of Change and Contingency

Reasoning	*Activities*	*Outcomes*
Techne—planning, how to make something (reproduction)	*Poiesis*—producing, making	Artifacts
Phronesis—deliberating on activities for the good (particular situation)	*Praxis*—acting, doing the good	Good Action

Techne. Unlike *theoria,* the purpose of which was to produce knowledge about the realm of the unchanging, *techne* and *phronesis* are types of practical reasoning used to produce practical knowledge about carrying out activity in the realm of the changing. *Techne* is the reasoning used in making or producing *(poiesis)* things and art. (Aristotle uses *'techne'* to refer to a way of reasoning about doing something; *'techne'* can also refer to the body of knowledge produced by *techne* reasoning, as was the case in its use in the chapter on technology.) *Phronesis* is the reasoning used to deliberate about good actions *(praxis).* *Poiesis* and *praxis* are two different kinds of activity governed by two different kinds of reasoning. "In the variable [earthly changing realm] are included both things made and things done; making and acting are different; . . . so that the reasoned state of capacity to act is different from the reasoned state of capacity to make" (NE 140a 1–5). "Action and making are different kinds of things" (NE 140b 3–4). Thus, there are two kinds of practice: *poiesis,* which is guided by *techne,* and *praxis,* which is guided by phronesis.

Poiesis is the activity in which a person brings something into being that did not exist before. Unlike natural changes, such as the changes that occur as a flower grows, changes in *poiesis* are brought about by human activity. *Poiesis* covers a range of activities from building houses and making shoes (construction, manufacture) to making a journey safely and curing illnesses. *Poesis* also includes art or craft activities in which natural materials are transformed into aesthetic or useful objects, such as a painting, a bowl, or a pair of earrings. *Techne* is the reasoning used to develop the knowledge of how to bring about a desired change, for example, transforming a lump of clay into a bowl for serving food. The goal of the action is established before production begins. The producer does not determine this end but comes to the task with the end already established. Knowing what end is to be accomplished, the producer can use *techne* to figure out the procedure that will transform the material into the desired object. The actual manufacture of the object *(poiesis)* follows the steps that have been worked out through *techne* reasoning.

To recapitulate, *techne* is the kind of reasoning that develops plans for the production of artifacts. *Poiesis* is the art or craft by which natural materials are made into aesthetic or useful objects. Once a plan has been developed through *techne,* it can be used repeatedly on the same type of materials and will consistently produce the same outcome. It can also be taught to others, who can then use it to make similar products. The activity of *poiesis* yields a product or result that is separate from the person who made it and is available to others for their use and evaluation. The worth of a *poiesis* activity can be judged by its consequences, that is, how well it serves its intended purpose.

Phronesis.   Aristotle's depiction of *techne* as productive knowledge is not unique in Greek thought (see the chapter on technology); however, the distinction he made between *techne* and *phronesis* was his point of departure from Plato's ethics, and as such it remains of considerable interest to modern philosophers (Dunne, 1993). *Phronesis* is the kind of reasoning used in knowing how to live well. The activity of living well is termed *"praxis"* by Aristotle. Both *poiesis* and *praxis* are practical activities; the former is the practice of making things, and the latter the practice of living fully. Because *praxis* is often translated as "practice" and *phronesis* as "practical wisdom," confusion can arise. Therefore, I will use the Greek terms to refer to the individual types of practice and the term *practice* to refer to the overall notion of human operation in the world.

With his use of *phronesis,* Aristotle inserts a "deviant" concept into the hierarchy of knowledge (Dunne, 1993, p. 245). Knowledge was understood to consist of facts learned from sensory experience or truths about the eternal objects. *Phronesis* is a different kind of knowledge: one that varies with situations, is receptive to particulars, and has a quality of improvisation. If, for example, the moral excellences of honesty and care are appropriate in a situation, *phronesis* indicates what action will manifest these life excellences in this particular instance. As the appropriate excellences will vary from case to case, so will the action prescribed by *phronesis*.

Unlike *techne*, *phronesis* is concerned with actions that relate to human beings. Its product is knowledge about actions that in and of themselves are expressions of the good life; it is not knowledge about how to produce things that stand alone. For example, care requires phronetic reasoning, because it is a practice whose doing is an end in itself; it is not simply a means to make over the person served. In *techne*, means developed to produce one artifact can be used again to produce similar objects. A set of rules that yields the intended product can be worked out and passed on to others. *Praxis*, however, is enacted in particular situations; there can be no general formula for doing good in every instance. Praxis requires sensitivity to the salient characteristics of a situation and judgment about how to proceed from there. *Praxis* cannot be learned from a book of instructions; proficiency in *praxis* comes from experience.

Phronetic Deliberation

The function of phronetic deliberation is to decide which moral concerns or excellences are appropriate to the situation one faces, and having done so, to choose actions that will manifest those concerns or excellences. Does the situation call for a courageous or honest response, or both? What actions will manifest courage and honesty in this particular situation? Phronetic deliberation produces knowledge about practical choices by integrating background understandings, felt meaning of a situation, imaginative scenarios, prior experiences, and perceptive awareness. It employs the type of thinking that combines and coordinates diverse elements to reach a conclusion. It retains the rationality of noncontradiction, so conclusions that are reached do not send mixed messages. However, its processes are not limited to formal deductions and mathematical calculations.

> Practical wisdom *[phronesis]* . . . is concerned with things human and things about which it is possible to deliberate; for we say this is above all the work of a man of practical wisdom, to deliberate well. . . . The man who is without qualification good at deliberating is the man who is capable of aiming in accordance with calculation at the best for man of things attainable by action. (1141b 8–15)

The operations of phronetic deliberation can be described as the three steps in the so-called practical syllogism: (a) a major premise—X is the excellence to be carried out; (b) a minor premise—Y is the means for carrying it out in this situation; and (c) a conclusion—Y should be done.

Wiggins (2001) has outlined a theory of the phronetic process. A person is confronted with a particular situation in which the question "What shall I do?" arises. The task is not usually seen as how to maximize some single value, but as how to respond now. Demands are made on one's practical perception to notice the salient aspects of the situation, but not all of the relevant features may "jump to the eye" (p. 291). The latter can be identified using the imagination to engage in reflection or thought experiments. This is the process of practical insight, "situational appreciation," or what Aristotle calls "perception."

> Practical wisdom *[phronesis]* is concerned with the ultimate particular, which is the object not of scientific knowledge but of perception—not the perception of qualities peculiar to one sense but a perception akin to that by which we perceive that the particular figure before us is a triangle; . . . though it is another kind of perception than that of the qualities peculiar to each sense. (NE 1142a 25–30)

Practical perception is a capacity to identify with clarity and discernment the features of a complex situation that are significant for determining the most appropriate action. It brings to the fore aspects of a situation that have gone unnoticed and gives one an intuitive sense of what is important for making a moral choice. Practical perception is cultivated through one's own experiences of moral choice and through observation of the choices made by those who possess practical wisdom. It expresses a person's commitment to the excellences of life.

In many situations, what should be done is not immediately obvious. Further specification is often needed. A starting point is to notice the relevant needs provisionally identified through perceptive insight. However, one must achieve a more specific understanding of what the situation requires before moving on and determining what action will meet those needs. Wiggins held that the most interesting and difficult parts of practical reasoning occur in the initial perception and in the move to further specification. Before one can determine what to do to meet a need, it is necessary to determine exactly what the need is.

Agents are not blank slates. They come to new situations with knowledge from their background, memories of what worked for them in similar situations in the past, and awareness of the general principles and rules for responding to this type of situation. However, phronetic deliberation requires that agents approach each new situation prepared to see what is different and unique about it. They need to consider the situation's specific composition, timing, and place and be ready for unexpected developments. Thus, agents do not enter situations with a method or algorithm for selecting which concerns are to be addressed. Phronetic deliberation requires that the particular situation be approached without preconceptions, as its aspects take priority over formal schemes and logically ordered diagnostic categories. "Indeed, a person's reflection on a new situation that confronts him may disrupt such order and fixity as had previously existed and bring a change in his evolving conception of the point, or the several or many points, of living or acting" (Wiggins, 2001, p. 292).

Once an agent comes to understand what the concern is or which excellence applies to a particular situation (the major premise), he or she begins to consider the specific means (the minor premise) to carry out that excellence. For example, after coming to the realization that a situation demands courage, the agent has to consider what would be the courageous thing to do in this particular case. After mulling over several possible actions, the agent may conclude that none of them is a good choice. Some of the alternatives considered may take too much time or require too many resources, or they may raise other concerns. If this is the case, the agent should refrain from taking action and reconsider whether the goal (acting courageously) can actually be carried out in this situation. As a result of this stepping back, the agent may decide to start over by considering a new goal, in which case it will be necessary to determine how this affects the salient features of the situation.

Wiggins's theoretical outline noted that phronetic deliberation does not lead to conclusive and certain choices. Choices usually have to be made on the basis of unfinished and inexact deliberative results. Because moral excellences have to be enacted in the human realm, they are carried out in circumstances that are mutable, indeterminate, and particular. The problem is not that the phronetic process lacks the precision and exactness of the physical sciences; "it should not even *try* for such precision" (Nussbaum, 2001a, p. 302). One cannot measure a situation with a carpenter's rule to calculate its exact dimensions. Its perception is like the sculptor's Lesbian ruler, which, being made of lead, bends according to the shape of each object. "For when the thing is indefinite, the rule also is indefinite, like the leaden rule used in making the Lesbian moulding; the rule adapts itself to the shape of the stone and is not rigid, and so too the decree is adapted to the facts" (NE 1137b 30–32). As the human realm is inexact, the process of making choices in this realm is necessarily inexact as well.

There are no formal criteria for comparing the potential good that may be derived from different actions. The choice of good or excellence to be manifested in a situation "is evaluated not for its unconditional acceptability, nor for embracing more considerations than its rivals, but for its adequacy to the situation" (Wiggins, 2001, p. 293). Aristotle has noted that the valued excellences are multiple and that agents are confronted with multiple possibilities of values to enact in particular situations. It is left to the discretion of the agent to choose the goals for each occasion, and consideration of the alternatives will contribute to the evolution in his or her view of the good life.

From the Wiggins outline, one might expect phronetic deliberation to be a slow process. However, in actuality the decision-making process is immediate and smooth. "It is possible to attain it [the good choice] by long deliberation while another man attains it quickly. Therefore in the former case we have not yet got excellence in deliberation, which is rightness with regard to the expedient—rightness in respect both of the end, the manner, and the time" (NE 1142b 25–27). Phronetic deliberation is not a skill that can be learned, as one learns the skill of making a bowl. It is an excellence in and of itself, as well as one of the values that constitutes a good life. Also, the choice determined by this process is for a particular agent at a certain time and in a specific place. Phronetic knowledge is not transferable to another as a substitute for his or her own deliberation. The right action for one person may not be right action for someone else in a similar situation. Furthermore, there is not a single right answer for each situation; the same goal can be reached through various courses of action.

Phronetic deliberation provides a means of choosing among various actions that can actually be carried out in a given situation. The action decided upon may be less than ideal, but at the specific time and place, a better one may not be possible. Sometimes the limits of possibility only allow for bad choices—the lesser of evils, so to speak—and any action taken will leave one with feelings of remorse or guilt for not having been able to find a better solution.

Improvisation

Aristotle presented only a sketch of phronetic reasoning in a single book of the *Nicomachean Ethics*. Focusing on how to choose a plan that would result in the correct practical action, he proposed that an agent with the proper dispositions and developed perceptive capacity can make the right choice through the use of deliberation. However, practitioners of care do not simply make a single choice and then carry it out. They are engaged with the people they serve over time. Over the course of weeks, months, or years, they continually have to make choices about what to do next. Aristotle provided a description of an initial phronetic decision. To depict the endless series of choices made by caregivers would require a panorama.

Practitioners of care act and then react upon observing responses to their actions. They engage in conversation with others who are also involved in choosing goal-directed actions. The to and fro, give and take of their person-to-person interaction places their choices in a constantly shifting context. The particular situation in which they initiated action changes into something different as a result of the other person's response. The practitioner's next action involves an adjustment to this change. During a single interactive process, innumerable choices must be made about what to do, and practitioners of care learn more about what to do as a session progresses. As one would expect, some of their phronetic choices do not bring about their intended result. The original plan may have to be replaced by a new one. Thus, phronetic reasoning involves more than simply deciding what to do in the beginning; practitioners have to monitor the responses to their choices and adjust subsequent actions accordingly.

The interaction between the caregiver and the other person, whose responses are not scripted, is like musical improvisation in which each player is attuned to and responsive to the other's performance. Caregivers are not like the members of an orchestra who play a musical score as it has been written. They are more like the members of a jazz duo who have to adjust their innovations to those of their partner. Neither part is determined in advance, but each depends on the evolving innovations of the other performer. Practitioners make choices within the give and take of a dynamic conversation. Aristotle's rather static description of *phronesis* does not capture the decision-making process that informs an ongoing reciprocal interaction. A supplement is needed to record the improvisations that occur during a situated sequence of phronetic choices.

Dewey—Learning in the Situation

In addition to phronetic improvisation, practitioners of care learn which choices are more likely to work within a session by trial and error. Some choices they make prove to be ineffective, leading away from the goal of the work rather than toward it. Dewey, one of the founders of American pragmatism who wrote more than two millennia after Aristotle, provided a theory of learning from practice that serves as a supplement to Aristotle's description of *phronesis*. While Aristotle was primarily concerned with initial decision making and action, Dewey was concerned with what happens after an action is carried out. He was especially interested in instances when the planned action does not bring about the intended result. From his investigations, Dewey developed a method of inquiry or learning in which negative results are used to reform the assumptions on which the original plan was based. This is followed by implementing new actions based on the revised assumptions. The process of revision continues until the altered assumptions produce an action that accomplishes the task.

Dewey wrote after the publication of Darwin's theory of evolution and after the new science had been adopted as the means to control nature. He shared with Aristotle the idea that human beings are special members of the animal kingdom with embodied intellectual capabilities. Interested in how these capabilities could be refined and directed to help people live more effectively, Dewey studied the ways in which everyday practical activities were carried out. Dewey found that everyday choices about what to do and how to do it come from background understandings that operate outside awareness. Aristotle, who was interested in cultural differences within the Hellenistic world, did not delve into the role of out-of-awareness background understandings in phronetic deliberation. Dewey, however, saw that a person's particular situational, cultural, and historical background defines the area in which practice is conducted. The internalized background usually provides sufficient knowledge for coping with everyday situations. However, one's background understandings are not static; they grow and change over time.

The richest opportunities for advancing practicing knowledge occur when one's action fails to produce the desired result. These opportunities occur either when an action taken in a new or unusual situation did not work or when background knowledge is found to be no longer effective in ordinary situations. When an activity is unsuccessful, ongoing action is disturbed or interrupted. Dewey called these breakdowns "indeterminate situations." The problems arising from an indeterminate situation initiate learning and inquiry. The latter is a reflective type of problem solving that serves to change an indeterminate situation into a determinate one; that is, inquiry is the process by which problems that do not yield to one's initial responses can be solved.

One begins inquiry after a practical action has failed to accomplish its intended task and the practitioner finds him- or herself in an indeterminate situation. The first step is to determine why the routine and habitual plan of action was not effective in this instance by considering the situation carefully and sorting out all the facts. This leads to ideas—that is, hypotheses and expectations—about new actions that might solve the problem. These ideas are conceived "on the basis of current facts and assumptions, or by virtue of established habits, or otherwise in an ongoing trial-and-error manner, . . . [to settle] on a course of action or mode of being which effectively solves the problem" (Burke, 1994, p. 145). However, the development of hypothesized solutions is not simply a matter of using a decision tree or another rule-governed process. Proposals for effective action can be built up analogically from what has worked in the past in similar situations, or they can result from a creative Gestalt shift in how the situation is viewed. From an initial notion, the inquiry proceeds to refine the concept until the proposed action assumes a form in which it can be applied and tested.

> A hypothesis, once suggested and entertained, is developed in relation to other conceptual structures until it receives a form in which it can instigate

and direct an experiment that will disclose precisely those conditions which have the maximum possible force in determining whether the hypothesis should be accepted or rejected. (Dewey, 1938, p. 112)

A hypothetical solution is tested by engaging in the proposed action. If the action solves the problem, it is judged to be effective. If it does not, the inquiry continues until a proposed solution works. The successful action is judged to be effective and to have "warranted assertibility" (Dewey, 1941/1998). Dewey's logic of inquiry was not a theory of truth in the same sense as modern philosophy's theories about the structure of reality. He was dealing specifically with the evaluation of actions that are proposed to bring about desired results in restricted situations (Burke, 1994).

Dewey's model of inquiry incorporated notions of experimentation in that something is tried and then the results are examined (Dewey, 1938). This kind of experimental inquiry is employed by practical problem solvers such as those engaged in crafts, as opposed to the experimentation carried out by scientists in laboratories who are removed from the everyday problems of life. Dewey regarded experimental inquiry as the most effective way to develop knowledge about how to accomplish things in the world. He held that it was the most recent and the most advanced approach to learning, experimental inquiry succeeded less effective means of solving problems that were handed down by tradition, based on authority, or derived from theory. Dewey said that the purpose of inquiry is not to provide an accurate description of the objects of the world and their properties, but rather to find ways to do things better. By finding solutions to problems through experimentation in the real world, the kind of inquiry favored by Dewey has improved the quality of life.

Aristotle depicted the craftsman's *techne* or knowledge as an intellectual process of figuring out how to shape the raw material into the desired form. He did not emphasize experimentation as a means of improving knowledge about how to make things (Dunne, 1993). For Dewey, it was experimental inquiry that elevated *techne* (knowledge about how to make things) to the modern level and thereby made it possible to provide services and produce goods that greatly benefited the human race.

Because the experimental method of inquiry had been so successful in advancing practice in the physical realm, Dewey proposed that it be applied to the human realm as well. He believed that this would lead to solutions for many personal and social problems. I do not interpret this as his advocating the technification of the human realm to the extent that decisions would be governed by general rules and technical-rational processes. His model of inquiry is essentially a method for developing more effective means of accomplishing what is worthwhile (or in Aristotle's terms, what is the excellent thing to do). Dewey's inquiry does not argue against the multiple values, particularity, and embodied knowing that constitute the human realm. It can be added to phronetic deliberation without distorting the aim of the latter, which is to do what is best in a particular situation for a particular person. Furthermore, inquiry can provide phronetic deliberation with the dimension of trial and error learning, through which decisions about more effective actions can be generated. Although Aristotle held that in phronetic deliberation one must think in advance about what action might be most effective, he did not indicate what to do if one's best thinking resulted in actions that proved unsuccessful. Dewey held that one can learn from failure and incorporate this knowledge into the next phronetic deliberation, thereby improving the chances of success.

The use of inquiry is not restricted to professional scientists only. It can be used by anyone deliberating about what to do in an indeterminate situation in everyday life. Dewey called the capacity to learn through doing "intelligence." Bernstein (1967) provides a description of Dewey's concept:

> [Intelligence] consists of keen observation, the ability to discount private practices in favor of a bias of objectivity, the ability to envision ideals by which we can satisfactorily resolve situations in which conflicts arise, the ability to formulate relevant hypotheses, and a willingness to revise them in light of new experiences. The intelligent person is sensitive to the practical demands of situations and knows how far to carry his deliberations. In those situations in which immediate action is demanded, the funded experience of the intelligent person guides his actions. (p. 126)

Intelligent inquiry is a not a hit-or-miss proposition. It is method for determining a problem and its solution through a progression of four steps: (a) experiencing an indeterminate situation; (b) identifying the problem; (c) determining a solution; and (d) carrying out the determined solution.

A person's practical knowledge develops and changes as he or she engages in problem solving through intelligent inquiry. By trying different approaches and learning which ones work and which do not, one accrues a fund of knowledge about what might be useful in future situations. Those who engage in phronetic deliberation informed by inquiry eventually become more efficient and successful practitioners.

Aristotle held that excellence in phronetic deliberation is developed through experience. Dewey believed that inquiry-based problem solving was a skill that could be developed and nurtured through education. He also believed that the ability to act rationally and intelligently could become internalized and function as the natural way in which a person approached decisions in indeterminate situations. In time this approach would no longer require deliberate reflection. "Experience is capable of incorporating rational control within itself" (Dewey, 1935/1960, p. 78).

Dewey and Aristotle shared the notion that not only was the kind of intelligent deliberation they described useful for individual decision making, but it could also be used by judicial and governmental bodies to determine which actions would effectively contribute to the accomplishment of a society's moral, aesthetic, and political aims. Part of Dewey's philosophical agenda was to make human action more intelligent so that people would engage more effectively with self, others, and the world. His view of intelligence, like Aristotle's, was more inclusive than the formal and calculative view of rationality presented by Plato and Descartes. For Dewey, intelligence is grounded in experience, not separate and distinct from it. It is a general way of thinking about engagement in the practical world that takes into account how ideas fare when tested in action.

Education

Phronetic deliberation is the disposition of those living a good or flourishing life to approach choices in the human realm by seeking the excellent thing to do. It is not something that one turns on and off, deciding to use it in one situation but not in another case. Phronetic deliberation is part of a person's character, essential to the context of his or her life.

Aristotle made a distinction between character training and the philosophical study of ethics. For the most part, character training is accomplished through a child's interactions with his or her parents and educators. Aristotle does not regard children as being brutish or mechanical, but open to modification. Through discourse and other forms of interaction, parents can teach their children to control their emotions and direct the desires to appropriate objects. The parent's love and the child's reciprocation can provide the basis for dispositions that form attachments to friends and the community. Parents and relatives who display good dispositions serve as models of a flourishing life. Children who have been abused or who have not experienced the love and care from adults often lack the foundation for character development. Aristotle held that it was the duty of the *polis* to provide for the shaping of children's capacity for thought and emotional health. "Now it is evident that that form of government is best in which every man, whoever he is, can act best and live happily" (*Politics,* Revised Oxford, trans., 1324a 22–23).

Aristotle believed that certain preparations were necessary if students were to benefit from philosophical instruction about living the good life. He doubted that those who lacked the foundation provided by character training would gain much from his teaching. Like others, he also held that those who were too disorderly to study should not attend school. Furthermore, Aristotle only accepted students with sufficient life experience to participate in discussions. He regarded young people as being unstable, distractible, and inconsistent in ethical behavior and felt they needed time to grow up before becoming his students (Nussbaum, 1994).

A philosophical education can provide only part of what a person needs to live a flourishing life; a prior foundation and readiness are also required. "Hence a young man is not a proper hearer of lectures on political science; for he is inexperienced in the actions that occur in life, but its discussions state from these and are about these; and, further, since he tends to follow his passions, his study will be in vain and unprofitable, because the end aimed at is not knowledge, but action" (NE 1095a 2–4). The purpose of Aristotle's instruction was to clarify each student's understanding of ethical matters. Because the good life is a social life with others in the community, the clarification involved an open-ended dialectical exchange among Aristotle and his students. While moral training can direct one's aim at the right target, intellectual scrutiny of the values of life can provide a clearer understanding of the right means for attaining the flourishing life.

Intellectual clarification is not an end in itself. The good life is an activity, not an intellectual exercise. It is *praxis,* the actions that concern the human realm that cannot be taught or learned from books. Choosing the right goal and the right means for a particular situation is not an innate ability, but one that requires cultivation. A person can become more accomplished in phronetic deliberation by reflecting on what he or she has done, and one's practical perception can be sharpened by discussing particular situations. However, the ability to make wiser *praxis* choices ultimately comes from practical experience. The true measure of intellectual clarification is the wisdom of future choices.

Living the Good Life

In order to describe the best way to live, Aristotle examined people who were living flourishing lives. When one looks at the lives of such people, it is apparent that they have not dedicated themselves to amassing the greatest amount of money or indulging in bodily pleasure. Rather, these people are living complete lives that express the fullness of their humanity. They have not denied their emotions or their appetites, nor have they denied their intellect. They do not struggle with every decision but have developed dispositions or characteristic ways of acting that manifest the human excellences. Among the human excellences named by Aristotle are courage, gentleness, generosity, munificence, friendliness, truthfulness, modesty, and righteous indignation.

One of the excellences is *phronesis,* a manner for deciding which excellence is appropriate to express in a particular situation, and *praxis* is the right action for expressing that excellence. Aristotle's recognition of a way of thinking and deciding about actions in the human realm is of utmost importance for the argument of this book. He differentiates it from the rule following rationality *(techne)* used in making *(poiesis)* artifacts and devices. *Phronesis* is rationality for decision making in the human realm where the particularity of individuals has priority. *Phronesis* rationality is a personal excellence, and the *praxis* it guides is a realization of the actor.

While I have focused on Aristotle's discussion of the use of *phronesis* to direct the actions of individuals, he noted that it was also appropriate for managing a household and for making judicial or political decisions. The administrative role of judges involves more than simply following the letter of the law. In reaching a verdict, they also take into account the particular circumstances of the violation. Administrators and legislators should consider which of the possible actions will bring about the desired result for the particular *polis* at this time in this context. Practitioners of care often serve individuals in environments dominated by technical rationality. Aristotle's *phronesis* provides caregivers with another rational approach for determining the best (most excellent) choice for the persons they are serving. Aristotle noted that choosing practical actions for the human realm requires a different kind of thinking than the one employed for making such choices in the natural realm. *Techne* is the proper rationality for developing knowledge to determine actions *(poiesis)* that deal with the physical realm; *phronesis* is the proper rationality for developing knowledge to determine actions *(praxis)* that deal with people. Dewey adds that intelligent inquiry can contribute to making better choices about means to attain ends for both *techne* and *phronesis*. Aristotle and Dewey both held that reasoning is more complex than simple calculative and logical thinking; it includes thinking that integrates intellect with feeling and that addresses particulars and conflicting values.

A technical-rational–based practice is informed by knowledge claims about the response of an examined aggregate of people to an intervention. It presupposes that in essential ways the response of all people of the aggregate's classification will resemble those of the examined aggregate. In this approach, practical decision making employs deductive reasoning to infer from the general knowledge claim what action should be taken in a particular situation. I have argued that because these presuppositions do not hold in practices of care another kind of reasoning is required to inform their decision making. The differences among people and situations are significant enough to make a difference in how practitioners of care need to judge what to do. They serve in situations of direct give and take between themselves and those they serve. Their reasoning has to be such that it can adjust to nuanced changes in the flow of each engaged interaction. Aristotle's *phronesis* provides an outline for the kind of reasoning needed for making practical judgments in the sphere of human interaction. With *phronesis* as a foundation, the next two chapters continue the building of a model of decision making appropriate for informing practitioner judgments. Chapter 6 explores the role of background processes in making judgments, and chapter 7 advances the idea of reflective understanding.

6

Embodied Reasoning

PRACTICES ARE ACTIVITIES engaged in by human beings, and there is a difference between practices that pertain to physical objects and those that pertain to other humans. Aristotle recognized this difference by making a distinction between *poiesis* or production activities and *praxis* or activities related to human beings. He also indicated that *poiesis* and *praxis* require different kinds of reasoning. Deciding what to do when making something *(poiesis)* calls for the kind of reasoning Aristotle called *"techne,"* which produces knowledge about the steps required for transforming raw materials into objects. Considering what action will accomplish the human good in a particular situation *(praxis)* requires the kind of thought he called *"phronesis"* in order to determine which actions of excellence are appropriate for a situation and which means will accomplish the good.

With the technification of contemporary culture, the distinction between practices that are appropriate for producing things and those that are appropriate for the human good has been blurred. *Techne,* in its contemporary guise as technical-rational thought, has become prevalent in both the physical and the human realms. In the latter, it has replaced *phronesis* as the means of determining how to enact the good in response to human needs. The institutions that oversee caregiving practices (hospitals, school districts, government agencies, and health insurance companies) govern their activities with technical-rational plans. These plans tend to emphasize control over costs and regard caregivers as the strategic means for achieving institutional goals. Little room is left for the practitioners of care to make phronetic judgments about the best way to meet the needs of the individuals they serve. As a result, systems are losing the flexibility provided by phronetically guided personal judgment to determine the most effective way to care for an individual with certain characteristics in a certain place at a certain time.

In the previous chapter, we returned to the time of Aristotle, who wrote before the mind-body split became dominant in Western thought. The purpose of this chapter is to augment Aristotle's description of phronetic reasoning with recent investigations that are consistent with and supportive of the notion of embodied reasoning. They provide an expanded view of reasoning (now called "cognition") as a bodily generated activity rather than a divine spark housed in the soul, or a type of formal calculation that can be done by the brain or another mechanism such as a computer. The chapter offers an alternative to mainstream contemporary theories of reasoning that divorce the thinking process from embodied interaction with the world. The chapter advances the position that reasoning is a bodily activity that incorporates one's background knowledge, emotional feeling, imaginative scenarios, and reflective cognition. The position draws on Epstein's notion of experiential thinking, Lakoff and Johnson's philosophy of the flesh, Gendlin's experiencing, and Damasio's embodied mind. The chapter concludes with a discussion of the connection between embodied thinking and phronetic thinking.

The view that limits rational thought to inferences using the rules of deductive logic or mathematical calculation is being challenged. In an expanded approach to rationality, reason means that one has "a motive or cause for acting or thinking in a particular way" (Bready, 1999) In *Thinking and Deciding*, Baron (1988) wrote, "The best kind of thinking, which we shall call rational thinking, is whatever helps us fulfill our personal goals" (p. 28). Toulmin (2001) called for a return to a more balanced idea of rationality. Contending that the idea of reason as deduction and calculation was an Enlightenment replacement for the more open Renaissance idea of reasonableness, he proposed that the future is not the province of those who are obsessed with formal rigor.

> It is a province, rather for reflective practitioners who are ready to act on their ideals. Warm hearts allied with cool heads seek a middle way between the extremes of abstract theory and personal impulse. The ideals of practical thinkers are more realistic than the optimistic daydreams of simple-minded calculators, who ignore the complexities of real life, or the pessimistic nightmares of their critics, who find these complexities a source of despair. (Toulmin, 2001, p. 214)

In recent decades, a new model of human thinking has challenged the notion that deductive reasoning is the superior method for all decision making. Derived from the examination of embodied and everyday thinking rather than the logic of formal argumentation, this model offers a more inclusive view of rationality and promotes the idea that different situations call for different kinds of thought. The new model augments the kind of phronetic thinking identified by Aristotle, who did not consider *phronesis* appropriate for determining what to do in all situations. It was not proposed as a replacement for *techne* reasoning when making choices about production but rather as an additional kind of reasoning to be used in *praxis* situations. Embodied rationality is not intended to supplant deductive reasoning but to expand the notion of what is reasonable in order to include other kinds of deliberative processes. However, embodied rationality is meant to establish phronetic thought as the most "reasonable" way for practitioners to make decisions involving interaction with those they serve.

The expanded view of phronetic reasoning derived from embodied rationality reveals it to be integrative and nonlinear. When engaged in it, agents draw on their values, feelings, and imagination; they incorporate their cultural understandings, personal experiences, training, and applicable scientific findings. It is deliberative processing that occurs both within and outside their conscious awareness. The phronetic process makes use of all one's sources of knowledge in reaching a decision about what should be done. Actions based on this kind of reasoning are not simply emotional displays or the performance of culturally dictated scripts; they are deliberated and reasoned responses. Phronetic reasoning leads to personalized choices in which both the agent and the recipient of service are taken into account. Thus, the outcome, unlike that of deductive reasoning, does not hold universally across actors.

Both Plato and Descartes depicted the mind as having two separate parts. According to these philosophers, the part in which deductive reasoning takes place is pure intellect, and the other part is infected with emotion and personal bias. Contrary to their perceptions, deductive and phronetic reasonings and other mental processes are all carried out in the same place. "People generally assume that one [phronetic decision making] and the other [deductive decision making] have entirely unrelated mechanisms, mentally and neurally" (Damasio, 1994, p. 168). Damasio suggested Descartes' notion that there were two separate kinds of thinking, one higher and the other lower, caused him to place formal decision making, which he regarded as the essence of humanness, outside the body, and the other kinds of thinking, which he regarded as characteristic of an animal nature, within the body. For Descartes, "one [formal decision making] stands for clarity of thought, deductive competence, algorithmicity, while the others connote murkiness and the less disciplined life of the passions" (Damasio, 1994, p. 168). Damasio considered this separation Descartes' mistake.

The remainder of this chapter provides outlines of four theories of embodied thinking—Epstein's, Lakoff and Johnson's, Gendlin's, and Damasio's. Taken together, these theories provide a foundation for phronetic thinking as well as an extension of its ideas.

EPSTEIN'S EXPERIENTIAL THINKING

Epstein (1980; 1993; 1994) differentiated two kinds of thinking processes—the experiential system and the "rational" system—which he connects with Aristotle's two types of thinking (1994, p. 712). The former has the characteristics associated with phronetic thinking, while the latter overlaps *techne* or technical-rational thinking. Epstein's use of the term *rational* for the formal way of thinking reflects the traditional notion that only formal and calculative thinking is rational. I have used 'rational' in a broader sense to cover both phronetic and *techne* thinking. Reserving 'rational' for *techne* thinking can imply that all nonformal thinking is irrational.

Although the experiential system operates primarily out of awareness, it is distinct from the unconscious thinking identified by Freud. In Freud's unconscious, primary processes distort unacceptable thoughts and desires to protect the ego. Experiential thinking, however, is a "fundamentally adaptive system that automatically, effortlessly, and intuitively organizes experience and directs behavior" (Epstein, 1994, p. 710). The search for a lost key provides an example of the background operation of the experiential system. After consciously retracing my movements and recalling places where the key might have been left, I check these places; but the key does not turn up. I give up the directed search and move on to writing a letter. I am no longer consciously concerned about the lost key. But while writing the letter, an image of the key and its location pops into my awareness. It was not a place I had thought to look; but when I get up and go to that place, I find the key. As I was writing the letter, experiential thinking about the key was occurring outside of my awareness. When it determined where the key was, it presented the answer to my awareness in the form of an image.

Terms such as *deliberation, deciding,* and *thinking* normally connote consciously directed processes. However, we also engage in deliberating and deciding in experiential thought. It may sound odd to talk about deliberation when we are not consciously aware that we are considering alternatives, but many of our everyday practical action choices are made without conscious direction. Experiential deliberation can work with the complexities of multiple and conflicting values and unique situations. It can make use of memories and culturally provided background understandings about the world and social relations. In some ways, experiential reasoning is more sophisticated and integrative than formal reasoning. It is not restricted by the conditions required for formal thought.

The traditional understanding in the West held that all thought occurred in consciousness and was available for reflective viewing. While some part of experiential thinking is available to reflection and examination in awareness, much of it lies beyond conscious reflection. Dreyfus and Dreyfus (1986) found

TABLE 6.1
Comparison of the Experiential and Rational Systems

Experiential system	*Rational system*
1. Holistic	1. Analytic
2. Affective: Pleasure-pain oriented, what feels good	2. Logical: Reason oriented (what is sensible)
3. Associationistic connections	3. Logical connections
4. Behavior mediated by "vibes" from past experiences	4. Behavior mediated by conscious appraisal of events
5. Encodes reality in concrete images, metaphors, and narratives	5. Encodes reality in abstract symbols, words, and numbers
6. More rapid processing: Oriented toward immediate action	6. Slower processing: Oriented toward delayed action
7. Slower to change: Changes with repetitive or intense experience	7. Changes more rapidly: Changes with speed of thought
8. More crudely differentiated. Broad generalization gradient; categorical thinking	8. More highly differentiated
9. More crudely integrated: Dissociative, emotional complexes; context-specific processing	9. More highly integrated: Cross-context processing
10. Experienced passively and preconsciously: We are seized by our emotions	10. Experienced actively and consciously: We are in control of our thoughts
11. Self-evidently valid: "Experiencing is believing"	11. Requires justification via logic and evidence

From: Epstein, S. (1991). Cognitive-Experiential Self-Theory: An Integrative Theory of Self. In R. C. Curtis (Ed.), *The relational self: Theoretical convergences in psychoanalysis and social psychology*. New York: Gilford. Used by permission.

that experts often cannot describe how they reach their decisions. We often cannot give a formal explanation of why we decided experientially to do or not to do something. Merleau-Ponty (1945/1962) provided an analogy to illustrate the inaccessibility of the depths of experiential thinking. He compared the reflective viewing of experiential thinking to a person looking down a well. The light penetrates a short distance into the upper portion of the well, allowing one to see what is there. However, whatever is beyond the lighted portion cannot be seen.

Experiential reasoning primarily involves thinking with images rather than words (Arnheim, 1969; Kosslyn, 1980). This is a departure from the position that thinking takes place primarily in language (for example, Margolis, 1997). Imaged reasoning is not limited to thinking within the rules of grammar and network of concepts provided by one's language. The images are a result of people's interactions with themselves, the world, and others, and they provide the primary content for experiential reasoning. The sources of the images are all the modes of perception, including interoception, proprioception, and exteroception. Experiential images are not limited to visual sights; they also include audio images of words and other sounds, images of tactile experiences, and images of tastes and odors. Imaged thinking retains the particularity of experiences while arranging them into categories.

Rosch (1978; 1999) noted that mental concepts can be organized around the image of a category prototype. The prototypes for categories are not universal but vary according to individual experiences. Prototype categories differ from the traditional definition in which membership in a category is determined by conforming to a number of necessary and sufficient properties. Prototypes allow for gradations of membership in a category. For example, a robin may serve as the prototype for the category of bird. While an eagle also belongs in this category, it is not equivalent to a robin. Deductive and calculative reasoning are based on traditional categories in which all members can be treated as being the same. For example, every person included in the diagnostic category "General Anxiety Disorder" is expected to have the same properties. Experiential thinking with imaged prototype categories preserves individual differences among the category members. "One of the philosophically cogent aspects of prototypes is that, far from being abstractions of a few defining attributes, they seem to be rich, imagistic, sensory full-bodied mental events that serve as reference points" (Rosch, 1999, p. 67).

The theory of experiential reasoning does not neglect language, which is still held to be the most sophisticated of human capacities. However, its significance is not derived from the notion that knowledge is stored as language or that thought necessarily occurs in language.

> The glories of language lie elsewhere, in the ability to translate, with precision, thoughts into words and sentences, and words and sentences into thought; in the ability to classify knowledge rapidly and economically under the protective umbrella of a word; and in the ability to express imaginary constructions or distant abstractions with an efficient simple word. (Damasio, 1999, p. 111)

Some experiential images are visual and auditory images of words, but experiential thinking primarily involves relating images, not language concepts. Experiential images are organized into categories that sometimes precede those presented by the concepts of a language. However, the concepts learned from language can add new and more abstract categories that provide further schemes for organizing experiential thought.

Experiential thinking also makes use of narrative logic in figuring out what to do. Unlike formal thinking, narrative thinking infers relationships in terms of their contribution to a goal. It organizes incidents in the form of a story in which the meaning of an event depends on when it occurred and in what context (Polkinghorne, 1988). The primary dimension of narrative thinking is temporality; it integrates the events of an unfolding situation in deliberation about what is to be done next. Mattingly (1991; 1998) held that clinical practitioners use narrative logic in deciding what to do in their work with patients.

Epstein's differentiation between experiential and "rational" thinking extends Aristotle's *phronesis-techne* distinction, but he does not restrict experiential thinking to choices about actions in the human realm. Neither does he address the issue about the appropriateness of "rational" thinking for deciding how to accomplish the good in dealing with a particular person. The distinctions Epstein makes concern different ways of thinking, not their suitability for specific kinds of tasks. One of the modes described would not be considered formal thinking, yet it captures many of the features of Aristotle's *phronesis*. According to Epstein, we use this mode for most of our everyday choices, whether they are for action in the physical or the human realm.

The experiential system (or *phronesis*) is not a less evolved way of thinking to be overruled by the more "rational" system when making decisions (Wilson, 2002). Rather, it is a highly evolved and adaptive system, which is neither inferior nor superior to formal, deductive thought. Each system has its advantages and disadvantages. Epstein described the experiential system as one that fosters fast and natural processing of information and is the source of intuitive wisdom and creativity. It is used in the give and take between practitioners of care and those they serve.

LAKOFF AND JOHNSON'S EMBODIED RATIONALITY

Lakoff (1987) and Johnson (1987) have argued that human thinking should be approached as a bodily activity. The computer model employed by cognitivism presents thinking as an independent operation that can be carried out on various platforms. When human beings engage in thinking, their thought has no special qualities that differentiate it from the thinking of machines. Dreyfus (1979) produced an early critique of cognitivism and its view that thinking is limited to the programmed manipulation of symbols, which have no inherent content meaningful to the human thinker. Dreyfus emphasized that human beings, unlike computers, have bodies that exist in time and space. Human thought contains the perspective of the thinker, and it cannot simply be transferred to a computer and retain the characteristics of actual embodied human thought.

In the decades since Dreyfus's critique, a second generation of cognitive science has taken its place beside the cognitivism of the first generation. The second generation holds that the mind is inherently embodied, although most thought occurs out of awareness, and abstract concepts are largely metaphorical (Varela, Thompson, & Rosch, 1991). The following description of second-generation cognitive psychology was provided by Lakoff and Johnson (1999):

> Second-generation cognitive science is in every respect a cognitive science of the embodied mind. Its findings reveal the central role of our embodied understanding in all aspects of meaning and in the structure and content of our thought. Meaning has to do with the ways in which we function meaningfully in the world and make sense of it via bodily and imaginative structures. This stands in contrast with the first-generation view that meaning is only an abstract relation among symbols (in one view) or between symbols and states of affairs in the world (in another view), having nothing to do with how our understanding is tied to the body. (p. 78)

Lakoff and Johnson pointed out that this new view of human reasoning "is not at all what the Western philosophical tradition had held it to be" (1999, p. 4). The traditional understanding of reason is in need of revision. Descartes' view that the mind is the seat of reason and that it is separate from and independent of the body is no longer accepted. Neither is his belief that people are capable of knowing everything about their minds through self-reflection. Finally, the view that reason is universal and operates according to invariant logical rules is incorrect.

In place of these traditional views, Lakoff and Johnson proposed that reason has the following set of characteristics (1999):

1. Reason arises from the nature of people's brains, bodies, and bodily experience. It is not disembodied, but the structure of reason comes from the details of human embodiment. Reason makes use of the same neural and cognitive operations that are used in people's sensory and motor systems. It is an activity that is dependent on the peculiarities of the organization of the human body.

2. Reason is evolutionary in that it makes use of, rather than transcends, those aspects of the human organism that are shared by other developed organisms. Reason makes use of forms of perceptual and motor inference

present in "lower" animals. Thus, reason is not a characteristic that separates humans from other animals, but places humans on a continuum with other developed forms of life.

3. Reason is not universal in the sense that it is not part of the structure of the universe. It is, however, a capacity shared by all human beings. What makes reasoning similar in people [are] the commonalities in the way human minds are embodied. Thus, reason does not strictly vary according to the language a person speaks.

4. Reason operates mostly out of awareness; it is not an exclusive property of conscious awareness.

5. Reason is not dispassionate, but is emotionally informed and engaged.

6. Reason does not function in a literal fashion, but functions largely through the use of metaphor and imagination. (p. 4)

In commenting on Dreyfus's *What Computers Can't Do* (1979), Collins (2000) expanded the idea of embodied knowing by adding the human beings' capacity for socialization. According to him, there are four types of knowledge: symbol-type, embodied, embrained, and encultured. The symbol-type is the kind of knowledge early computer-based models attributed to human mental abilities. Collins used spell-checking programs to illustrate this ability. Spell checking involves comparing typed groups of alphabetic signs with those on a list of grouped alphabetic signs loaded in the computer. If a typed group of letters does not match any group on the list, it is flagged as a misspelled word. The computer is indifferent to the identity of the author. The ability to spell check can be transferred between computers simply by loading it on disks and reloading it on to another computer. While either a human brain or silicon chip can serve as the hardware for spell checking, the problem with the symbol-type model is that it does not know the meaning attached to a group of alphabetic signs. If an author writes, "If one spells "mistake" with the letters *m i s s t a k e*, it is a mistake," the spell checker will flag the second word as an error.

Because so many human abilities are individually embodied and cannot be transferred directly to another person, the computer model is inadequate to account for them all. For example, the ability to ride a bicycle is carried in one's body as muscular responses to maintaining balance. Furthermore, human knowledge of the world is a function of the particular shape and needs of our bodies. Organisms interact with their environments in terms of their embodied needs and the opportunities (and dangers) presented in their environment to meet those needs (Gibson, 1979). For example, if a person has been standing too long, he or she will seek a place to sit. A chair, a tabletop, a railing, or anything that will serve as a place to sit will do. What is perceived is a function of the organism's characteristics, needs, and abilities. A meal that satisfies the hunger of an insect will not afford the same relief for a human being. Relief ultimately depends on what is available in the environment. If a person wishes to sit, he or she will consider the options for doing so. Is there a chair, a table-top, or a railing? Thus, what is experienced perceptually is a consequence of an organism's needs (the subject) and what is available (the object).

The symbol-type model of human knowing is inadequate, not only because we engage the world through the particular kind of bodies we have, but also because of the particular kind of brains we have. The chemicals that make up the human brain and the structural arrangement of our brains affect the type of mental abilities we have. Attempts have been made to emulate the structure of the brain with computer models using connections of "neural nets." In these models, the computer is presented with a task, and the neurons fire randomly. When they hit on the output, the firings that produced that output are strengthened. The model uses a simple reinforcement theory to strengthen desired responses. The computer does not have to be programmed on how to respond in advance; it "learns" how to do so from feedback. Although the connectionist models emulate human abilities to learn from experience, Collins noted that their stimulus-response training does not enable them to adapt to new situations as human beings do.

Collins (2000) proposed that people's abilities are related to the kind of bodies and brains they have, and the most important of these abilities relates to the human capacity for "socialness." "Socialness is the capacity of humans . . . which enables them to attain social fluency in one or more cul-tures" (p. 193). Socialness gives one the ability to know what counts by relat-ing things to the whole context.

> To know what counts one has to understand the whole context. "Rubbish" and "antique" are categories that continually shift both in time and space. Even something as ephemeral as the newspaper changes its value as the events it records changes. Most issues of yesterday's newspaper are rubbish, but those recording momentous events, such as great victories or crimes, gain a sentimental value, or become memorabilia or collectors' items. (Collins, 2000, p. 192)

Socialness is the human capacity to have a background of experiences that have meaning as they relate to and are distinguished from everything that makes up our understandings of ourselves, others, and the world.

GENDLIN'S EXPERIENCING

Phronetic reasoning and reflective understanding are activities that draw on and make use of the special embodied abilities of human beings. Unlike technical-rational decision making, their deliberation cannot be given over to computers. Traditional models have envisioned human thought as having a logical structure resembling that of formal argument or mathematical calculation. More recently, thought has been depicted as having a linguistic structure. This is in keeping with the notion that human thinking proceeds through the grammatical structures of language. Lacan (1968) proposed that unconscious thought was not structured by condensation, displacement, and symbolism, but was "structured like language." Gendlin (1962; Levin, 1997) held that formal and verbal models failed to capture the richness and complexity of human thought. Like the other embodiment theorists, he held that most human thinking happens in the background, out of awareness.

Gendlin is a psychotherapist and a philosopher. He worked with Rogers at the University of Chicago, and his ideas have special relevance for extending Aristotle's idea of phronetic reasoning. Focusing on experiential meaning and disagreeing with linguistic pragmatism, Gendlin holds that experience is not a culturally imposed construction; rather, it is the result of a more fundamental interaction between a person and the world. His basic thesis is that the source of speech and action is experience (or *experiencing,* a term he uses to emphasize the fact that experience is an ongoing process, not a thing). Gendlin's experiencing can be related to the kind of embodied thinking described above, but it should be differentiated from thinking as a conscious, logical process. Experiencing is our interaction with life situations and the visceral meanings these situations have for us. It consists of a more complex order than the concepts and distinctions inherent in language. Speech and action are partial expressions of the intricate multiplicity of experiencing, but experiencing is always greater than what one can say about it. Words become meaningful as they are used to communicate and reflect on an aspect of one's felt experience. Gendlin's theory of felt meaning reverses the notion that conceptual distinctions and structures are the determinants of speech and actions. Instead, he held that words and phrases are drawn out of experiencing. Language is an open and enabling system, not a closed and determinant one.

Gendlin first presented his theory of embodied felt meaning in *Experiencing and the Creation of Meaning* (1962), in which he argued its superiority to the then-predominant ideas of logical positivism. In his more recent works, Gendlin has addressed reductive analytic philosophy and the linguistic idealism of postmodern writers. Taking the middle road, he focuses on what has been overlooked by both these positions—*bodily felt meaning*. He uses this term to refer to the kind of nonconscious awareness people have of their practical and background understanding of themselves, others, and the world. In Gendlin's view, most human activity is not the result of conscious deliberation; it flows directly from felt meaning instead.

Gendlin, however, distinguished between bodily, experiential understanding and reflective, verbal thought. Embodied understanding functions below the level of conscious awareness and is more intricate than thought carried out in reflection. It is an amalgamation of emotions, memories, spatial and temporal locations, the felt presence of other people and things, and language. Embodied understanding is not static but dynamic; it is continuously integrating new exchanges between person and world. Human practice is primarily a consequence of the intricate experiential understanding and secondarily a consequence of the grammatically organized conceptual apparatus of a linguistic system.

According to the theory that thought occurs linguistically, it was believed that people who speak different languages would experience the world differently. This notion led to the idea that the experiences of people who speak different languages are incommensurate, and therefore, they cannot understand one another. However, Gendlin noted that because all human beings have the same bodily form, at certain levels people have a set of common desires and experiences. Thus, even those who speak different languages can understand and appreciate one another's basic life experiences.

Gendlin described the texture of experiential understanding as "more than conceptual patterns (distinctions, differences, comparisons, similarities, generalities, schemes, figures, categories, cognitions, cultural and social forms)" (1997, p. 3). Because felt meaning is too intricate to be expressed through the concepts and formations of language, Gendlin uses the ellipsis mark ". . . ." to refer to embodied understanding. The ". . . ." is the source of the creation of meaning. Rosch (1978), who developed the notion of prototype concepts, presented the idea that a nonconceptual background exists below conceptual thinking. Her idea supplements Gendlin's notion that experiential understanding is more intricate than concepts. The cognitive models do not recognize that there can be such a thing as nonconceptual thinking.

> There is no way that a cognitivist system can deal with the non-conceptual. Yet it is just in those experiences that people find meaning and integrity in their lives. In cognitivism such things must be relegated to a separate sphere where they are either denied to exist or put fundamentally beyond the reach of cognitive science. In the new view [embodied thinking] proposed here, the non-conceptual is inherently part of mind-world situations, perhaps of every situation. No science of human existence can afford to straight-facedly exclude what is most meaningful to life. (Rosch, 1978, p. 75)

Gendlin used the example of a poet at work to illustrate the way intricate nonconceptual thought becomes expressed in concepts. The poet uses and discards different words and sentences trying to find ones that will convey the meaning she wishes to express. Finally, she comes upon the metaphor or figure of speech that articulates the felt meaning. In this example, the felt meaning functions implicitly by eluding capture until the right words come along to express the poet's feelings. A felt meaning does not have a decisive boundary or sharp configuration, yet it is informative. Reflective understanding used by caregivers follows a process similar to that of a poet trying to find the right word to express her thoughts. Practitioners feel what they want to do, but "try out" imagined scenarios, discarding those that do not quite convey what they feel until they find one that expresses it. They then put this scenario into action.

It is difficult to describe the intricate and complex operations and structure of embodied background thinking within the literal meaning of words. Descriptions of the background (itself a metaphor) are usually given as metaphors or analogies. Gadamer used the spatial metaphor *horizon* to depict the breadth of the background in which thought occurs. Gendlin wanted to extend the spatial meaning of 'horizon' to include a temporal dimension. He held that people's background horizon extends back into the past through the body's openness to remembrances and forward into the future through imagined scenarios. Depicting the background as having a past and a future captures and deepens the reflective-understanding notion that the background retains and draws upon prior situational encounters. Schrag (1986) urged caution in using the metaphors *horizon* and *field* to connote characteristics of the background. In his opinion, they are too visually weighted and give privilege to experiential phenomena that are known through sight (see also Jay, 1994; Levin, 1993). Schrag also proposed the metaphorical use of the term *texture* to characterize the "structure" of the intricacy of embodied thinking. 'Texture' creates an image of the background of a fabric woven from interlaced processes.

Another visual metaphor for the intricacy of embodied understanding is the rhizome, which has been used by Eco, Deleuze and Guattari, and Cunningham to capture the idea of its complex entanglement. A rhizome is the intricate, interconnected rootlike network that anchors mosses to surfaces and through which they absorb nourishment. Cunningham (1998) explained:

> The tangle of roots and tubers characteristic of rhizomes is meant to suggest a semiosic space where (1) every point can and must have the possibility of being connected with every other point, raising the possibility of an infinite juxtaposition; (2) there are no fixed points or positions, only connections and relationships; (3) the space is dynamic and growing, such that if a portion of the rhizome is broken off at any point it could be reconnected at another point without changing the original potential for juxtaposition; (4) there is no hierarchy or genealogy contained as where some points are inevitably

superordinate or prior to others; and (5) the rhizome is a whole with no outside or inside, beginning or end, border or periphery, but is rather an open network in all of its dimensions. (p. 829)

Making practical decisions through phronetic and reflective-understanding processes involves embodied thinking. For the most part, this occurs outside of conscious awareness, and as Gendlin noted, it draws from the breadth of one's understanding of the world and the depth of one's past and imagined future actions. Embodied thinking is more complex and integral than the logical models proposed by the philosophers who followed Descartes as well as those proposed by contemporary cognitivists. The combination of nonconceptual and emotional understandings results in greater sensitivity to the intricacies of the human realm. Therefore, embodied thinking enables the practitioner to consider actions using open processes that will produce more appropriate action responses to particular people than the calculative procedures based on scientifically validated general knowledge statements.

DAMASIO'S EMBODIED-ENACTIVE MODEL

Psychologists such as Epstein and Gendlin, linguists such as Lakoff, and philosophers such as Johnson have contributed to the development of the embodied model of thinking. Additional influence has come from explorations in neurology that make use of scientific theories dealing with situations of flux, such as nonlinear dynamic systems, self-organizing states, and dissipative structures. As a result, thinking processes are being viewed as emerged systems enacted by situated agents (Ellis, 1999). In what is now termed the "embodied-enactive model," thought is understood to be a synthesis of the body, the environment, and the interaction between them.

> This new synthesis seeks a close and explicit relationship between brain mechanisms, their existence within an organism, and a surrounding world within which there is an unceasing coupling. Hence this view highlights the role of the agent's actions and interests, the way the organism enacts its being, adapting with plasticity to the environment over time. (Roy, Petitot, Pachoud, & Varela, 1999, p. 61)

The embodied-enactment approach questions the relevance of the computational and connectionist's representational explanation of cognition. The notion of representation retains the flavor of a subject-object dichotomy. A person's sense apparatus is bombarded with information from objects in the environment, such as their length, color, movement, sound, and so on. The senses encode this information as symbolic forms, which they send to the brain. In the brain, these symbols stand for or represent the real objects. Thought is the manager of these representations, and cognition is held to be the symbolic representation of a pregiven world by a pregiven mind (Varela et al., 1991, p. 9).

The term *enactive* serves to emphasize the alternate view that cognition is an enactment between a person and the environment that produces an experiential world on the basis of his or her interests, plans, and history of activity. The world of experience is an interior construction of the body, not a reproduction of an external reality (Bolles, 1991; Maturana & Varela, 1998). Cognition is an activity of the whole embodied person in meaningful interaction with the self, others, and world. It is not limited to conscious thought but includes the body's internal regulation of life processes as well as its emotional sensitivity and openness to cues that are experienced outside of awareness (see Bargh & Chartland, 1999; Wegner & Wheatley, 1999).

The embodied-enactment approach has drawn on the work of philosophers who have studied experiential appearances, such as Husserl and Merleau-Ponty (Petitot et al., 1999). Merleau-Ponty's investigations of embodiment are particularly important resources (Varela et al., 1991), as are Gibson's (1979) explorations of affordances. Topics once considered the purview of philosophy—consciousness, self, volition, emotion, feeling, and imagination—are now being investigated by neurologists. Neurologist Damasio's explorations provide an example of a contemporary scientific investigation of these topics. His research illustrates the results of neurological investigations undertaken from an embodied-enactive perspective.

Damasio's method of investigation, like Merleau-Ponty's (1947/1964), involved the observation of patients with brain injuries. By knowing what part of the brain's activity is impaired and what experiences have been changed as a result of the injury, it is possible to make connections between certain kinds of brain activity and certain kinds of experience. Unlike Merleau-Ponty, Damasio had access to the new scanning devices that show the location of brain activity as a person is engaged in thinking. He also made use of the explanatory power of new theories of causal relationships to account for neural processes; for example, chaos theory, nonlinear feed-forward and feed-backward causation, emergent and self-organizing system causation.

As organisms living within the structure of their bodies, human beings undergo continuous change. The bodily processes are constantly monitored by the neural system, which communicates with the body through two systems: neural circuits and biochemical changes. Neural circuits carry signals to the brain and from the brain to every part of the body. Biochemical changes operate through the bloodstream, which circulates chemical signals such as hormones, neurotransmitters, and modulators throughout the body.

Thought. For Damasio, "having a mind" means that an organism forms neural representations that can become images, that it can manipulate these images in a process called "thought," and that it can use thought to influence activity by anticipating the consequences of an action. Mind, therefore, arises from activity in neural circuits, but "the mind is embodied in the full sense of the term, not just embrained" (1994, p. 118). Damasio's view that the mind is derived from the entire organism as an ensemble is in opposition to the dualistic view that mind is located in an otherworldly sphere, as well as the more current view that it resides in or around the brain. According to him, "mind is probably not conceivable without some sort of *embodiment*" (1994, p. 134).

In disagreement with philosophers who hold that thought occurs through language, Damasio maintains that "thought is made largely of images" (1994, p. 106). Words and arbitrary symbols, including those used in inner speech or those mentally rehearsed before writing, exist as auditory or visual images in our awareness. Feelings that occurred during the original experience are retained by the image during thought. Damasio believes that these feeling-loaded images, which he refers to as "dispositional representations," constitute the full repository of human knowledge, whether innate or acquired by experience. However, he does not use the term *representation* in the traditional sense to mean an image of an external reality.

> The problem with the term representation is . . . the implication that, somehow the mental image or neural pattern *represents*, in mind and in brain, with some degree of fidelity, the object to which the representation refers, as if the structure of the object were replicated in the representation. When I use the word representation, I make no such suggestion. (1999, p. 320)

"While there is an external reality, what we know of it would come through the agency of the body proper in action, via representations of its perturbances" (1994, p. 235). People never know how faithful their knowledge is to absolute reality. What they do have is a consistency in the constructions of reality that people's brains make and share. Damasio (1994) uses the idea of cats to illustrate his point:

> Consider our idea of cats: we must construct *some* picture of how our organism tends to be modified by a class of entities that we will come to know as cats, and we need to do that consistently, both individually and in the human collective in which we live. Those systematic, consistent representations of cats are real in themselves. Our minds are real, our images of cats are real, our feelings about cats are real. It is just that such a mental, neural, biological reality happens to be *our* reality. Frogs or birds looking at cats see them differently, and so do cats themselves. (p. 235)

Emotion. Damasio has summarized his investigations in two books, *Descartes' Error* (1994) and *The Feeling of What Happens* (1999). The title of the first book refers to Descartes' belief that the mind was separate from the body. Its theme is that emotion is integral to the processes of reasoning and decision making and that the traditional notion that emotion always hinders clear thinking is wrong. Damasio emphasized the body's homeostasis, which are the coordinated and largely automated processes that maintain steady internal states in living organisms. Feeling is the experience of the continuous changes taking place in the body. A human being continuously feels, in the background of his experience, the homeostatically regulated changes that result from his body's monitoring of its basic life processes. "[These background feelings are] minimalist in tone and beat, the feeling of life itself, the sense of being" (1994, p. 150).

Emotions are bodily changes resulting from the monitoring of internal changes that exceed the homeostatic limits and from changing perceptual experiences of the world. They constitute an innate part of the body's regulating system. "Emotions are part of the bioregulatory devices with which we come equipped to survive" (1999, p. 53). One of the functions of emotions is to regulate the internal state of an organism to prepare it for a specific reaction. The biological reaction might be to flee, to become immobile, or to engage in a pleasurable activity. If, for example, the reaction is to flee, emotion is the embodied signal to increase blood flow to the arteries in the legs so that the muscles receive extra oxygen and glucose. Because the body interacts continuously with its internal and external environment, emotional responsiveness is always present at varying levels. Humans can temper their emotionally generated actions through mental processes, such as deliberative decision making or recalling the consequences of such actions in the past.

Damasio held that feelings are always connected with the mental image that initiated the emotional response. "A feeling depends on the juxtaposition of an image of the body [the emotional response] to an image of something else, such as the visual image of a face or the auditory image of a melody" (1994, p. 145). Recalled images are composites of the entire body's changes, including emotional responses that have occurred in past situations. Thus, when an image is recalled, it is accompanied by the feeling that was originally connected with it. For example, when one recalls a beloved individual, not only does a perceptual image of the person come to mind, but also the warm feelings the image evokes. The emotional or somatic feelings first brought forth by an experience are the consequence of socialization through which one learns which are normal responses to certain images or situations. For example, a child can be socialized to feel fear when approached by a stranger. Damasio said that when a person has attached a feeling to a class of images, it is "somatically marked." "Somatic markers are thus acquired by experience, under the control of an internal preference system and under the influence of an external set of circumstances which include not only entities and events with which the organism must interact, but also social conventions and ethical rules." (Damasio, 1994, p. 179).

According to Damasio, what is stored in the mind is not the original perceptual image per se; rather, it is a representation of the "firing patterns which trigger the momentary reconstruction" of the original perceptual experience by "activation of the neural firing patterns largely in the same early sensory cortices where the firing patterns corresponding to the perceptual representations once occurred" (Damasio, 1994, p. 102). When an image is recalled, it is simply a momentary reconstruction, not a replica or exact reproduction of the earlier experience. How close the recalled image is to the original depends on the circumstances in which the original image was learned and the circumstances under which it is recalled.

Action. As felt images accumulate throughout a lifetime, they are categorized with somatically marked images from previous experiences of a similar nature (Lakoff, 1987). When one is confronted with a new experience that calls for a choice, the situation is identified analogically as belonging to one of these categories. The identification, which most often occurs out of awareness, initiates a process in which a number of stored images flash through awareness. Each recalled image is accompanied by an emotional or somatic feeling connected to the original experience. The flashing images present a series of scenarios about what might happen if the person were to take the same action in the present situation. "To our consciousness, the scenarios are made of multiple imaginary scenes, not really a smooth film, but rather pictorial flashes of key images in those scenes, jump cut from one frame to another, in quick juxtapositions" (1994, p. 170). The emotional or somatic feelings evoked by these scenarios serve to guide choices of action in the current situation. "When the bad outcome connected with a given response option comes into mind, however fleetingly, you experience an unpleasant gut feeling" (p.173). A recalled felt image focuses attention on the possible negative or positive outcome of its reenactment and serves "as an automated alarm signal which says: Beware of danger ahead" (p. 173) or "Go for it!" (p. 180).

Often people are not fully conscious of the emotional or somatic feelings that influence their decision. The entire process of identifying a situation by category based on previous experience, the flashing of recalled felt images that remind one of the consequences of actions taken in the past, and the selection of an action for the present is quick and mainly out of awareness. This results in the feeling that an action has been chosen because it was the right thing to do. Damasio noted that this process has erroneously been called "intuition," "the mysterious mechanism by which we arrive at the solution of a problem *without* reasoning toward it" (1994, p. 188). The feelings generated by somatic markers are particularly effective in guiding personal and social choices. Decisions influenced by these feelings "align themselves readily with the notions of rationality and practical reason" (p. 168). Damasio is not suggesting that feeling can be substituted for reason in making decisions but that it provides a support system without which reason cannot operate properly.

Damasio's (1994; 1999) view of practical decision making is that it is experientially based, drawing on images from a person's past encounters and enactments in the world. These are images of organism/environmental involvements that include both the person's relationship to some environmental object or activity and the changes this relationship has produced. Images are not merely visual but include all manner of internal and external sensing; for example, sounds, taste, smell, and touch. People learn about the world by engaging it and use what they have learned to decide what to do in similar situations. One's repertoire of practical knowledge consists of the accumulation of the images, conveniently categorized with their feelings attached. When recalled, they provide an array of past actions that may be taken in the present. These possible actions are accompanied by feelings that warn against or lend support for their reenactment. In this way, recalled felt images predict the outcome of potential actions and provide guidance on what to do.

Self. Damasio addressed the relation of a person's experiences of self and consciousness to the body's neurobiology in *The Feeling of What Happens* (1999). Watt (2000) called this book a landmark and stated in his review, "I suspect that much of Damasio's more original terminology . . . will quickly become part of the basic lexicon in consciousness neuroscience in many quarters, due to the sheer force of his ideas and the volume of original thought in this work" (p. 72). In this book, Damasio held that consciousness depends not only on the bodily representation of objects but also on the representation of a primitive self. The latter representation is derived from the manner in which the body is being altered by interaction with objects. Consciousness requires the brain to represent the interaction between objects and the self.

Damasio developed a theory in which three levels of self are tied to the neurological structures and activities of the body. The first level, which he identifies as the protoself, has its roots in systems that regulate the homeostasis of the body's life functions. They provide a stable anchor for the protoself's biological and dynamic representation of the state of the organism. The protoself is connected to the deepest levels of the body's functioning and is the source of the unconscious feeling that one is alive.

The second level is the core self, which results from sensing changes in the protoself that are being initiated by a worldly object and a person's sensing of that object. The core self is the preverbal awareness of the mapping of subject-object connections, the self that is engaged in the formation of somatic marking that links the interaction in a situation with the body's emotional response. The core self provides the body's ability to engage emotionally and purposefully with something in the present and construct an image of it.

The third level is the extended self, which "extends" the body's interaction with the world through reciprocal processing among short-term memory, working memory, and long-term memory. It is also involved in the semantic translations of initially wordless knowledge about interactions with the world. Extensions of the self gain access to these memories as a supplement to the core self's immediate experience of the body's interactions. The extended self is not a creation of language but a level of bodily activity that draws on and integrates emotionally charged past and present images of the body's encounters with the world. It has the ability to translate the body's nonverbal images into verbal meaning.

> In the case of humans the second-order nonverbal narrative of [core] consciousness can be converted into language immediately. One might call it the third-order [extended consciousness]. In addition to the story that signifies the act of knowing and attributes it to the newly minted core self, the human brain also generates an automatic verbal version of the story. I have no way of stopping that verbal translation, neither do you. Whatever plays in the nonverbal tracks of our minds is rapidly translated into words and sentences. That is in the nature of the human, languaged creature. (Damasio, 1999, p. 185)

The activities of the extended self allow for the production of what Damasio called the "autobiographical self," which extends into a remembered past and an anticipated future. The extended self has access to a rich and increasingly extensive set of images over a person's life span. Materializing sometimes in the background and sometimes in the foreground, these images inform one's interpretation of current events and how to respond to them.

In his books, Damasio explained how the structures and organization of the neurological system support his views on consciousness, self, and thought. He situates the self throughout layers of monitoring activity in which the body is continuously engaged. These layers include the monitoring of basic life operations, present interactions with the world, and the extended monitoring that depends on memory and thought. He rejects the idea of the self as a homunculus that observes the body or an executive that manipulates symbols according to logical rules.

Damasio brings a different perspective to the deliberative process of making practical decisions by phronetic and reflective-understanding practical means. As a neurologist, he can speak authoritatively about brain functions and neuronal activity, but his descriptions of mental functioning are consistent with the other models in this section. Therefore, they lend further support to a model of phronetic reasoning in which action choices are embodied, involve emotional and cognitive processes, and draw on the full life experience of practitioners.

CONCLUSION

Practitioners of care deal with the complexity of individual human beings. They need to think about what to do in order to provide individually tailored responses that take into account the time, the place, and the personal histories of the people they serve as well as their own strengths and weaknesses. The mainstream models of reasoned human thought are the traditional model represented by Descartes and his philosophical heirs and contemporary cognitivism. The traditional Descartean model pictures the mind as a nonbodily entity whose processes follow the logic of deductive argumentation; the contemporary cognitivist model, which continues down the same path, limits thinking to programmed calculations of meaningless groups of signs. According to both models, the only legitimate way to make decisions regarding practical actions is by deductive calculation. Any kind of thought that does not conform to logical and calculative operations has been dismissed as being irrational. These two models leave no room for phronetic thinking.

With the advance toward an embodied model of reasoning, approaches that employ the phronetic process have gained legitimacy for making decisions about practice in the human realm. Philosophical differences notwithstanding, these approaches have the following things in common: They take place within a shared embodied and culturally informed background; they are mainly derived through processes that operate out of awareness; they are emotionally informed; and they integrate concerns about multiple values and particular needs.

The embodied model of thinking does not encourage practitioners of care to ignore scientifically validated knowledge statements that relate to their practice, nor does it provide an excuse for not being well trained. It requires practitioners to think for themselves. Even if certain techniques or programs have produced higher mean scores for particular groups under experimental conditions, this does not mean that they should be followed blindly or slavishly. Practitioners need to reflect on possible actions and attend to their feelings about them; they need to take care in monitoring the responses to the things to do; and they need to be clear about the goals they hope to accomplish.

The book began with a discussion of the controversy between technical and judgment approaches to the practices of care. The technical approach comes from an extension of practical decision making from the physical realm to the human realm. It has become the dominant approach to problem solving in contemporary society and is an expression of the technification of Western culture. To find a viable nontechnical alternative, it was necessary to venture out of contemporary society and return to the culture of classical Greece and the texts of Aristotle. Aristotle had also called for the recognition of an additional way to make decisions about actions in the human realm; he called this approach *"phronesis."* Returning to the present, it was noted that the model of embodied thinking shares many themes about deliberation with Aristotle's sketch of phronesis. The next chapter completes the development of a model for practitioner judgment by integrating the themes of background knowing and phronetic thinking with Gadamer's idea of understanding and situated reflection.

7

Reflective Understanding
and Practitioner Judgment

THE ACTIONS OF PRACTITIONERS of care occur in personal interactions with
those they serve. Effective decisions about what to do require a type of reasoning that is responsive to the specific aspects of a situation and sensitive to
changes taking place in that situation. Aristotle's description of *phronesis* provided an outline for an understanding-reflective kind of reasoning that meets
these requirements. Practitioners are embodied and social beings. Reflective
understanding is an integrating process that draws upon understandings
gained from the body's interaction with the world and from the accumulated
wisdom of the culture. The last chapter was an investigation of the embodied
dimension of reflective understanding; this chapter inquires about its cultural
and reflective dimensions.

Practice always takes place within a cultural context. In practices of care
neither the practitioner nor the one served enters as a blank slate. Both bring
with them backgrounds of internalized cultural understandings and accumulated personal experiences. Their thinking takes place within their background
understandings and not in a realm of pure thought insulated from personal
and social context.

The first part of the chapter explores the idea of background understanding and its role in phronetic reasoning. Practitioner judgment, however, is not
simply a matter of expressing unconscious or internalized background knowledge. The chapter's second part adds the notion of reflective understanding to
the idea of background to build a reasoning model that informs practitioner
judgment. In this model practitioners monitor and reflect on the effect of their
background informed actions on achieving their desired goal and adjust their
actions accordingly. The model is based on Gadamer's hermeneutic theory of

understanding texts. Gadamer uses the term *horizon* for background understandings. He says that because we act within a horizon, in our initial encounter with a situation our actions are informed by a prejudgment of what is salient. However, through a dialogic interaction with another, we reflectively enlarge our understanding of the situation and notice new action possibilities. This model of practical reasoning is called "reflective understanding," and it provides the kind of judgments required by care givers who personally interact with those they serve.

PRACTICE AND THE BACKGROUND

The technical-rational approach is derived from an Enlightenment view of people as rational, conscious subjects who stand over and against the world. Although this view retains currency in mainstream contemporary Western society, it was challenged in the past century by some social scientists and philosophers who depicted people as being engaged in practical interaction with the world. Philosophical inquiry has turned its attention from the epistemological problem of how one can know with certainty what the world really is to the problem of practices (Rorty, 1979). "The major philosophical achievements of the century are now widely interpreted as assertions about practices" (Turner, 1994, p. 1).

Social science studies have found that everyday practices do not ordinarily issue from conscious, rational calculation; instead, they flow from background understandings that are culturally embedded. Current philosophies investigating practice have the following general themes: (a) practices are expressions of out-of-awareness background understandings about the world and about how to accomplish things; (b) background understandings are internalized by people through socialization processes; (c) cultures maintain and disseminate their understandings through their rituals, languages, and institutions; and (d) cultures differ in their understandings about the world and about how to accomplish things. People's inherited backgrounds provide them with a pretheoretical understanding that gives them a sense about others, the world, and themselves. It functions by providing an immediate understanding of what is to be done and by identifying useful equipment for accomplishing tasks. The background's fore-structuring or preunderstanding serves to order people's experience of the world and others.

The background is not a set of logically ordered rules about what to do and when to do it but is a holistic web of understandings about how to go about and get things done in the world. Although it is agreed that the background does not have a logical order, there are different views on the kind of organization and attributes it does have. One view holds that the background is an internalization of a culture's language with its conceptual and grammatical attributes (for example, Rorty, 1991). Another view contends that the background is made up of embodied skills and habits (for example, Dreyfus, in Stern, 2000). Others describe the background as a composite of linguistic and embodied understandings; for example, Kuhn's notion of paradigm (1970), Polanyi's idea of tacit knowledge (1962), and Gendlin's view of integral understanding (1997). It seems to me that the composite position is more capable of capturing the fullness and intricacy of the background.

Everyday practice is nondeliberative. Emanating from our backgrounds, it effectively guides us through life, and with it we are able to accomplish our ordinary tasks. However, when one is confronted by obstacles or complex problems, the background cannot always provide the solution. At these times, we employ the reflective mode of understanding to adjust our activities, or we deliberate about what is to be done by using the technical-rational method. These secondary modes do not replace the background; they are simply extensions of it. The background remains and serves as the foundation for reflective and deliberative decisions.

The idea that out-of-awareness mental activity governs everyday practice is relatively recent in Western philosophy. The traditional view held that mental activity only occurred within conscious awareness. Ellenberger (1970) wrote about the growing interest in nonconscious mental activity that began in the 1800s. At the beginning of the twentieth century, Freud was impressed by the nonconscious thinking he observed in hypnotized patients. From the notion of nonconscious thought, he created his psychoanalytic theory in which these unconscious operations managed to keep consciously unacceptable thoughts and desires out of awareness. The unconscious operations did not employ the rational processes of conscious thought, but instead used processes such as condensation, displacement, and symbolism. Through these processes, it diverted a person's unacceptable thoughts into harmless slips of the tongue or dream images. Wilson (2002) speculates that for many decades problems with Freud's views stood in the way of academic psychology's investigations of unconscious processes.

In the early decades of the past century, American academic psychology turned away from the study of mental processes. In its classical conditioning model, it assumed out-of-awareness mental processes that transferred responses from an unconditioned response (tearing in the presence of onion juice) to conditioned responses (tearing at the sound of a bell). In his operate conditioning model, Thorndike assumed that out-of-awareness mental tendencies to act in a certain way were formed when an action was reinforced. In recent cognitive psychology, the mind is depicted as a complex computer, capable of making out-of-awareness calculations; however, this view has difficulty in accounting for the experienced meaningfulness of mental activity (Searle, 1983).

Freud and academic psychology's early learning theories regarded out-of-awareness mental activity as a deficient mode of thought when compared to conscious, rational thought; and cognitive psychology considers it to be logically ordered but without meaning. These views had little influence on the development of background theories, in which the background is seen as a person's primary and original opening on the world and the source of practical activity. The background gives sense to the world, others, and self. The rational, calculative conscious processes prized by prior philosophers are understood by background theorists to be a derivative form of thinking. Rationally governed practical decisions require that aspects be abstracted from the original flow of the background before its logical deductive operations can be performed.

Two philosophers, Dewey and Heidegger, brought to the fore the importance of understanding practice through the operations of people's background (Polkinghorne, 2000). Although both wrote during the first half of the twentieth century, it appears that they developed their ideas about background practice independently. Each sought to transform philosophy by overthrowing the traditional notion that human beings are subjects whose link to the world is forged through representations that appear in the mind. In this understanding, people were like the players of computer games in which images appear on the screens in front of them. Bodily movements are directed in a manner similar to the way game players move the handles and push the buttons to move characters about on the screen. From the perspective of the traditional model of human beings, the central problem for philosophy is epistemology; that is, the relationship between what appears on the screen of consciousness (the theater of the mind) and the world as it actually is.

Although their agendas were different, both Dewey and Heidegger refocused philosophical inquiry on the Continent and in America on the practical, everyday engagement of people with the world. Dewey's purpose for doing this was to develop an understanding of practical intelligence that could serve as the basis for education and also used by social scientists and citizens to solve the problems of a democratic society. Heidegger's project was the understanding of Being, and his investigation of everyday human practice was a means of discovering how Being is disclosed within human existence. By excerpting ideas from their overall projects, one can detect several themes in their understanding of the functions of the background.

Functions of the Background

When people find themselves in a situation, their backgrounds serve to interpret situations and to suggest actions that are responsive to them. It is the background that gives meaning to experiences and informs activity. Dewey believed that human mental processes are an organically evolved attribute, the purpose of which is to guide people in effectively encountering their environment. Burke (1994) delineates Dewey's view of everyday human functioning as follows:

> The basic picture, generally speaking, is that of the given organism/environment system performing a wide range of operations as a normal matter of course—scanning, probing, ingesting, discharging, adapting to, approaching, avoiding, or otherwise moving about and altering things in routine ways, in order to maintain itself. This applies not just to simple biological systems but also characterizes an individual human being's normal activities—from simple things like moving the cup to one's lips to drink from it without dribbling liquid all over the place, or walking down a hallway without careening into the walls, to long-range activities like being in love, pursuing a career, owning a home, managing the budget. . . . Such ongoing activities just *are* interactions which constitute some manner of organism/environment integration. (p. 23)

Practice is performed by carrying out one's background understandings of how to complete tasks. Thus, ordinary accomplishments in the world are not the result of applying theoretical propositions or generalized scientific laws to particular situations. People's backgrounds provide a sense of what to do to achieve an intended result. This sense takes the form of "how-to" knowledge, rather than knowledge "about" something or "what" something is. Dewey (1922) described these different forms of knowledge:

> We may . . . be said to know-how by means of our habits. . . . We walk and read aloud, we get off and on streetcars, we dress and undress, and do a thousand useful acts without thinking of them. We know something, namely, how to do them. . . . If we choose to call [this] knowledge . . . then other things also called knowledge, knowledge of and *about*-things, knowledge *that* things are thus and so, knowledge that involves reflection and conscious appreciation, remains of the different sort. (pp. 177–78)

Dewey proposed that people ordinarily engage the world through learned habits that operate out of awareness. The background habits work sufficiently well so that people generally accomplish their everyday tasks. Dewey called the situations in which background or habitual understanding was successful in accomplishing tasks "determinate" situations.

Heidegger, using a different vocabulary, referred to everyday activity that functions well without deliberate thematic awareness as "circumspection." He wrote that circumspection is unobtrusive and *unthought*.

'Unthought' means that it is not thematically apprehended for deliberate thinking about things; instead, in circumspection, we find our bearing in regard to them. . . . When we enter here through the door, we do not apprehend the seats, and the same holds for the doorknob. Nevertheless, they are there in this peculiar way: we go by them circumspective, avoid them circumspectively, . . . and the like. (1927/1982, p. 163)

In circumspection, a person is functioning in the mode of "absorbed coping." However, when absorbed coping breaks down, a person has to change to "deliberate coping." Deliberate coping involves reflective planning, in which the locus of decision making is switched from out of awareness into awareness.

In Dreyfus's commentary on Heidegger's *Being and Time* (1991), he describes Heidegger's view of the background. The background "enables us to make sense of things" and "provides the conditions necessary for people to pick out objects, to understand themselves as subjects, and generally, to make sense of the world and of their lives" (p. 4). The background has four functions. First, it makes the world intelligible. "Things are not encountered as isolated occurrent entities to which we attach isolated function predicates. . . . [N]othing is intelligible to us unless it first shows up as already integrated into our world, fitting into our coping practice" (pp. 114–15). Because of our background, things immediately appear to us as meaningful. Second, through the background we experience the things of the world in an integrated and holistic way, not as isolated objects. Third, much of our understanding consists simply in our skills for doing things and for getting around in the world. Fourth, human beings respond, not simply to objects, but to situations; our activity is grounded in a background of practices, not a set of mental rules.

The Situated Focus of the Background

The background has a weblike, holistic organization that connects and integrates its vast network of pretheoretical knowledge about how to do things. Thus, we do not experience objects in the world as bits and pieces, but as contextualized interconnections. Humans are always engaged with the world by being in some specific circumstance or situation. Dewey noted that the background does not present the world as a whole. Instead, it adjusts its focus to the here and now. It shows the situation as being textured and layered with interconnections among its parts. Surrounding the center of focus is an aureole of understandings about the broader context. The background provides understandings that enable a person to decide what actions to take from a range of possibilities and places practices within the context of the situation. For example, if the situation calls for the construction of a bookcase, the background indicates what tools are needed, the normal ways in which these tools are used, the way tools in general are used, the more inclusive purpose of the undertaking (such as setting up an office), and the other links that give breadth and depth to one's understanding of the task.

Dewey (1896) held that the significance provided by the background of an event depends on its context. He used the example of noise to emphasize the importance of context: "If one is reading a book, if one is hunting, if one is watching in a dark place on a lonely night, if one is performing a chemical experiment, in each case, [a] noise has a very different psychical value; it is a different experience" (p. 361). Heidegger made a similar point about the attunement of the background to particular tasks. For example, a hammer can be viewed in different ways, depending on the task that is to be accomplished. If one's project is to nail two boards together, the hammer is seen as a tool appropriate to the task; if one's project is to keep the wind from blowing a door closed, the hammer is regarded as a makeshift doorstop. The background attends to and absorbs itself into the task at hand and presents what is significant for that task.

> Being-in-the-world, according to our interpretation hitherto, amounts to a nonthematic circumspective absorption in references or assignments constitutive for the availableness of an equipmental whole. Any concern is already as it is, because of some familiarity with the world. In this familiarity Dasein [human being] can lose itself in what it encounters within the world. (Heidegger, 1927/1962, p. 107)

Gurwitsch (1979), a student of Heidegger, emphasized that background thinking does not conform to an external formal structure but is guided by the situation in which a person is acting.

> What is imposed on us to do is not determined by us as someone standing outside the situation simply looking on at it; what occurs and is imposed are rather prescribed by the situation and its own structure; and we do more and greater justice to it the more we let ourselves be guided by it, i.e., the less reserved we are in immersing ourselves in it and subordinating ourselves to it. We find ourselves in a situation and are interwoven with it, encompassed by it, indeed just "absorbed" into it. (p. 67)

Because one's background understanding focuses itself on accomplishing a particular task in a particular situation, its manifestation differs depending on the task and the place and time in which the task is to be carried out. Background knowledge configures itself according to specific contextual or situational needs; it does not bring to the fore the totality of all that it holds.

The Background Operates out of Awareness

As a person's background informs understanding and action, it normally functions outside of awareness. People ordinarily engage in practical, everyday tasks without consciously calculating what to do. The practices of doing something most often flow through human activity without the actors themselves becoming reflectively aware of their performances. For the most part, people engage in everyday practices without having to mull over what to do. Bernstein (1967) wrote about Dewey's view: "Most of our lives consist of experiences that are not primarily cognitive. We are creatures who are continually involved in doing, enjoying, suffering" (p. 63). The background, however, is not housed in a mental compartment removed from conscious thought; it remains present and operative within what appears to be strictly consciously directed thinking. Neither is the background separated from the body; it spreads to the extremities and permeates the skilled movements involved in a person's engagement with the world. For example, the background dictates the appropriate distance one should stand from others. "[Background] knowledge . . . lives in the muscles, not in consciousness (Dewey, 1922, p. 347).

When practices are performed out of the background, they are rapid and smooth. They resemble what Csikszentmihalyi (1990) called "flow." There is total concentration on the task. "People become so involved in what they are doing that the activity becomes spontaneous, almost automatic; they stop being aware of themselves as separate from the actions they are performing" (p. 53). Practitioners (like athletes) can have the experience of "being in a zone" or "in a groove," where they are not aware of deciding what to do, but are completely caught up in doing it successfully.

The Source of the Background

The primary source from which people gain their background understandings is their culture. One is either born or thrust into a culture that has already developed and is maintaining its understanding of how the world works and how people can cope with it. A basic function of a culture is to transmit to its members accumulated wisdom about how to function successfully. People internalize and incorporate the transmitted cultural wisdom so that it becomes the foundation of their ordinary functioning. Cultures transmit knowledge to their new members through socialization processes. It is an essential characteristic of humans to accept or be initiated into their culture's interpretations of self, others, and the world.

Dewey agreed that one's background understanding is transmitted to individuals from their culture. He (1935/1960) wrote:

[The practical know-how or background] denotes the cumulative informa-tion of the past, not merely the individual's own past but the social past, transmitted through language and even more through apprenticeship in var-ious crafts, so far as this information was condensed in matter-of-fact gen-eralizations about how do certain things like building a house, making the statue, leading an army, or knowing what to expect under given circum-stances. (pp. 71–72)

Dewey also believed that personal experiences add to and individualize back-ground knowledge. An individual's experiences can modify and sometimes produce a Gestalt transformation within his or her background network. Dewey noted that people are not simply passive recipients of their culture's perspective but are open to new learning and creative reformulations of their background's interpretive preunderstandings. Thus, an individual's back-ground evolves and changes through new life experiences. Dewey's agenda was an optimistic one, and he believed that an individual's and a society's background understanding could become more effective at solving problems through intelligent inquiry.

Because the understanding of the world and how to get things done varies among cultures and historical periods, background-enacted practices differ among cultural groups. People do not choose their background; it is formed in them through culturally enacted transmittal processes. Heidegger's interest was directed to the way in which different backgrounds disclose and conceal Being.

[The] everyday way in which things have been interpreted is one into which Dasein [human being] has grown in the first instance, with never a possibil-ity of extrication. In it, out of it, against it, all genuine understanding, inter-preting and communicating, all re-discovering and appropriating anew, are performed. In no case is a Dasein untouched and unseduced by this way in which things have been interpreted. . . . The dominance of the public way in which things have been interpreted has already been decisive even for the possibilities of having a mood—that is, for the basic way in which Dasein lets the world "matter" to it. (Heidegger, 1927/1962, p. 213)

Heidegger held that people take shelter in the background practices of their cultures. The background is an expression of the ordinary way in which the world is presented and the way people of a culture are expected to carry out actions. Doing what one is expected to do is a retreat from the unsettling and uncanny feeling *(angst)* that results from an awareness that one's life is finite and has no inherent meaning. Facing this awareness allows a person a degree of freedom to make his or her own choices and to live more intensely.

Heidegger was particularly concerned about the concealment of Being that is present in contemporary technological culture with its technical-rational understanding (see chapter 2).

Dewey and Heidegger's views about the role of the background in practice have influenced many more recent writers concerned with practice. Rorty has developed a language pragmatism that makes use of Dewey's ideas. Heidegger's influence is found in the work of many Continental philosophers who came after him; for example, in Merleau-Ponty's phenomenology of the body, in Gadamer's notion of prejudgment, and in Foucault's, Bourdeau's, and Certeau's analyses of practice in contemporary society.

Recent Investigations of the Background and Practice

A separate view of the background came out of French developments in the philosophy of science. Writing in the middle decades of the past century, Bachelard proposed that scientific activity was historically situated and did not arrive at final truths. In his view, it moved dialectically by correction and rectification of past errors (Thiboutot & Martinez, 1999). Bachelard's ideas were similar to those proposed later by Kuhn (1970). He also influenced Polanyi (1962), whose investigations of scientific discoveries led him to propose the concept of 'tacit knowing'. Tacit knowing functions out of awareness and is rooted in the body. Tacit knowledge develops through personal interaction with the world, and without intention or awareness, it integrates and synthesizes experiences into patterns. Knowledge of the world is not given simply through impersonal formal thinking; rather, an indispensable part of knowledge development is tacit thought. Polanyi argued that competence is gained through the tacit dimensions of interactions with the world. He believed that language conveys only part of what people perceive and know and that this tacit knowledge is the key component in competent human action.

Recently, Sternberg and Horvath (1999) edited a book based on Polanyi's ideas about the operation of tacit thinking in the performance of professional practices.

> People know more than they can tell. Personal knowledge is so thoroughly grounded in experience that it cannot be expressed in its fullness. In the last 30 years the term *tacit knowledge* has come to stand for this type of human knowledge—knowledge that is bound up in the activity and effort that produced it. (p. ix)

The Sternberg and Horvath volume, which approaches tacit knowledge more as a product of personal experiences than as the result of the internalization of cultural understandings, advances the following notions. Tacit knowledge is embedded in people and "acquired largely from experience" (p. 233) It recognizes a present situation as analogous to previous ones. Furthermore, tacit knowledge is "procedural knowledge that guides behavior but that is not readily available for introspection" (p. 231), and it is intimately related to action and relevant to the attainment of goals that people value. Tacit understanding is also a source of individual differences because it is a consequence of personal experiences with the world. It is not static but develops and changes as people engage in and learn from their new actions. Sternberg and Horvath held that people can shift from tacitly suggested actions developed out of awareness to a reflective examination in order to determine whether the analogy from past experience is appropriate to the present situation.

In a chapter of the Sternberg and Horvath book, Torff (1999) describes the function of tacit knowing in teaching. He observes that teachers have a tacit understanding about how to teach based on their prior experiences as students and also on the successes and failures of their teaching careers. "[Teachers'] intuitive/tacit conceptions about education intermingle with the concepts and practices presented in courses in teacher education" (1999, p. 195). Torff also points out that students have experiential tacit understanding of subject matter and teachers should take this into account when working with them.

Recently, other investigations have been conducted by psychologists about nonconscious processes. Terms such as *implicit, preattentive,* and *automatic* are used for these processes. The rather thin term *automatic* has gained some dominance in recent articles. These investigations picture awareness as a container with only a small capacity. Once the container has been filled, there is no longer any room for conscious thought, so nonconscious thought takes over. The findings of these psychologists have been reported in the *American Psychologist.* According to an article by Park (1999), "The source of behavioral control comes not from active awareness but from subtle cues in the environment and from thought processes and information not readily available to consciousness" (p. 461).

> There are mental activations of which we are unaware and environmental cues to which we are not consciously attending that have a profound effect on our behavior and that help explain the complex puzzle of human motivation and actions that are seemingly inexplicable, even to the individual performing the action. (p. 461)

In the same volume, Bargh and Chartrand (1999) wrote: "Much of social behavior occurs without conscious choice or involvement" (p. 468). They contend that awareness has a limited capacity and that people "use up this limited self-regulatory resource" (p. 464). When this happens, "conscious self-regulatory acts can only occur sparingly and for a short time" (p. 476). Bargh and Chartrand noted that a study by Baumeister, Bratslavsky, Muraven, and Tice (1998) found that awareness plays a causal role only about 5 percent of the time. Because conscious thought depletes the capacity for awareness, it can occur only rarely in the course of a person's day.

Wilson (2002) provided an overview of the recent psychological studies of the mental processes operating out of awareness. He proposed that Freud's view of the unconscious as a storehouse of primitive thought was too limited. Instead, the unconscious is "mental processes that are inaccessible to consciousness but that influence judgments, feelings, or behavior" (p. 22). Wilson proposed that the mind is made up of two systems: the adaptive unconscious and consciousness. The adaptive unconscious is composed of multiple systems that quickly detect patterns in the environment and signals whether they are threatening or not. Consciousness is a single system and functions in a slower, more controlled manner. It "can provide a more detailed analysis of the environment, catching errors made by the initial, quick analysis" (p. 50). The adaptive unconscious deals with the here-and-now, while consciousness focuses on long-term planning.

Summary

The idea of background knowledge challenges the traditional view that all thinking occurs in consciousness. Much of what we do in our everyday practices is a consequence of notions operating in the background of our awareness. Our background informs us how the world operates and how to get things done in it. We are born into an already present understanding about the world, about social organization and relationships, and about what a person is. Through acculturation we assimilate these understandings, and they become our own. It is through the background that we find meaning in the world. The background operates in ways analogous to language (which is incorporated as part of our background). The grammar and vocabulary of a language exist already before a person learns to speak it. Language is internalized and functions out of awareness, producing well-formed sentences and meaningful phrases. Marks on paper such as *c, a, t,* show up as meaningful words. Because a background is shared by the members of a culture, they experience a common world.

The background provides the setting for individual and group practices. These practices themselves are absorbed into one's background as habits, bodily movements, and ways of thinking about things. Our backgrounds are always with us, enabling us to function. There is no way to remove ourselves from our backgrounds, as if by doing so we could engage in "pure" thought, unencumbered by culture, language, and body.

REFLECTIVE-UNDERSTANDING REASONING

Reflective-understanding reasoning is the kind of thinking that informs the judgments of practitioners of care. It differs from technical-rational thinking that calls for the use of conscious, deductive thought to determine correct practices. Through the technical-rational mode, one arrives at decisions about practical actions by employing inference to move from scientifically validated knowledge statements to conclusions about what to do. Reflective understanding incorporates the idea of background operations. It acknowledges that much of practice is determined by nonconscious operations, which draw on complexly organized, internal understandings about the world and about what to do to get things done. However, the reflection-understanding approach holds that, in itself, background knowledge is inadequate for informing practitioner judgment. The reflective-understanding model adds to the ideas of the background as an active reflective process when making practitioner choices. Reflective thinking, however, needs to be distinguished from technical-rational thinking. Reflection is a dialogic engagement with a situation in which a practice is being carried out. It results in an increasing understanding of the unfolding situation. From this enlarged understanding, other possible actions become apparent. The reflective-understanding mode of practice fits best with human situations in which practitioners of care make action choices.

Gadamer and Reflective Understanding

The reflective-understanding mode of informing practice judgments comes into play when actors notice that the actions flowing from their background are not moving them toward the desired goal. When a practice has led to an impasse or veered off course, people can switch to a reflective mode and consider different actions. In reflection, the operations of practical decision making become more deliberate and methodical. Gadamer (1960/1975) provided an analysis of the operations of understanding that can be adapted for use in describing the process of reflective-understanding practice. Understanding uses a different kind of thought than is used for developing scientific knowledge. Aristotle distinguished the thinking used for producing things *(techne)* and that used in performing moral actions *(phronesis)*. Appropriating this distinction, Gadamer linked understanding with phronetic thinking. As he was opposed to the extension of the technical-rational mode into the realm of moral and social practices, a purpose of his work was to propose an alternative approach for practice in the human realm. He found this approach in the humanities, where knowledge was developed through a part-whole or hermeneutic way of thinking. As an exemplar for this kind of knowing, Gadamer chose the reading of texts.

Gadamer accepted the notion that people approach texts (or situations) out of their background understanding. They do not experience phenomena in a direct or brute fashion but as already having been given a meaningful interpretation by their background. The background sets an interpretive framework in which the meaning of natural events and human actions is displayed. "On the hermeneutic account this interpretive framework is not primarily of our own making but is taken over by us from the tradition of which we are part" (Healy, 1996, p. 160). Because human knowledge is always conditioned by the knower's background, it occurs within a fore-understanding or prejudgment about its object.

One cannot rise above the human condition and establish a nonhuman viewpoint from which to look upon the world. However, one's background is not a closed system. Unlike radical background theorists, Gadamer held that people's background understandings do not remain static but evolve and deepen over time. This change is the result of reflection on practices that have been successful as well as those that have not. Gadamer (1986/1994) described the changes that occur in people's background understandings as follows:

> The historical movement of human life consists in the fact that it is never absolutely bound to any one standpoint, and hence can never have a truly closed horizon. The horizon is, rather, the something into which we move and that moves with us. Horizons change for a person who is moving. Thus the horizon of the past, out of which all human life lives and which exists in the form of tradition, is always in motion. The surrounding horizon is not set in motion by historical consciousness. But in it motion becomes aware of itself. (p. 304)

Thus, practitioners are not bound by the understanding provided by their backgrounds. Through reflective understanding they are able to consider new or different practices. One can abstract from Gadamer's writing a four-step process for reflective understanding: (a) a problem occurs with a practice; (b) one questions the prior understanding of the situation; (c) new understandings are considered and deliberated about; and (d) a new understanding is appropriated and serves to inform practice.

A Problematic. Gadamer held that changes in understanding a situation or person are inaugurated by a problem. A reflective inquiry is initiated only when people admit that they lack knowledge or when they experience the need to go beyond their present understanding. Gadamer (1986/1994) cited the Socratic notion that "he knows that he does not know *(docta ignorantia)*" as the impetus for investigation:

> Recognizing that an object is different, and not as we first thought, obviously presupposes the question whether it was this or that. From a logical point of view, the openness essential to experience is precisely the openness of being either this or that. It has the structure of the question. . . . [This is] the knowledge of not knowing. This is the famous Socratic *docta ignorantia* which, amid the most extreme negativity of doubt, opens up the way to true superiority of questioning. (p. 362)

Posing Questions. Once people recognize the inadequacy or intrinsic limitations of their prereflective background understanding, improvement in understanding depends on their willingness to question their former way of engaging the situation. They need to take a radically open stance in which questions can be raised about any part of their background. Inquirers, however, cannot remove themselves entirely from their own tradition. In order to look objectively at one's background understanding and see possibilities that lie beyond it, it is necessary to realize that one's interpretation of a situation is just that: an interpretation, and not a mirror image. Gadamer coined the term *effective historical consciousness* to describe the state of awareness that one stands in a tradition and is affected by it. Because of this, reflection occurs within the context of one's background, not outside it.

One learns from situations only by asking and answering questions about them. Therefore, improvement in background understanding is primarily dependent on asking the right questions. The formulation of questions progresses through stages from an unfocused "feeling" that asks about the adequacy of the received interpretation to a more explicit questioning intended to solicit answers through a worldly response. As answers are received, questions are often modified and sharpened to produce a "new series of questions better attuned to the particularities of the subject matter" (Healy, 1996, 165). Gadamer's questioning process is an iterative and dialectic process whereby answers to initial questions produce further questions that require further testing.

"The ability to ask the right questions about the topic under investigation is something of an art, an art which above all requires insight and good judgment (or better, *phronesis*) as a condition of its possibility" (Healy, 1993, pp. 166–67). Framing questions that lead to an enlarged understanding is a creative process that cannot be reduced to a set of rules. Gadamer proposes that individuals who are experienced with the subject of an inquiry are more likely, because of their experientially developed enlarged understanding, to formulate questions that are better attuned to the phenomena. A methodical movement through a set of algorithmic steps does not produce an appropriate question or hypothesis. (Gadamer reserved the term *method* to refer to regular and systematic procedures used in the sciences.) According to Gadamer (1986/1994):

The priority of the question in knowledge shows how fundamentally the idea of method is limited for knowledge, which has been the starting point for our argument as a whole. There is no such thing as a method of learning to ask questions, of learning to see what is questionable. On the contrary, the example of Socrates teaches that the important thing is the knowledge that one does not know. (p. 365)

Deliberation. For Gadamer, questions lead to answers when they are submitted to the test of experience. In addition to being willing to question one's background's preunderstanding, inquirers need to be open to situational responses to their questions. Reflection requires a question-focused encounter with a recalcitrant experience, and experience becomes the arbiter between competing understandings. The process of questioning-testing-questioning again is an inherent tool, chipping away like an adz at the background's texture. Thus, the background possesses a mechanism for self-correction. Gadamer wanted to bring this process to light so that it might be used more effectively to increase understanding of the world, others, and situations, and consequently produce more successful decisions for practice.

As formulation of questions is not governed by rules, neither is the testing of questions. The traditional concept of 'inquiry' proposes that answers to questions require exact adherence to the rules of a research method. For Gadamer, discovering an enlarged truth about a situation is not a function of using a method correctly. One may be taught how to investigate an object by the object itself. The title of Gadamer's major publication, *Truth and Method,* refers to his position that uncovering the truth about a situation is a more open and creative process than simply following the algorithmic steps laid out in a method. Understanding is more likely to be clouded or distorted than it is to be enlarged by strictly following the requirements of a predetermined method. Gadamer again emphasized that openness is essential to all aspects of hermeneutic reflection: (a) openness to the problematic of a background interpretation; (b) openness to a reappraisal of all aspects of the initial background understanding; (c) openness to framing questions that show up different aspects of the situation; and (d) openness to how the testing of questions is to be carried out.

Gadamer objected to the notion that the inquirer must assume the role of a disinterested spectator that is emphasized in the scientific understanding of validation. Many elements of the traditional scientific method are designed to liberate inquirers from their biases and subjective beliefs so that the object is seen in its pure objectivity. Gadamer believed that it is neither possible nor desirable to seek to view the object from "nowhere." Hermeneutic reflection always takes place within one's textured background and the situation always appears embedded in a particular context. Understanding is derived from the active participation of inquirers with the situated subject matter on which they are reflecting.

This presentation of Gadamer's view has focused, thus far, on a single inquirer who accomplishes his or her work by entering into a dialogue with a situation. The dialogue consists of the inquirer posing enlarged possible interpretations and the situation responding by displaying itself in a fuller way. The single inquirer dialogue takes place *in foro interno* (in the court of consciousness).

Gadamer also explained how several reflectors working together can develop an increased understanding of a situation conversationally. In conversation, inquiry is expanded from a personal, single subject's inquiry to an intersubjective, multiple-horizoned inquiry. Gadamer (1986/1994) offered the following description of conversational reflection:

> To conduct a conversation means to allow oneself to be conducted by the subject matter to which the partners in the dialogue are oriented. It requires that one does not try to argue the other person down but that one really considers the weight of the other's opinion. Hence it is an art of testing. But the art of testing is the art of questioning. For we have seen that to question means to lay open, to place in the open. As against the fixity of opinions, questioning makes the object and all its possibilities fluid. . . . Dialectic consists not in trying to discover the weakness of what is said, but in bringing out its real strength. It is not the art of arguing (which can make a strong case out of a weak one) but the art of thinking (which can strengthen objections by referring to the subject matter). (p. 367)

Dialogic conversation requires that the participants be committed to coming to an understanding beyond that maintained in their present backgrounds. The participants need to respect the understandings of each other and be open to questioning their own prejudgments. Through dialogic conversation, the fusion of the participants' horizons or backgrounds leads to a more "truthful" or enlarged understanding of their situation. However, the development of understanding of a situation never reaches complete fullness. Rather, each new level of understanding that is reached reveals new possibilities that must be investigated. Gadamer emphasized that respect for the other is the essence of conversational reflection. Moreover, the situation, like a fellow inquirer, is to be respected and viewed as the source of enlarged understanding.

Appropriation. Gadamer's idea of appropriation differs from the notion of technical application in which general knowledge is applied to a particular situation. Reflection does not produce universal or general truths about how to do things. What is understood now that was not before is situation specific. Reflection, however, is not complete until its enlarged understanding informs action. The purpose of reflective understanding is to move practice along to its goal. If movement through the process stops at a point where the situation is understood more fully but does not result in renewed action, it remains simply a mental exercise. The point of reflective understanding is to open up one's background for new possible actions.

Gadamer used the interpretation of a law to illustrate the application of an enlarged understanding. To understand a law completely requires more than knowing what the words mean. It is necessary to understand how the law is to be applied in the particular situation under consideration. Correct application of a law must be faithful to its "original meaning" or spirit, but one must also "take account of the change in circumstances and hence define afresh the normative function of the law" (1986/1994, p. 327). Hermeneutic reflection involves not only a grasp of the essential meaning in a situation but also how that meaning informs present practice. Gadamer derives the meaning of application from his notion that the true purpose of understanding is to inform an individual how to act in his or her present situation.

By breaking down the reflective-understanding mode of practical decision making, the process appears more complex and lengthy than it is when carried out. As Schön observes in the next section, the transition from background practice to reflective-understanding practice is smooth and occurs within an ongoing practice performance. It is a temporary transition in which alternative responses are quickly mulled over and then enacted. If the considered alternatives move the practice forward, the actor reengages in the background mode. If they do not, it may be necessary to retreat to a technical-rational mode of deciding, in which case the actor will employ the deductive mode of action planning. However, in actual practice both the reflective-understanding and technical-rational modes continue to focus on the practice at hand and make use of the background's assumptions about the workings of the world.

Reflection-in-Action

Schön (1983) has also investigated reflective understanding in practitioner judgment. Like Gadamer, he understood that the shift to a reflective mode occurs when the consequences of background-informed practice are not sufficient to achieve the intended goal. Schön wrote:

> [Reflection occurs] when there is some puzzling, or troubling, or interesting phenomenon with which the individual is trying to deal. As he tries to make sense of it, he also reflects on the understandings which have been implicit in his action, understandings which he surfaces, criticizes, restructures, and embodies in further action. (p. 50)

The kind of reflection that interested Schön is reflection-in-action. His notion differs from the idea that reflection involves a "stop-and-think" pause in a "region of withdrawal" (Arendt, 1971, p. 97). In that kind of reflection, one breaks off from whatever he or she has been doing, steps back, and reasons with words about what has gone wrong and what might be done to correct the problem. However, Schön's reflection-in-action takes place in the midst of action, in the action-present, and does not necessarily involve thinking in words. Schön provided the following example:

> Think of a basketball player's instant maneuvering in response to an opponent's surprising move, or a jazz pianist's on-line improvisation on the melody she has just heard the trumpet play. Such performers think of what they are doing while doing it, without the use of words. (1992, p. 125)

Reflection-in-action can also take place in verbal encounters, yet even here it does not involve a withdrawal into theoretical thinking to decide what will be said next. Examples of this are the improvisations that make up a good conversation and practitioners' sensible on-the-spot responses to unexpected questions or statements from students or clients. Schön held that reflection-in-action is a Deweylike fleeting "episode of inquiry that arises momentarily in the midst of a flow or action, and then disappears, giving way to some new event, leaving in its wake, perhaps, a more stable view of the situation" (1992, p. 125).

Schön believed that a substantial part of practitioner expertise, and probably the most important part, comes in the form of "knowledge-*in*-action," which can be distinguished from "knowledge-*for*-action." Knowledge-*for*-action can be acquired from books or colleagues, but knowledge-*in*-action is acquired from the experience of performing an actual task. As the practitioner is generally unable to articulate what knowledge-*in*-action involves, outside observers cannot write it up so that it can be taught to others. Knowledge-*in*-action is a product of each practitioner's unique history of personal experience. Schön's (1988) description of reflection-in-action parallels the characteristics of reflective understanding decision making:

> When someone reflects-in-action, he becomes a researcher in the practice context. He is not dependent on the categories of established theory and technique, but constructs a new theory of the unique case. . . . He does not keep means and ends separate, but defines them interactively as he frames a problematic decision which he must later convert to action. . . . Thus, reflection-in-action can proceed, even in situations of uncertainty and uniqueness, because it is not bound by the dichotomies of Technical Rationality. (p. 76)

Knowledge-in-action is not limited to professional practice situations; it also functions in personal practices, such as writing. Authors engage in rapid thought experiments to create images of possible words to express their feelings and ideas.

Professional practitioners most often receive their basic training in practice in university settings, where they are instructed that proper practice is the application of the knowledge generated by the practitioners of research. Schön (1983) identified this as the dominant view of practice. He wrote:

> How comes it that in the second half of the twentieth century we find in our universities, embedded not only in men's minds but in the institutions themselves, a dominant view of professional [practicing] knowledge as the application of scientific theory and technique to the instrumental problems of practice? (p. 30)

Schön saw the dominance of technical rationality in the practicing professions as the consequence of the move to place practitioner training in the universities. This move brought about a separation of research from practice and the adaptation of the academic view of science as the way to understand and refine practice. In this model, the function of the university is to develop generalized and systematic knowledge that satisfies its particular epistemological values and then to transmit it to students so that they can apply it in their practice situations.

Schön distinguished practitioner reflection-in-action from technical rationality. He held that the professions have approached practice primarily from the perspective of technical rationality. In this view "professional activity consists of instrumental problem solving made rigorous by the application of scientific theory and technique" (1988, p. 60). Schön viewed the technical model of practice as limited: "In order to solve a problem by the application of existing theory or technique, a practitioner must be able to map those categories onto features of the practice situation" (1983, p. 41). However, the individuals served often fall outside the categories of application, and the problems and goals of practice change during the course of working with clients and students. Practitioners cannot simply follow a set of rules but need to reflect-in-action and adjust what they do on the move if they are to help clients achieve their goals.

Validation and Reflective Understanding

Two approaches to caregiver practice have been proposed: the technical and the judgment. It has been argued each of these approaches requires its own kind of reasoning for making decisions in practice. The technical approach requires technical-rational thinking, which involves the processes of deductive logic and calculation; and the judgment approach requires reflective-understanding thinking, which draws on background and dialogic reflection. Each approach also deals with the issue of validation of practice decisions in a different way. In practices the idea of validity is about doing the correct action or sets of action to produce the desired outcome. Technical and judgment practices approach the determination of correct action differently. In technical practice correct actions are determined prior to their implementation; in judgment practice correct actions are determined in the situation.

In technical practice, practitioners draw on a set of previously determined rules or techniques to be applied in various types of situations. A valid or correct action is one that follows the rules laid out for the situation they confront. Errors arise when the practitioners misdiagnose the type of situation and thereby apply the wrong set of rules. If they have applied the correct set of rules, their practice is valid, even if the desired result is not achieved. The responsibility for bringing about desired outcomes is not so much the practitioner but the constructors of the sets of rules. The practitioner is simply following the called for action rules.

The rules are held to be correct when they have been submitted to and passed the test of scientific scrutiny. If the scrutiny is correctly executed, the proposed rules are said to be validated. The term *validate* in reference to scientific scrutiny has a specialized meaning. It refers to the correct implementation of the research design. This design consists of trying a set of rules on an experimental group of participants but not on a control group. If the experimental group has a higher mean score on an outcome measure than the control group, it suggests that the technique is effective; that is, it has been scientifically validated. However, for a set of rules to be officially listed as scientifically validated, it has to pass the scrutiny of several independent experiments. Validity is a function of following the approved scrutiny steps. The participant aggregate needs to consist of members randomly selected from the population (or be equivalent to a random selection), the instruments must produce accurate measurement and be reliable, and the statistical analyses have to account for error and variance. Technical practice is valid if the practitioner enacts a validated set of rules.

Actions in judgment practice, at the most basic level, are valid if they move the caring process forward. The validity of an action cannot be known in advance. Validity is determined by its effectiveness in a particular situation at a particular time. Whether or not a judgment about what to do was valid becomes known after the fact. Practitioners of care must monitor the effect of their judgments continuously. Determining the validity of judgments is an essential and ongoing part of the caring process. When actions prove ineffective or do not advance the process adequately, practitioners need to engage in reflective understanding to enlarge their perceptive understanding of the situation and consider other possible actions.

Practitioners of care most often have to make judgments on the spur of the moment. They must decide what to do while interacting with those they serve, and there is no time for a full-scale deliberation in which all the options are weighed. Most often practitioners' responses flow directly out of their background understanding without passing through awareness. When adjustments are made through reflective understanding, they are carried out in action without interrupting the flow of interaction (Schön, 1983).

Practitioners of care, who directly interact with others, work "in situations in which we run out of rules" (Brown, 1988, p. 139) and where there is no rule-governed way to make the right or valid decisions that will best meet the needs of those they serve. This does not entail that actions based on practitioner judgment are arbitrary or irrational. Judgment operates out of the background of the practitioner; it is neither presuppositionless nor independent of the person making the judgment. Two different practitioners can make different judgments in similar situations and both be correct. The means to the goals sought by practitioners of care have equifinality; that is, there are equal means for achieving the same outcome. Judgment is not infallible, nor do its conclusions necessarily follow from the "facts" of the situation.

Brown (1988) said that to defend judgment against accusations that it produces biased and impulsive choices, one must distinguish judgments from unconsidered choices. He held that a key factor in reliable judgment is expertise in the area in which the judgment is made. Expertise is acquired through training and practice. Brown also said that novice practitioners should avail themselves of rules of application, if such are available, until they attain a level of expertise. He defined expertise as the internalization of the rules to such an extent that they no longer require conscious application but function in the background as tacit knowledge (p. 163).

According to Brown, reliable judgment also requires the acquisition of a "way of seeing" in which the salient details of a situation serve to inform correct judgment. Aristotle (see chapter 5) also believed that perceiving what is significant is an important component of good judgment. "Trained judgment brings with it the ability to recognize the salient features of a situation, the relevant constellation of operative factors and patterns, their harmony or disharmony, and the weight that they should have in a particular context" (Healy, 1993, p. 4).

Because practitioners of care make judgments within situations, they do not have time to stop an interaction to consult with others. However, practice judgments can be examined with others. This communal examination can take place before or after a practice engagement. Before entering a practice situation, practitioners can discuss possible strategies and plans of interaction with the one to be served. After an engagement, practice decisions can be reflected on with others about alternate choices that could have been made.

Because in-situation judgments are not infallible and possible valid choices overlooked, judgments can be submitted to an expert community; Brown held that validation of judgment decisions should have an intersubjective dimension. Healy (1993) suggested that "the most promising current approach [of intersubjective validation] is, . . . the model advocated by Habermas. Habermas suggests that it is possible to reconstruct the judgment process and draw out the nondeductive reasons for what was done. I think he is overly optimistic about this. When experts have been pressed to give the reasons for their judgments, they often produce textbook reasons that bear little resemblance to how they actually decided.

Like Weber, Habermas (1968/1970) believed that the new science that produced technology is inherently oriented to possible technical control of society. Technological thinking governs the sphere of work or purposive-rational action. Validation of empirical claims and explanations relating to the sphere of work focus on determination of whether or not the claim resulted from following the rules or algorithm of research correctly. Habermas identified another sphere of action that is only possible among humans: symbolic interaction. Symbolic interaction is not governed by rules, and this is the sphere in which judgment operates.

Because symbolic interactions and judgments are not rule governed, they cannot be validated in the same way as purposive-rational actions. Habermas proposed that judgments in the symbolic interaction sphere should be validated by presenting arguments to a group of experts in the area of the judgments. Evidence in support of each position also would be given. Habermas believed that a kind of nonrule-governed rationality inherent in the communication process would guide the group to a correct consensus. However, for communicative rationality to have the desired effect, the process must approach what he called "the ideal speech situation." In the ideal speech situation, no obstacles stand in the way of a free and just exchange of views and the goal of achieving truth. Only the cogency or soundness of argument and its warrants influence the group's decision. Although Habermas (1981/1984) admitted that the ideal speech situation exists as a potentiality rather than as an actuality, he held that it serves as a point from which to evaluate any particular decision about the validity or truth of a claim in the sphere of symbolic interaction.

Habermas believed that by performing an action or practice in the human realm, one implies that it was the correct thing to do and could give reasons for having done it. These are not the same kind of reasons required for a knowledge claim about the physical realm. Thus, when presenting a knowledge claim in the form of a journal article to reviewers, one is expected to provide a demonstration. A demonstration differs from an argument in that demonstrations offer logical or mathematical proof in which the claim necessarily follows from the given data (Perelman, 1979). The reviewers do not question the logic of calculation, only whether the calculations have been carried out accurately. When presenting a claim that one made a correct judgment to a group, such as a review board, one has to argue that given the information available and the circumstances, it was the right thing to do. Because judgments are not the result of mathematical calculations or deductive demonstrations, their correctness or validation is a matter of convincing other experts that the judgment was reasonable in that setting at that time; that is to say, they might have made the same decision themselves.

Reconstructive reviews are often useful for increasing practitioners' background understanding and bringing other things they might have done to their attention. Practitioner supervision often takes this form. However, when one is engaged in service with another, the judgment approach to practice should always include a monitoring process.

CONCLUSION

This book arose out of the concern that practitioners of care are being asked by their governments, institutions, and agencies, as well as by insurance companies, to limit their activities to those that have been scientifically validated through experimentation to produce desired effects. Practitioners of care have responded that such limitations are not in the best interests of the people they serve. They argue that sets of techniques and programs found to improve mean scores of some groups are not sensitive enough to the differences of skills and strengths among those who serve or individual differences among those served. The issue has usually been framed as a debate between scientists and practitioners about which group knows best how to serve people in need (Beutler, Williams, Wakefield, & Entwistle, 1995). This frame is too narrow to address the question. This book has been an effort to enlarge the frame so that the general notion of human practice could be examined. Backing away from the immediacy of the debate and the limited perspectives of both sides provided a broader view of the issue.

From a more distanced view, practice was seen to include the innumerable activities in which people engage to affect changes in something. Many of the things we do relate to changing the materials of the physical world. From building superhighways to building a tree house, we engage in practices to rearrange, transform, and control our natural environment. Some of the practices for dealing with materials are very sophisticated, such as building a space ship, and some are naïve, such as assembling a book case from bricks and boards. There seems not to be much debate about these practices. As a culture, we accept the idea that science can provide the answers to questions about the best way to accomplish projects in the physical realm. Debates sometimes arise over which scientist has the best answer, but we still look to science. Debates also arise over the interpretation of science, such as the consequences of cutting down old-growth forests or the effect of fluorocarbons on the ozone.

Using this enlarged frame, chapter 2 traced the growth in the power of human beings to control nature and the surge that occurred when controlled observation was combined with technical-rational thinking. Choices determined by technical-rational deduction based on the knowledge generated by science have served humanity well and have led to the technological transformation of the world. The technical accomplishments encouraged the belief that the reality that appears through the lens of science is all that exists. The new science that produced high technology has been transformed from a method for shaping nature into a worldview; it has pushed aside other ways of thinking and alternative views of reality to assume the position of authority on the way things are.

During the last century the technical-rational method of controlling nature penetrated the human realm and has come to be regarded as the only legitimate and rational method for deciding what to do. It has been extended from decisions about dealing with physical objects to those related to human beings. Technical-rational practical decision making is held to produce the same efficient and effective results for human entities as it does for physical entities. Decisions that relied on human situated judgments are derided as error ridden, biased, and nonrational or irrational. I have used the term *technification* to refer to the spread in our culture of technical decision making to the human realm.

Among those who practice in the human realm are the practitioners of care. Their practices take place in direct person-to-person interaction. Among the practices of care are teaching, social work, nursing, and psychotherapy. Their practices are concerned with assisting people in various ways. Practitioners of care are under pressure to conform to the dominant cultural themes of means-end rationality and ordered efficiency. The institutions that control payment for their services are exemplars of means-end thinking and technological understanding. They have demanded that practice become more technological, and the disciplines have responded by shifting their research and training to a technologically driven practice. Researchers are focusing on the development of scientifically supported or validated sets of techniques as a means of responding to human problems. Instrumental or technical-rational reasoning, which is geared to determining the most efficient and cost-effective means of achieving a goal, has come to dominate the institutional thinking about practices of care.

I have argued that the procedures used to determine the best way for accomplishing goals with materials are not appropriate for accomplishing goals with people. Most of the literature about practice does not distinguish between practices for changing nature and practices for assisting people, yet such a distinction is essential for determining how practices of care should be conducted. The extension of technical-rational thinking to the human realm is problematic because of differences between the physical and the human realms. Moreover, in certain situations, such as the practice of care, technical-rational thinking can have harmful results.

> The primacy of instrumental reason is . . . evident in the prestige and aura that surround technology, and makes us believe that we should seek technological solutions even when something very different is called for. We see this often enough in the realm of politics, as Bellah and his colleagues forcefully argue in their . . . book. But it also invades other domains, such as medicine. Benner has argued in a number of important works that the technological approach in medicine has often sidelined the kind of care that involves treating the patient as a whole person with a life story, and not as the locus of a technical problem. (Taylor, 1991, p. 6)

The practices of care require a kind of decision making appropriate to the human realm in which they operate. I have proposed that these practices need to rely on practitioner judgment informed by a reflective understanding of the changing situations in which they are performed. The ideas for reflective understanding were assembled from Aristotle's notion of *phronesis* as an alternative to deductive reasoning for deliberating about practice in the human realm, from Dewey's idea of learning in-situation from the effect of an action, from the understanding of the role of background in practice decision making, and from Gadamer's description of dialogic engagement. Reflective understanding draws on the full human capacities for interacting with other persons. It involves an integration of previous personal and cultural learning, of imagined scenarios of responses to an action, and of emotional reading of possible actions in the situation. In reflective understanding the practitioner is attuned to the salient features of a specific situation and responsive to the nuanced changes that are occurring during an interchange. It is a decision process that adapts to the particular complex situations in which practitioners of care serve.

The following chapter is a case study about the effect of technification on the field of psychotherapy, but similar tales could be told about other fields of caregiving. The social institutions in which the practices of care operate have become more "businesslike"; that is to say, they have adopted the cost-effective values of technical-rational thinking. To create a space in which they can function according to strategic planning, they want the practices of care to become predictable technologies. They want them to take on another form in which the implementation of specific techniques will produce predictable results.

As we live in an age of technification, we have three options: (a) we can move out of technically managed social institutions; (b) we can remain in these institutions and look for opportunities to engage in caring practice; or (c) we can change the view of management about what constitutes effective care and how it is accomplished.

Moving out of the system is not a viable choice for most of us. Some teachers who are seeking places that support the practice of judgment-based caring instruction believe charter schools and private educational institutions may provide such an environment. Some nurses are changing to private nursing or leaving the profession entirely. Some psychotherapists are limiting their practices to clients who can afford to pay for their services. In a recent article in *USA Today*, a psychotherapist (Schwarzchild, 1999) wrote about his decision to "get out of the managed care system before it gets me." He wrote: "I don't know whether I'll be able to make a living on my own terms. I can't compete financially with nothing-out-of-the-patient's pocket insurance plans. Instead, I'll have to offer that old-fashioned commodity managed care companies seem to have forgotten about: real service to my customers." However, those most in need of the services provided by practitioners of care must come to the managed institutions for help because they have no other choice.

The second option is to remain in the technically managed institutions and seek opportunities to extend caring responses to those in need. Certeau held that there were places within the bounded space of strategically managed organizations in which individuals can express themselves. He used the example of *la perruque* to illustrate how people can remain in the system yet still engage in judgment-based caring practices. *La perruque* ("the wig") is a worker's way of disguising his own work as work for the employer. It is not pilfering in that nothing of value is taken. It is not absenteeism in that the worker is on the job. It "may be as simple a matter as a secretary's writing a love letter on 'company time' or as complex as a cabinet maker's 'borrowing' a lathe to make a piece of furniture for his living room" (de Certeau, 1980/1988, p. 25). It is a matter of diverting time (not goods) for work that is "free, creative, and precisely not directed toward profit" (p. 25). Certeau called for tactical thinking as a means of self-expression within the system. The tactical act "ties together (moral) freedom, (esthetic) creation, and a (practical) act—three elements already present in the practice of '*la perruque*,' that modern-day example of everyday tactic" (p. 26). This option calls for practitioner resistance to giving in to the dominant structure.

The third option is to convince managers that they will "get the most bang for the buck" by allowing practitioners of care to use their judgment in how to best respond to the needs of those they serve. Noddings (1996) wrote that "teachers, after their initial apprenticeship, must be allowed to exercise their professional judgment in all classroom matters" (p. 169). This does not mean that practitioners of care should not be held responsible for what they accomplish.

> Teachers should be asked to account for every failure, to suggest what might be done for every child experiencing difficulty, and to explain what they have done for each child in their care, but they should be free to decide how to conduct their own teaching. I really believe teachers need to be adamant on this. (Noddings, 1996, p. 169)

The purpose of this book is to present an argument for allowing practitioners of care to judge what actions are most appropriate for accomplishing the goals of their practice. The argument is based on the position that human beings are diverse, context sensitive, historical, and undergoing change. They are coactors in caring interaction, not docile and passive productions of technically administered interventions (Bohart & Tallman, 1999). Thus, effective practices of care require in-situation judgments about what is to be done at a particular time, in a particular situation, with a particular person.

8

A Case Study

Psychotherapy

IN THE PAST FOUR CENTURIES, the Western world has produced transformations of nature that would have been inconceivable to our forbears. Our technical progress can be attributed directly to the advent of the new science. The new science has made it possible for human beings to build a series of new physical environments, each believed to be better than the one before. This has brought us a new vision of reality in which the world appears as a reflection of the new science's own image. When people apply logical and calculative thinking to make decisions, they tend to view the world as ordered, law abiding, and comprehensible. It has come to the point that this view is now accepted as the only true perspective rather than one of many.

As the focus of the new worldview widens to encompass the human realm in its entirety, ideals and values that have been central in our cultural traditions are in danger of disappearing from the picture. Among the most important of these is the significance of each individual. With the growing tendency to look at things as instances of a kind, subtle variations may go unnoticed or be ignored. Even in practices of care, human beings are sometimes categorized, cataloged, and treated as a type. In 1959, Snow (see 1970) identified a tension in our culture between the contrasting views of the world presented in the sciences and the humanities. Looking back over more than four decades, it is apparent that the perspective of science has become increasingly more powerful, and the perspective of the humanities has continued to lose ground.

In our society, the contest between the two opposing views is taking place in the practices of care. I have framed this contest as a conflict between the technical approach and the judgment approach to the delivery of services of care. The technical approach looks at care through the lens of science, while the judgment approach looks at it through the lens of the humanities. The two approaches use different ways of thinking about the practice of care: technical-rational thinking for the former and reflective-understanding thinking for the latter.

This chapter is a case study of the tension between these approaches in a single practice of care: psychotherapy. While psychotherapy encompasses the work of several professional groups—for example, marriage and family therapists, licensed clinical social workers, and school psychologists—this study will focus on psychotherapy delivered by licensed clinical and counseling psychologists.

A case study has the form of a story or narrative. It is a historical account with a beginning, middle, and end, and it traces the development of how and why something moved from a starting point to a denouement or conclusion. In précis, this story is about the attempt to change psychotherapy into a technified practice. The protagonists are the practitioners of psychotherapy and the academic discipline of psychology. In an oversimplified characterization, psychotherapy can be identified as representing the view of the humanities and academic psychology as representing the view of science. Until the 1960s, these disciplines existed as relatively separate enterprises, each operating in its own field of values. They were equal partners at the beginning of their interaction, but over time academic psychology assumed the dominant role. As a result, psychology wanted to change psychotherapy into something with which it could be more comfortable living. Psychotherapy resisted this pressure to change and tried to maintain the identity it had established before entering into the relationship with psychology. However, in the past decade, psychology gained a powerful ally (managed care corporations) in its attempt to make psychotherapy more like itself.

Functioning in the broader Western culture, both psychotherapy and academic psychology have been influenced by the increasing dominance of the technical-rational way of thinking about practice. They can be looked on as fields, in Bourdieu's sense, within the culture, each having a set of rules by which its game is played and a set of established values about how capital is accumulated. Individual practitioners exercise strategies from their repertoires of dispositions as a means for getting ahead in their respective fields. There are certain membership boundaries that must be observed, and entry into the fields requires a certain amount of accumulated social capital. Since the 1970s, a state license has been required to practice psychotherapy, and a doctoral degree is a prerequisite for the licensing examination. To begin a career in academic psychology, one must first be hired by an institution of higher education and then obtain tenure.

These two fields originated at approximately the same time during the latter decades of the nineteenth century. Acceptance of Descartes' religious ideas had begun to wane, as Darwin's evolutionary theory was gradually beginning to replace the notion of soul with that of mind. In this period of great intellectual growth, psychotherapy was developed as a means to care for mentally distressed individuals, and psychology was established as a scientific discipline to study the mind. The relationship between the two fields can be divided into three phases: (a) The early phase from 1890 to 1950, when there was little connection between the two fields, their common interest in the mind notwithstanding; (b) the middle phase from 1950 to 1990, when they were associated in an uneasy partnership; and (c) the current phase from 1990 to the present, during which scientific psychology has made a concerted effort to become the dominant partner.

THE FIRST PHASE: 1890–1950

Psychotherapy originated in the late nineteenth century in the context of treating *neurasthenia*. This term was used to describe an array of symptoms that appeared to have no obvious organic cause. Some of the symptoms of neurasthenia included chronic fatigue and weakness, loss of memory, paralysis, insomnia, and general aches and pains. In 1895, Freud published *Studies in Hysteria*, in which he described a cathartic conversational therapy for the treatment of the hysterical symptoms of neurasthenia as reported in a previous coauthored work (1895/1966). During the early decades of this period the dominant approach to psychotherapy was based on Freud's theory of psychoanalysis or its adaptations by ego psychologists and object relation therapists (Mitchell & Black, 1995). However, academic psychology held that Freud's theories and its revisions were not susceptible to scientific validation, and therefore they could not be included within the science of psychology. The major cultural impact of psychoanalysis was in literature and the humanities (Polkinghorne, 2001).

Some academically trained psychologists were engaged in clinical practices during this period. For the most part, their practice involved nonpsychoanalytic counseling and therapy. In 1896, Witmer (Reisman, 1991) initiated psychological counseling for children, a practice that grew into the child guidance movement. In the period's later decades Rogers introduced a nondirective approach to counseling, and Thorne introduced a more directive eclectic approach. Nevertheless, in the main, the clinical activity of psychologists was separate from the discipline's research practice. (An exception was Roger's early research on counseling practice; see below.)

The birth of scientific psychology occurred in 1874. This was the year Wundt published his *Principles of Physiological Psychology* (1874/1904) and

Brentano published *Psychology from an Empirical Standpoint* (1874/1995). Both Wundt and Brentano were proposing that consciousness could be studied with scientific methods; however, they disagreed as to what the appropriate scientific methods were. Wundt held that psychology should adopt the method used by physiology. A physical stimulus (a sound, weight, or color) is presented to a trained subject. Using inner perception, the subject then reports the changes that occurred in his or her consciousness. By comparing the changes in the stimuli with the changes in consciousness, consistent mathematical patterns can be identified. Brentano proposed that a special method was needed to study consciousness. His method involved self-examination of the activity of consciousness through inner perception. Brentano's method became the forerunner of Continental philosophy; however, Wundt's method was exported to the United States, where it was heralded as the basis of American scientific psychology (Polkinghorne, 2003).

Several decades after the adaptation of Wundt's method and the introduction of functionalist explanations of mental activity, the focus of psychological investigations in the United States shifted from the study of the mind to the study of observable behavior. The scientific investigations of nature called for the use of publicly observable data, and because mental operations were not publicly observable, in order for psychology to become a "real" science, the study of the mind had to be abandoned (Smith, 1986). One of the beliefs of functionalism had been that the human mind did not differ significantly from the minds of other animals. Behaviorism retained this belief, and its studies focused on the observations of animal behavior to test theories of learning. This was the period of "rat psychology," and research on psychotherapy was not an important part of its program.

Applied psychology was used primarily in the administration of diagnostic tests in educational institutions, businesses, and mental asylums. It developed instruments to measure intelligence and vocational interests. The value of these instruments was displayed during World War I when they were used by psychologists to determine the suitability of new recruits for specific jobs. The repertoire of vocational inventories was increased and used to counsel people on career choices. However, during this period, psychotherapy (as opposed to counseling) was deemed a medical practice, and only physicians could receive insurance payments for providing psychotherapeutic services (Danziger, 1979).

THE SECOND PHASE: 1950–1990

Midway through the twentieth century, a transformation began to occur in the relationship between academic psychology and psychotherapy. The demand for psychotherapeutic services increased dramatically, and the hegemony of psychodynamic theories along with the medical domination of psychotherapy came to an end. By 1990, psychoanalysis was only a marginal part of the practice of psychotherapy. States had started licensing psychologists, thereby making them eligible to receive insurance payments as providers of psychotherapy. As more academic psychologists engaged in the practice of psychotherapy, the discipline turned its attention to the scientific study of psychotherapy and how it would train those entering the field.

Although training in applied or clinical psychology had been available prior to World War II (Routh, 2000), the postwar demand for mental health services prompted some psychology departments to create programs for this purpose. A conference held in Boulder, Colorado, in 1949 established the training model for these new programs. Existing graduate programs in psychology focused primarily on research training; the model for the applied programs kept the focus on research but added training in applied skills. Hence it was conceptualized as a scientist-practitioner model intended to form an equal partnership between academic research in psychology and the practice of psychotherapy.

In actuality, the scientist-practitioner model turned out to be a scientist model that generated findings to be implemented by practitioners. Psychology created a division of labor in which some (working primarily in the academy) served as researchers, developing a body of knowledge that others (working primarily in the field) who served as practitioners applied. Although practitioners were expected to utilize the findings of academic research instrumentally, most did not. As the appliers of knowledge, they were of a lower standing than the researchers who actually developed knowledge.

To gain entry into the field of psychotherapy, students had to earn a degree from the academy. During the four or five years required for this undertaking, they were expected to become acculturated into the values of the academy and its commitment to technical-rational thinking. They were also taught to acknowledge academic research findings as the authority for their future practice. Having been instructed in research methods, like Certeau's consumers of research, they could read the research journals and familiarize themselves with the latest findings. They were taught not to trust in the reliability of the experiential understandings derived from practice. Coming from trial and error or anecdotal experience, such knowledge had not been validated by the rigorous methods of academic science and therefore was not to be used for guiding actions and interventions. Students were expected to learn that practice based on personal experience is unsystematic and produces unpredictable results.

However, as students left the academy, they were inducted by their supervisors into a new community, their community of practice. It was there that their professional identities were formed through associations with other practitioners in the field and from their own experiences as practicing psychotherapists. Their community of practice had values that were different from those of the academy. Here, psychotherapy was understood to be an individuated practice that requires sensitivity to differences and mastery that comes from situated learning (Lave & Wenger, 1991).

The idea of psychotherapy as an applied discipline in which one is expected to utilize research findings instrumentally did not catch on with its practitioners. Although instrumental utilization was stressed in their training, most did not accept the idea, relying primarily on practical experience-based understanding in their ongoing interactions with clients. Many practitioners did not find the kind of knowledge they were asked to utilize instrumentally to be particularly useful. Probability statements about the relation among variables abstracted from their contexts did not seem applicable to the kinds of decisions they had to make in their practice with individual clients. They realized that in actual situations they had to be guided by their sensitivity and their instantaneous, experientially derived responses to what was happening at the moment. Practitioners readily admitted that they seldom perused research findings published in journals to determine what to do with their clients. Instead, they reported that they relied on their own experiences, their discussions with fellow practitioners, and case histories written by others.

Morrow-Bradley and Elliott (1986) surveyed APA Division 29 (Psychotherapy) members about their production and utilization of psychotherapy research. The source of information about psychotherapy that practitioners found most useful was their ongoing experience with clients; "only 10% reported psychotherapy research articles or presentations as their primary source of information" (p. 191). Barlow (1981) described the differences between the belief that practice should consist of the application of research-generated findings and the actual performances of practitioners:

> At present, clinical research has little or no influence on clinical practice. This state of affairs should be particularly distressing to a discipline whose goal over the last 30 years has been to produce professionals who would integrate the methods of science with clinical practice to produce new knowledge. (p. 147)

During this second phase, as psychotherapists did not find the research literature directly applicable to their work, they developed a second knowledge base. This body of knowledge consisted primarily of case histories passed on orally by colleagues and supervisors and ones that were published, for example, those collected by Wedding and Corsini (1979) and Freud's descriptions of his work with clients. This second knowledge base provided psychotherapists with descriptions of situated judgments that were made in practice with individual clients. It furnished therapists with vicarious experiences that could be integrated into their backgrounds and drawn on in their own work. Training in psychotherapy was primarily accomplished through apprenticeships (Lave & Wenger, 1991) in clinical settings. Supervisors assisted trainees by reflecting on the judgments the trainees made in working with clients. Therapists were taught to monitor their clients' responses and to improvise and make adjustments in their sessions. Development was not the mastery of a predetermined set of techniques; it was basically a matter of experiential learning.

As practitioners mature and gain experience, they rely less on the technical model and more on the human judgment model in deciding what actions to use with clients. Skovholt and Rønnestad (1992) conducted an interview study of the development of counseling psychologists over the course of their careers. Counselors between sixty and seventy years of age who had practiced from twenty-five to thirty-five years reported that over time their awareness of the complexity of human existence had grown continuously. These counselors no longer adhered to simple rules of treatment but relied increasingly on their experienced-based understandings and accumulated wisdom. During this phase, psychotherapy was being practiced by psychologists trained in academic settings in which the field is governed by technical-rational thinking. However, once they had left the academy and established a practice, their actions were drawn from their accumulated background and from reflective understanding generated within a particular situation. Rogers' description of his work with clients captures the tone of psychotherapy during this second phase.

> I let myself go into the immediacy of the relationship where it is my total organism which takes over and is sensitive to relationship, not simply my consciousness. I am not consciously responding in a planful or analytic way, but simply in an unreflective way to the other individual, my reaction being based (but not consciously) on my total organismic sensitivity to this other person. (quoted in May, 1958, p. 82)

During the second phase, academic psychology introduced its own approach to psychotherapy. Behavioral therapy was based on a theory of learning and involved a set of desensitization techniques that were intended to reduce the anxiety aroused by the objects of phobias. At the time, academic research on psychotherapy focused on the interactions between the therapist and the client (Hill & Corbett, 1993). For example, Rogers used research designs from academic psychology to seek a correlation between therapists' actions to recognize, clarify, and accept their clients' feelings and clients' change from negative to positive feelings. Academic studies of practice were based on academic psychology's assumptions about the nature of science. They brought to light particular elements from a number of sessions conducted by different practitioners to determine if one or more of the practitioner behaviors would prove particularly effective in bringing about a desired change. The purpose of the research was to identify empirical generalizations that held across practice situations so that a therapist could use the identified behavior in working with a client and produce the desired change thereby.

Psychotherapists' use of academic research during this phase can be categorized in three groups: (a) no utilization, (b) a conceptual utilization, and (c) psychotherapy as the application of research findings. Cohen, Sargent, and Sechrest (1986) reported that about one-third of those responding to their survey placed themselves in the "no connection" position. For them, in-situation judgment determined their practice. They "did not believe that even the general research literature had affected their professional practice." Furthermore, these practitioners reported that research literature has "little application to day to day practice" (p. 204) and that most research is too simplistic and irrelevant for their purposes.

The second group, which was larger than the first, took a conceptual utilization position. They believed that the ideas and findings of research can provide an important part of the information to draw upon in making in-situation judgments about how to proceed with a particular client at a particular time. Conceptual utilization refers to the general effect of research training on clinical practice—thinking more critically, sharpening one's observational skills, and taking empirical data more seriously. On one hand, practitioners with this view held that dismissing academic research outright would reduce the fund of knowledge they could draw upon to formulate the best possible plan of action. As they saw it, the findings of academic research extended their background stock beyond the limits of their own personal experiences. On the other hand, if they were to dismiss their own experientially developed store of knowledge (which is what the academy would have them do), this would diminish their capacity to adjust their responses to each particular practicing situation. Conceptual utilization acknowledges the necessity of in-situation judgment for making appropriate decisions for individual clients at particular times; but it also recognizes that academic research, when integrated into practitioners' background knowledge, can be useful for making in-situation judgments.

The group holding the third position took an instrumental stance toward the utilization of research. Believing that practitioners' in-situation judgment was often erroneous and based only on anecdotal experiences, they held that practitioners should base their decision on knowledge generated by researcher-validated studies. For example, if a research article reported that a particular technique had been effective with a certain type of client; practitioners working with that population should use the research-validated technique. Cohen and colleagues reported that the third group was considerably smaller than the other two. When studies showed that practitioners were guided by personal experience and consultation with professional colleagues rather than the academy's research findings, the proposed solution was for a training program in the academy to place greater emphasis on the importance of using research findings to guide professional practice (Peterson, 1991).

THE THIRD PHASE: 1990–THE PRESENT

In the 1990s, the way in which health care costs were managed changed considerably. During the second phase, insurance plans indemnified their holders to reimburse providers for their services, and many of these plans were quite generous in their coverage of psychotherapy. For example, the insurance plan covering federal employees would reimburse 80 percent of the cost for up to twenty psychotherapy sessions per year. The therapist and client themselves determined the number of sessions that were needed, and insurers exercised little direct control over their decision. This fiscal arrangement gave health care providers significant autonomy in working with their clients.

Then, in response to escalating costs, insurance companies began replacing the old indemnity policies with a system that limited payment to services the company deemed medically necessary. Health care, which generally had been delivered by nonprofit organizations, was moved into the for-profit sphere where it was transformed into an industry. As a result, these corporations began applying the technical-rational approach to decision making as a means of maximizing profits. For some time, health care lingered outside the canopy of technified management, which was becoming increasingly dominant in business and government. Eventually it was lured inside, and health care providers lost their autonomy upon becoming employees or contractors of corporations.

The expanding technification of health care changed the balance between academic psychology and psychotherapy that existed in the second phase of their relationship. Decisions about what psychotherapy services clients needed as well as who could deliver these services were taken out of the hands of practitioners and turned over to utilization review boards established by the insurance companies. Within the mandate to control costs, services were limited to what was medically necessary for a patient to return to a functional level on the job, in school, or as a member of his or her family. Once this reduced purpose was accomplished, insurance companies were reluctant to authorize additional care (Tuttle & Woods, 1997).

All health care providers—physicians, dentists, rehabilitation therapists, and so on—have been affected by the changes in health care financing. Psychotherapists are among those most affected. Insurance companies had suspected for some time that much of what they were paying for in psychotherapy did not meet the criterion of medical necessity. They do not consider it their responsibility to help people achieve self-actualization or deal with problems of living. Although many people go through periods of psychological distress such as anxiety and nervousness, these conditions do not usually impair their lives to such an extent that they require psychotherapy. They are still able to "love and work," just not as effectively as they might (Johnson, 1995). Thus, the insurance industry determined that psychotherapeutic care would only be covered when a person was too dysfunctional to work or perform activities of daily living (ADLs). Tuttle and Woods (1997) provided an assessment of the situation psychotherapists faced:

> The "psychebusiness" experienced unprecedented growth during the 1960s, 1970s, and 1980s. We are now undergoing the purposeful downsizing of a business that is part of industrialization. Therapists are going out of business, accepting lower or flattened incomes, working part-time for agencies, or becoming employees of managed care systems. This is part of a political and social climate in which all forms of service delivery are subject to cynicism and to questions as to whether the service is needed, and if so, how it can be delivered more efficiently. (p. 21)

With the technification of health care management, both the therapeutic effectiveness and the cost-effectiveness of psychotherapy were called into question. Health care corporations wanted evidence in the form of outcome studies that would verify the results of medical procedures and drug treatments. Academic psychology responded by refocusing its research from process to outcome studies. Treatment and control group studies were carried out to demonstrate that therapeutic techniques resulted in a reduction of symptoms. To control for variations in the delivery of the techniques by different therapists, the treatments were manualized. Insurance companies would only pay for treatments that had been shown empirically to reduce the symptoms of diagnosed disorders. Other modes of treatment were considered experimental and therefore not reimbursable. Moreover, as psychotherapy was competing with other health care needs, it was not enough to present research showing that that it was effective therapeutically. Now there also had to be proof that it was cost-effective (Fraser, 1996).

Studies of the efficacy of psychotherapy were modeled on the double blind research design used to test drug treatments. These designs called for comparison groups in which the members are "blind" as to whether they are being given the active drug or a placebo, and those administering the drug also are "blind" as to which they are dispensing. Efficacy studies of psychotherapy treatments cannot be blind in this sense because the therapist knows he or she is delivering the therapy. These studies are designed to determine that a specific treatment is efficacious, and improvement in the client is not the result of specific skills or sensitivity on the part of a particular therapist. At first, the efficacy studies found that sets of cognitive-behavioral techniques produced the desired outcomes for clients in several diagnostic categories. However, additional studies found that other kinds of treatments for the same categories were also efficacious.

Seligman (1995) reported the results of a study conducted by *Consumer Reports* in which individuals who had received psychotherapy were asked afterward whether the experience had been helpful. Participants differed in their assessments according to the credentials of the therapist, but they did not report that the particular mode of treatment made a difference. Although the *Consumer Reports* effectiveness study has significant flaws (as do the efficacy studies), it suggests that effectiveness of psychotherapy is not based on the administration of a set of particular techniques for individuals with specific diagnoses.

During the second phase, even though academic researchers strongly encouraged therapists to use only scientifically validated treatments, for the most part therapists continued to rely on experience and consultation with colleagues to guide their practice. When the rules changed in terms of what services would be covered by health insurance, the researchers' recommendations had additional leverage. Researchers continued to stress the importance of practitioners limiting their therapeutic actions to empirically supported sets of techniques (Nathan & Goran, 1998). They considered this absolutely necessary if psychotherapy was to survive under the new conditions,

A third-phase utilization study by Beutler and others (1995) confirmed that the scientist-practitioner model remained basically a one-way model. Researchers continued to expect therapists to be guided by their research, rather than vice versa. Butler and his colleagues did find that practitioner interest in research findings had increased from the level reported in second-phase studies conducted by Morrow-Bradley and Elliott (1986) and Cohen (1986).

The attempt to technify psychotherapy as a means of justifying its continued coverage under health insurance created a number of problems. Some commonly held beliefs did not hold up under scrutiny. For example, the notion that psychotherapy must be long term in order to be effective was not supported (Austad, 1996); neither was the notion that doctoral training is necessary for one to be an effective therapist. The results from Wampold's (2001; 1997) studies are even more problematic. Wampold rearranged the sequence in which manualized techniques were delivered, dropped some of the techniques from the prescribed set, and did a metaanalysis of previous studies. Interestingly, he found support for the notion that most kinds of therapy produce similar results. Judging from recent research, it seems to be a mistake to model psychotherapy as a medical intervention when a drug or treatment is able to cure or control a certain disorder. An alternative view is to emphasize the common core of psychotherapy practice that assists clients in their recovery and growth. In essence, academic researchers have come to two conflicting conclusions: one supports the technical approach to practice; the other gives support to the practitioner-judgment approach.

The academic field and psycotherapy have retained a basic difference in their views about the predictability of human behavior. The former holds that for knowledge to be considered scientific, it must allow for prediction. In the latter, the production of predictive knowledge only holds when one aggregates enough individual scores. Attempts to predict individual behavior have been notoriously unsuccessful. Dawes (1994) contended that scientific training ought to make us aware of how little can be predicted about human behavior rather than leading us to believe that we can foretell which techniques will produce what effects. "No personal skill has yet been developed—or assessment instrument devised—that allows us to predict who will change, when, and how" (p. 27). Hagen (1997) also cited studies indicating that attempts to predict the future behavior of individual violent criminals were more often incorrect than correct.

The issue separating academic psychology from psychotherapy is not science versus practice but practice versus practice, that is, what should inform practice. Technical practice assumes that human behavior is predictable, and therefore practice should take advantage of this characteristic and do those things that have been shown to produce a particular result. Judgment practice assumes that human behavior is open-ended, so practice should respond to the changing actions of particular clients in therapy. Advanced knowledge is not useful for predicting what will happen, but it provides a background of possible ways of responding to what does happen.

The contemporary technical cultural milieu that has assimilated the practices of care wants practitioners to know in advance which actions will produce the desired outcomes. It wants to know the costs of delivering those actions so that managers can anticipate and control their costs. Their goal is to imbue the entire system with strategic thinking, including the way in which decisions are made in the delivery of services. Attempts to develop a psychotherapy that maintains the control over costs and services required in a strategically ordered system have been less than successful. The concern is that if psychotherapy cannot accommodate the need for management controls, it will not be included in health insurance payment plans. This is management's ultimate form of control.

The dictates of health managers who have the power to decide which modes of treatment are covered and for what period of time have convinced some therapists that managed care is destroying the practice of psychotherapy. Shore, a cofounder of the Coalition of Mental Health Professionals and Consumers, sent a letter to the APA Council of Representatives on January 23, 1995, in which he stated that managed care:

> is destroying much of what our profession has built over the past 100 years and is defying the values we believe are essential for quality care. I, as many others, feel I cannot practice ethically or with any sense of personal dignity under a managed care system. Many good psychologists are being forced out of work because they refuse to under-treat people or to comply with the betrayal of their patient's trust. Others are already preparing to leave the field, demoralized and in utter despair because of what is happening to patients, treatment, morals, ethics, to themselves as human beings and as professionals. . . . We are working against great odds to try to stop a giant from destroying all we hold dear. (quoted in Austad, 1996, pp. 36–37)

Woolfolk (1998) argued that the humanistic tradition of psychotherapy as self-exploration and personal growth should not be lost in the movement to a "psychotechnology represented by short-term, manualized treatment" and the effort to "'medicalize' psychotherapy [and] to reduce it to a healing technology based on somatic medicine" (p. xvii).

REFERENCES

Abbey, R. (2000). *Charles Taylor*. Princeton, NJ: Princeton University Press.

Ahearne, J. (1995). *Michel de Certeau: Interpretation and its other*. Stanford: Stanford University Press.

Arendt, H. (1958). *The human condition*. Chicago: University of Chicago Press.

Arendt, H. (1971). *The life of the mind: Thinking*. New York: Harcourt, Brace, Jovanovich.

Aristotle. (trans. 1950). *The ethics of Aristotle* (D. P. Chase, Trans.). New York: E. P. Dutton.

Arnheim, R. (1969). *Visual thinking*. Berkeley: University of California Press.

Austad, C. S. (1996). *Is long-term psychotherapy unethical?* San Francisco: Jossey-Bass.

Bachelard, G. (1958). *The poetics of space* (M. Jolas, Trans.). New York: Orion.

Bacon, F. (1620/1994). *Novem Organum* (P. Urbach & J. Gibson, Trans.). Chicago: Open Court.

Bargh, J. A., & Chartland, T. L. (1999). The unbearable automaticity of being. American *Psychologist, 54,* 462–479.

Barlow, D. H. (1981). On the relation of clinical research to clinical practice. The *Journal of Consulting and Clinical Psychology, 49,* 147–155.

Baron, J. (1988). *Thinking and deciding*. Cambrindge, MA: Cambridge University Press.

Baumeister, R. F., Bratslavsky, E., Muraven, M., & Tice, D. M. (1998). Ego depletion: Is the active self a limited resource? *Journal of Personality and Social Psychology, 74,* 1252–1265.

Becker, C. L. (1932). *The heavenly city of eighteenth-century philosophers*. New Haven: Yale University Press.

Bernasconi, R. (1989). Heidegger's destruction of phronesis. *The Southern Journal of Philosophy, 28* (Supplement), 127–153.

Bernstein, R. J. (1967). *John Dewey*. New York: Washington Square.

Bernstein, R. J. (1992). *The new constellation: The ethical-political horizons of modernity/postmodernity*. Cambridge, MA: MIT Press.

Beutler, L. E., Williams, R. E., Wakefield, P. J., & Entwistle, S. R. (1995). Bridging scientist and practitioner perspectives in clinical psychology. *American Psychologist, 50*(12), 984–994.

Bohart, A. C., & Tallman, K. (1999). *How clients make therapy work: The process of active self-healing.* Washington, D.C.: American Psychological Association.

Bolles, E. B. (1991). *A second way of knowing.* New York: Prentice-Hall.

Bourdieu, P. (1968). Structuralism and theory of sociological knowledge. *Social Research, 35*(4), 681–706.

Bourdieu, P. (1972/1977). *Outline of a theory of practice* (R. Nice, Trans.). Cambridge, England: Cambridge University Press.

Bourdieu, P. (1980/1990). *The logic of practice* (R. Nice, Trans.). Stanford: Stanford University Press.

Bourdieu, P. (1984). *Distinction: A social critique of the judgment of taste* (R. Nice, Trans.). Cambridge, MA: Harvard University Press.

Bourdieu, P. (1987/1990). *In other words: Essays towards a reflexive sociology* (M. Adamson, Trans.). Cambridge, England: Polity.

Bourdieu, P., Chambordedon, J.-C., & Passeron, J.-C. (1991). *The craft of sociology: Epistemological preliminaries* (2nd ed.). New York: Walter de Gruyter.

Bourdieu, P., & Wacquant, L. J. D. (1992). *An invitation to reflexive sociology.* Chicago: University of Chicago Press.

Bready, R. (Ed.). (1999). *Microsoft encarta world dictionary.* Redmond, WA: Microsoft.

Brentano, F. (1874/1995). *Psychology from an empirical standpoint* (A. C. Rancurello, D. B. Terrel, & L. L. McAlister, Trans.). New York: Routledge.

Brown, D. E. (1991). *Human universals.* New York: McGraw-Hill.

Brown, H. I. (1988). *Rationality.* New York: Routledge.

Browning, D. (Ed.). (1965). *Philosophers of process.* New York: Random House.

Buchanan, I. (2000). *Michel de Certeau: Cultural theorist.* Thousand Oaks, CA: Sage.

Burke, T. (1994). *Dewey's new logic: A reply to Russell.* Chicago: University of Chicago Press.

Caws, P. (2000). *Structuralism: A philosophy for the human sciences.* Amherst, NY: Humanity Books.

Chopra, D. (1989). *Quantum healing: Exploring the frontiers of mind/body medicine.* New York: Bantam.

Cohen, L. H., Sargent, M. M., & Sechrest, L. B. (1986). Use of psychotherapy research by professional psychologists. *American Psychologist, 41,* 198–206.

Collins, H. M. (2000). Knowledge, embodiment, and the question of artificial intelligence. In M. A. Wrathall & J. Malpas (Eds.), *Heidegger, coping, and cognitive science: Essays in honor of Hubert L. Dreyfus* (Vol. 1, pp. 179–195). Cambridge, MA: MIT Press.

Collins, J. (1993). Determination and contradiction: An appreciation and critique of the work of Pierre Bourdieu on language and education. In C. Calhoun, E. LiPuma, & M. Postone (Eds.), *Bourdieu: Critical perspectives* (pp. 116–138). Chicago: University of Chicago Press.

Csikszentmihalyi, M. (1990). *Flow: The psychology of optimal experience.* New York: HarperCollins.

Cunningham, D. J. (1998). Cognition as semiosis. *Theory and Psychology, 8*(6), 827–840.

Damasio, A. (1994). *Decartes' error: Emotion, reason, and the human brain.* New York: Avon.

Damasio, A. (1999). *The feeling of what happens: Body and emotion in the making of consciousness.* New York: Harcourt Brace.

Danziger, K. (1979). The social origins of modern psychology. In A. R. Buss (Ed.), *Psychology in social context* (pp. 27–45). Chicago: University of Chicago Press.

Dawes, R. M. (1994). *House of cards: Psychology and psychotherapy built on myth.* New York: Free Press.

de Certeau, M. (1980/1988). *The practice of everyday life* (S. Randall, Trans.). Berkeley: University of California Press.

Descartes, R. (1637/1955). Discourse on the method of rightly conducting the reason (E. S. Haldane & G. R. T. Ross, Trans.), *Philosophical works of Descartes* (Vol. 1, pp. 79–130). New York: Dover.

Dewey, J. (1896). The reflex arc concept in psychology. *Psychological Review, 3* (July), 357–370.

Dewey, J. (1922). *Human nature and conduct: An introduction to social psychology.* New York: Henry Holt.

Dewey, J. (1935/1960). An empirical survey of empiricisms. In R. J. Bernstein (Ed.), *John Dewey on experience, nature, and freedom* (pp. 70–87). New York: Liberal Arts Press.

Dewey, J. (1938). *Logic: The theory of inquiry.* New York: Henry Holt.

Dewey, J. (1941/1998). Propositions, warrented assertibility, and truth. In L. A. Hickman & T. M. Alexander (Eds.), *The essential Dewey: Vol. 2. Ethics, logic, psychology* (pp. 201–212). Bloomington: Indiana University Press.

Diamond, R. M. (1999). *Aligning faculty rewards with institution mission.* Jaffrey, NH: Anker.

Dostal, R. J. (1993). Time and phenomenology in Husserl and Heidegger. In C. Guignon (Ed.), *The Cambridge companion to Heidegger* (pp. 141–169). Cambridge, England: Cambridge University Press.

Dreyfus, H. L. (1979). *What computers can't do: The limits of artificial intelligence* (rev. ed.). New York: Harper & Row.

Dreyfus, H. L. (1991). *Being-in-the-world: A commentary on Heidegger's* Being and Time. Cambridge, MA: MIT Press.

Dreyfus, H. L., & Dreyfus, S. E. (1986). *Mind over machine: The power of human intuition and expertise in the era of the computer.* New York: Free Press.

Drucker, P. F. (1997). The first technological revolution. In T. S. Reynolds & S. H. Cutcliffe (Eds.), *Technology and the West: A historical anthology from Technology and Culture* (pp. 39–47). Chicago: University of Chicago Press.

Dunne, J. (1993). *Back to the rough ground: Practical judgment and the lure of technique.* Notre Dame, IN: University of Notre Dame Press.

Dupuy, J.-P. (1994/2000). *The mechanization of the mind: On the origins of cognitive science* (M. B. DeBevoise, Trans.). Princeton: Princeton University Press.

Ellenberger, H. F. (1970). *The discovery of the unconscious: The history and evolution of dynamic psychiatry.* New York: Basic Books.

Ellis, R. D. (1999). Integrating neuroscience and phenomenology in the study of consciousness. *Journal of Phenomenological Psychology, 30*(1), 18–47.

Ellul, J. (1964). *The technological society.* New York: Alfred A. Knopf.

Elster, J. (2000). Rationality, economy, and society. In S. Turner (Ed.), *The Cambridge companion to Weber* (pp. 21–41). Cambridge, England: Cambridge University Press.

Epstein, S. (1980). The self-concept: A review and the proposal of an integrated theory of personality. In E. Staub (Ed.), *Personality: Basic aspects and current research* (pp. 81–132). Engelwood Cliffs, NJ: Prentice-Hall.

Epstein, S. (1993). Implications of cognitive-experiential self-theory for personality and development. In D. C. Funder, R. D. Parke, C. Tomlinson-Keasey, & K. Widaman (Eds.), *Studying lives through time: Personality and development* (pp. 399–434). Washington, DC: American Psychological Association.

Epstein, S. (1994). Integration of the cognitive and the psychodynamic unconscious. *American Psychologist, 49*(8), 709–724.

Erikson, E. H. (1959). *Identity and the life cycle* (Vol. 1). New York: International Universities Press.

Faust, D. (1984). *The limits of scientific reasoning.* Minneapolis: University of Minnesota Press.

Feenberg, A. (2000). Constructivism and technology critique: Replies to critics. *Inquiry, 43* (June), 25–38.

Feldenkrais, M. (1997). *Body and mature behavior: A study of anxiety, sex, gravitation and learning.* New York: International Universities Press.

Flores, F. (2000). Heideggerian thinking and the transformation of business practice. In M. A. Wrathall & J. Malpas (Eds.), *Heidegger, coping, and cognitive science: Essays in honor of Hubert L. Dreyfus* (Vol. 2, pp. 271–291). Cambridge, MA: MIT Press.

Foucault, M. (1966/1971). *The order of things: An archaeology of the human sciences* (A. Sheridan, Trans.). New York: Pantheon.

Foucault, M. (1969/1973). *The archaeology of knowledge* (A. M. S. Smith, Trans.). New York: Vintage Books.

Foucault, M. (1975/1979). *Discipline and punish: The birth of the prison* (A. Sheridan, Trans.). Harmondsworth, Middlesex, England: Penguin Books.

Fraser, J. S. (1996). All that glitters is not always gold: Medical offest effects and managed behavioral health care. *Professional Psychology: Research and Practice, 27,* 335–344.

Freud, S. (1895/1966). *Studies in hysteria*. New York: Avon.

Freud, S. (1900/1965). *Interpretation of dreams*. New York: Avon.

Gadamer, H.-G. (1960/1975). *Truth and method* (G. B. J. Cumming, Trans.). New York: Seabury.

Gadamer, H.-G. (1963/1975). The problem of historical consciousness. *Graduate Faculty Philosophy Journal, 5*(1), 8–52.

Gadamer, H.-G. (1986/1994). *Truth and method: Second revised edition* (J. W. D. G. Marshall, Trans. 2nd, rev. ed.). New York: Seabury Press.

Gallagher, S. (1993). The place of phronesis in postmodern hermeneutics. *Philosophy Today, 37*(3), 298–305.

Gardner, H. (1985). *The mind's new science*. New York: Basic Books.

Garnham, A., & Oakhill, J. (1994). *Thinking and reasoning*. Oxford: Blackwell.

Garrison, J. (2002, April 21). Irresistible force of a techer's will [on line]. *Los Angeles Times*.

Geertz, C. (1955). *After the fact: Two countries, four decades, one anthropologist*. Cambridge, MA: Harvard University Press.

Gendlin, E. T. (1962). *Experiencing and the creation of meaning*. Glencoe: Free Press.

Gendlin, E. T. (1997). How philosophy cannot appeal to experience, and how it can. In D. M. Levin (Ed.), *Language beyond postmodernism: Saying and thinking in Gendlin's philosophy* (pp. 3–41). Evanston, IL: Northwestern University Press.

Gibson, J. J. (1979). *The ecological approach to visual perception*. Hillsdale, NJ: Lawrence Erlbaum.

Gleick, J. (1987). *Chaos: Making a new science*. New York: Viking.

Gurwitsch, A. (1979). *Human encounters in the social world*. Pittsburgh: Duquesne University Press.

Habermas, J. (1968/1970). *Toward a rational society: Student protest, science, and politics* (J. J. Shapiro, Trans.). Boston: Beacon Press.

Habermas, J. (1981/1984). *The Theory of Communicative Action, Vol. 1, Reason and the Rationalization of Society* (T. McCarthy, Trans.). Boston: Beacon Press.

Habermas, J. (1983). *Philosophical-political profiles* (F. G. Lawrence, Trans.). Cambridge, MA: MIT Press.

Hagen, M. A. (1997). *Whores of the court: The fraud of psychiatric testimony*. New York: Regan Books.

Hatab, L. J. (2000). *Ethics and finitude: Heideggerian contributions to moral philosophy*. Lanham, MD: Rowman & Littlefield.

Hawkes, T. (1977). *Structuralism and semiotics*. Berkeley: University of California Press.

Healy, P. (1993). Rationality, judgment, and critical inquiry. *The Electronic Journal of Analytic Philosophy, 1*(3).

Healy, P. (1996). Situated rationality and hermeneutic understanding: A Gadamerian approach to rationality. *International Philosophical Quarterly, 36*(2), 155–171.

Hegel, G. W. (1807/1967). *The phenomenology of mind* (J. B. Baillie, Trans.). New York: Harper & Row.

Heidegger, M. (1927/1962). *Being and time* (J. M. E. Robinson, Trans.). New York: Harper & Brothers.

Heidegger, M. (1927/1982). *The basic problems of phenomenology* (A. Hofstader, Trans.). Bloomington: Indiana University Press.

Heidegger, M. (1954/1977). The question concerning technology (W. Lovitt, Trans.), *The question concerning technology and other essays* (pp. 3–35). New York: Harper & Row.

Heidegger, M. (1959/1966). *Discourse on thinking* (J. M. Anderson & E. H. Freund, Trans.). New York: Harper & Row.

Heidegger, M. (1966/1976). "Only a god can save us," *Der Spiegel*'s interview with Martin Heidegger. *Philosophy Today, 4*(4), 278.

Hill, C. E., & Corbett, M. M. (1993). A perspective on the history of process and outcome research in counseling psychology. *Journal of Counseling Psychology, 40*(1), 3–24.

Hobbes, T. (1651/1958). *Leviathan.* New York: Library of Liberal Arts.

Holland, D., Lachicotte, W., Jr., Skinner, D., & Cain, C. (1998). *Identity and agency in cultural worlds.* Cambridge, MA: Harvard University Press.

Hollis, M. (1996). Philosophy of social science. In N. Bunnin & E. P. Tsui-James (Eds.), *The Blackwell companion to philosophy* (pp. 358–387). Oxford: Blackwell.

Hoy, D. C. (1999). Critical resistance: Foucault and Bourdieu. In G. Weiss & H. F. Haber (Eds.), *Perspectives on embodiment: The intersections of nature and culture* (pp. 3–22). New York: Routledge.

Hume, D. (1748). An inquiry concerning human understanding. In V. C. Chappell (Ed.), *The philosophy of David Hume* (pp. 313–391). New York: Modern Library.

Hutchinson, D. S. (1995). Ethics. In J. Barnes (Ed.), *The Cambridge Companion to Aristotle* (pp. 195–232). Cambridge, England: Cambridge University Press.

Ihde, D. (1990). *Technology and the lifeworld: From garden to earth.* Bloomington: Indiana University Press.

Ihde, D. (1993). *Postphenomenology: Essays in the postmodern context.* Evanston: Northwestern University Press.

Inden, R. (1990). *Imaging India.* Oxford: Blackwell.

Jakobson, R., & Halle, M. (1956). *Foundamentals of language.* The Hague: Mouton.

Jantsch, E. (1980). *The self-organizing universe: Scientific and human implications of the emerging paradigm of evolution.* Oxford: Pergamon.

Jay, M. (1994). *Downcast eyes: The denigration of vision in twentieth-century French thought.* Berkeley: University of California Press.

Johnson, L. D. (1995). *Psychotherapy in the age of accountability.* New York: W. W. Norton.

Johnson, M. (1987). *The body in the mind: The bodily basis of meaning, imagination, and reason.* Chicago: University of Chicago Press.

Jones, W. T. (1969). *A history of Western philosophy: The classical mind* (2nd ed.). New York: Harcourt, Brace, & World.

Jorgensen, K. (1996). *Pay for results: A practical guide to effective employee compensation.* Santa Monica: Merritt.

Kahneman, D., Slovic, P., & Tversky, A. (Eds.). (1982). *Judgment under uncertainty: Heuristics and biases.* Cambridge, England: Cambridge University Press.

Kahneman, D., & Tversky, A. (1972). Subjective probability: A judgment of representativeness. *Cognitive Psychology, 3,* 430–454.

Klockars, K. (1998). *Sartre's anthropology as a hermeneutics of practice.* Brookfiled, VT: Ashgate.

Kosslyn, S. M. (1980). *Image and mind.* Cambridge, MA: Harvard University Press.

Krogh, T. (1998). *Technology and rationality.* Brookfiled, England: Ashgate.

Kuhn, T. S. (1970). *The structure of scientific revolutions* (2nd ed.). Chicago: University of Chicago Press.

Lacan, J. (1968). *The language of the self: The function of language in psychoanalysis* (A. Wilden, Trans.). New York: Dell.

Lakoff, G. (1987). *Women, fire, and dangerous things: What categories reveal about the mind.* Chicago: University of Chicago Press.

Lakoff, G., & Johnson, M. (1999). *Philosophy in the flesh: The embodied mind and its challenge to Western thought.* New York: Basic Books.

Lakoff, G., & and Núñez, R. E. (2000). *Where mathematics come from: How the embodied mind brings mathematics into being.* New York: Basic Books.

Lave, J., & Wenger, E. (1991). *Situated learning: Legitimate peripheral participation.* Cambridge, England: Cambridge University Press.

Lawler, E. E., III. (1990). *Strategic pay: Aligning organizational and pay systems.* San Francisco: Jossey-Bass.

Lawler, E. E., III. (1994). *Motivation in work organizations.* San Francisco: Jossey-Bass.

Leach, E. (1974). *Claude Lévi-Strauss* (rev. ed.). Harmondsworth, Middlesex, England: Penguin Books.

Levin, D. M. (Ed.). (1997). *Language beyond postmodernism: Saying and thinking in Gendlin's philosophy.* Evanston, IL: Northwestern University Press.

Lévi-Strauss, C. (1955/1961). *Triste Tropiques* (J. Russell, Trans.). New York: Atheneum.

Lévi-Strauss, C. (1958/1963). *Structural anthropology* (C. J. B. G. Schoepf, Trans. rev. ed.). New York: Basic Books.

Lévi-Strauss, C. (1962/1972). *The savage mind.* Chicago: University of Chicago Press.

Malpas, J. (2003). Martin Heidegger. In R.C. Solomon & D. Sherman (Eds.), *The Blackwell guide to Continental philosophy.* Malden, MA: Blackwell.

Mandler, G. (1984). *Mind and body: Psychology of emotion and stress.* New York: W. W. Norton.

Margolis, J. (1997). Language as lingual. In D. M. Levin (Ed.), *Language beyond postmodernism: Saying and thinking in Gendlin's philosophy* (pp. 321–338). Evanston, IL: Northwestern University Press.

Mattingly, C. (1991). The narrative nature of clinical reasoning. *American Journal of Occupational Therapy, 45*(11), 998–1005.

Mattingly, C. (1998). *Healing dramas and clinical plots: The narrative structure of experience*. Cambridge, England: Cambridge University Press.

Maturana, H. R., & Varela, F. J. (1998). *The tree of knowledge: The biological roots of human understanding* (rev. ed.). Boston: Shambhala.

May, R. (1958). Contributions of existential psychotherapy. In R. May & E. Angel & H. Ellenberger (Eds.), *Existence: A new dimension in psychiatry and psychology* (pp. 37–91). New York: Basic Books.

McGowan, J. (1991). *Postmodernism and its critics*. Ithica, NY: Cornell University Press.

McKeon, R. (1947). *Introduction to Aristotle* (Oxford, Trans.). New York: Modern Library.

Merleau-Ponty, M. (1942/1963). *The structure of behavior* (A. L. Fisher, Trans.). Boston: Beacon Press.

Merleau-Ponty, M. (1945/1962). *Phenomenology of perception* (C. Smith, Trans.). New York: Humanities.

Merleau-Ponty, M. (1947/1964). The primacy of perception and its philosophical consequences (J. M. Edie, Trans.). In M. Merleau-Ponty (Ed.), *Primacy of perception* (pp. 12–42). Evanston: Northwestern University Press.

Miller, J. G. (1978). *Living systems*. New York: McGraw-Hill.

Mitchell, S. A., & Black, M. J. (1995). *Freud and beyond: A history of modern psychoanalytic thought*. New York: Basic Books.

Morrow-Bradley, C., & Elliott, R. (1986). Utilization of psychotherapy research by practicing psychotherapists. *American Psychologist, 41*, 188–206.

Nathan, P. E., & Goran, J. M. (1998). *Treatments that work—and what convinces us they do, A guide to treatments that work* (pp. 3–25). New York: Oxford University Press.

Nicolis, G., & Prigogine, I. (1989). *Exploring complexity: An introduction*. New York: W. H. Freeman.

Noddings, N. (1996). The caring professional. In S. Gordon, P. Benner, & N. Noddings (Eds.), *Caregiving: Readings in knowledge, practice, ethics, and politics* (pp. 160–172). Philadelphia: University of Pennsylvania Press.

Nussbaum, M. C. (1990). *Love's knowledge: Essays on philosophy and literature*. Oxford: Oxford University Press.

Nussbaum, M. C. (1994). *The therapy of desire: Theory and practice in Hellenistic ethics* (rev. ed.). Princeton: Princeton University Press.

Nussbaum, M. C. (2001a). *The fragility of goodness: Luck and ethics in Greek tragedy and philosophy* (rev. ed.). Cambridge, England: Cambridge University Press.

Nussbaum, M. C. (2001b). A science of practical reasoning. In E. Millgram (Ed.), *Varities of practical reasoning* (pp. 153–202). Cambridge, MA: MIT Press.

Nussbaum, M. C. (2001c). *Upheavals of thought: The intelligence of emotions* (rev. ed.). Cambridge, England: Cambridge University Press.

Ornstein, R. (1993). *The roots of the self*. San Francisco: Harper.

Ortner, S. B. (1999). Introduction. In S. B. Ortner (Ed.), *The fate of "culture"* (pp. 1–13). Berkeley: University of California Press.

Park, D. C. (1999). Acts of will? *American Psychologist, 54*(7), 461–461.

Perelman, C. (1979). The new rhetoric: A theory of practical reasoning (W. Kluback, Trans.). In C. Perelman (Ed.), *The new rhetoric and the humanities* (pp. 1–42). Dordrecht, Holland: D. Reidel.

Peterson, D. R. (1991). Connection and disconnection of research and practice in the education of professional psychologists. *American Psychologist, 41,* 188–206.

Petitot, J., Varela, F. J., Pachoud, B., & Roy, J.-M. (Eds.). (1999). *Naturalizing phenomenology: Issues in contemporay phenomenology and cognitive science.* Stanford: Stanford University Press.

Philipse, H. (1998). *Heidegger's philosophy of being: A critical interpretation.* Princeton: Princeton University Press.

Piaget, J., & Inhelder, B. (1969). *The psychology of the child.* New York: Basic Books.

Plato. (trans. 1961). *The collected dialogues of Plato* (E. Hamilton & H. Cairns, Trans.). Princeton: Princeton University Press.

Plomin, R. (1990). *Nature and nurture: An introduction to human behavioral genetics.* Pacific Grove, CA: Brooks/Cole.

Polansky, R. (2000). "Phronesis" on tour: Cultural adaptability of Aristotelian ethical notions. *Kennedy Institute of Ethics Journal, 10*(4), 323–336.

Polanyi, M. (1962). *Personal knowledge.* Chicago: University of Chicago Press.

Polkinghorne, D. E. (1988). *Narrative knowing and the human sciences.* Albany: State University of New York Press.

Polkinghorne, D. E. (1999). Traditional research and psychotherapy practice. *The Journal of Clinical Psychology, 55*(12), 1429–1440.

Polkinghorne, D. E. (2000). Psychological inquiry and the pragmatic and hermeneutic tradtions. *Theory and Psychology, 10*(4), 453–479.

Polkinghorne, D. E. (2001). Managing payments for psychological care. In B. D. Slife, R. N. Williams, & S. H. Barlow (Eds.), *Critical issues in psychotherapy: Translating new ideas into practice* (pp. 121–139). Thousand Oaks, CA: Sage.

Polkinghorne, D. E. (2003). Franz Brentano's *Psychology from an Empirical Standpoint.* In R. J. Sternberg (Ed.), *The anatomy of impact: What has made the great works of psychology great?* Washington, D.C.: American Psychological Association.

Popper, K. R. (1959). *The logic of scientific discovery.* New York: Basic Books.

Prigogine, I., & Stengers, I. (1984). *Order out of chaos: Man's new dialogue with nature.* New York: Bantam.

Putnam, H. (1978). *Meaning and the moral sciences.* London: Routledge & Kegan Paul.

Reisman, J. M. (1991). *A history of clinical psychology* (2nd ed.). New York: Hemisphere.

Reynolds, T. S., & Cutcliffe, S. H. (1997). Technology in the preindustrial West. In T. S. Reynolds & S. H. Cutcliffe (Eds.), *Technology and the West: A historical anthology from Technology and Culture* (pp. 23–38). Chicago: University of Chicago Press.

Ricoeur, P. (1984). *Time and narrative* (Vol. 1). Chicago: University of Chicago Press.

Ricoeur, P. (1992). *Oneself as another* (K. Blamey, Trans.). Chicago: Chicago University Press.

Rorty, R. (1979). *Philosophy and the mirror of nature*. Princeton, NJ: Princeton University Press.

Rorty, R. (1991). *Objectivity, relativism, and truth: Philosophical papers* (Vol. 1). Cambridge, England: Cambridge University Press.

Rosch, E. (1978). Principles of categorization. In E. Rosch & B. Lloyd (Eds.), *Cognition and categorization* (pp. 27–48). Hillsdale, NJ: Erlbaum.

Rosch, E. (1999). Reclaiming concepts. In R. Nùñez & W. J. Freeman (Eds.), *Reclaiming cognition: The primacy of action, intention and emotion* (pp. 61–78). Bowling Green, OH: Imprint Academic.

Routh, D. K. (2000). Clinical psychology training: A history of ideas and practices prior to 1946. *American Psychologist, 55*(2), 236–241.

Roy, J.-M., Petitot, J., Pachoud, B., & Varela, F. J. (1999). Beyond the gap: An introduction to naturalizing phenomenology. In J. Petitot, F. J. Varela, B. Pachoud, & J.-M. Roy (Eds.), *Naturalizing phenomenology: Issues in contemporay phenomenology and cognitive science* (pp. 1–80). Stanford, CA: Stanford University Press.

Safranski, R. (1994/1998). *Martin Heidegger: Between good and evil* (E. Osers, Trans.). Cambridge, MA: Harvard University Press.

Sartre, J.-P. (1943/1965). *Being and nothingness: An essay in pheomenological ontology* (H. E. Barnes, Trans. special abridged ed.). New York: Citadel.

Sarup, M. (1993). *An introductory guide to post-structuralism and postmodernism* (2nd ed.). Athens: University of Georgia Press.

Sassower, R. (1997). *Technoscience angst:Ethics and responsibility*. Minneapolis: University of Minnesota Press.

Saussure, F. de. (1907–1911/1966). *Course in general linguistics* (W. Baskin, Trans.). New York: McGraw-Hill.

Scaff, L. A. (2000). Weber on the cultural situation of the modern age. In S. Turner (Ed.), *The Cambridge companion to Weber* (pp. 99–116). Cambridge, England: Cambridge University Press.

Schön, D. A. (1983). *The reflective practitioner*. New York: Basic Books.

Schön, D. A. (1988). From technical rationality to reflection-in-action. In J. Dowie & A. Elstein (Eds.), *Professional judgment: A reader in clinical decision making* (pp. 60–77). Cambridge, England: Cambridge University Press.

Schön, D. A. (1992). The theory of inquiry: Dewey's legacy to education. *Curriculum Inquiry, 22*(2), 119–139.

Schrag, C. O. (1986). *Communicative praxis and the space of subjectivity*. Bloomington: Indiana University Press.

Schwarzchild, M. (1999, August 2). Getting out before the system gets to me. *USA Today*.

Searle, J. R. (1983). *Intentionality: An essay in the philosophy of mind*. Cambridge, England: Cambridge University Press.

Seligman, M. E. P. (1995). The effectiveness of psychotherapy: The Consumer Reports study. *American Psychologist, 50*(12), 965–974.

Seung, R. K. (1982). *Structuralism and hermeneutics*. New York: Columbia University Press.

Sharp, L. (1952). Steel axes for Stone Age Australians. In Y. Cohen (Ed.), *Man in adaptation: The cultural present* (2nd ed., pp. 116–127). Chicago: Aldine.

Sica, A. (2000). Rationalization and culture. In S. Turner (Ed.), *The Cambridge companion to Weber* (pp. 42–58). Cambridge, England: Cambridge University Press.

Simpson, J. (Ed.). (2002). *Oxford English Dictionary* (3rd ed.). Oxford: Oxford University Press.

Skovholt, T. M., & Rønnestad, M. H. (1992). *The evolving professional self: Stages and themes in therapist and counselor development*. New York: John Wiley & Sons.

Smith, L. D. (1986). *Behaviorism and logical positivism: A reassessment of the alliance*. Stanford, CA: Stanford University Press.

Snow, C. P. (1970). *The two cultures and a second look*. Cambridge, England: Cambridge University Press.

Stern, D. (2000). Practices, practical holism, and background practices. In M. A. Wrathall & J. Malpas (Eds.), *Heidegger, coping, and cognitive science: Essays in honor of Hubert L. Dreyfus* (Vol. 2, pp. 53–68). Cambridge, MA: MIT Press.

Sternberg, R. J., & Horvath, J. A. (Eds.). (1999). *Tacit knowledge in professional practice: Research and practitioner perspectives*. Mahwah, NJ: Lawrence Erlbaum.

Stich, S. (1985). *From folk psychology to cognitive science: The case against belief*. Cambridge, MA: MIT Press.

Sussman, G. (1997). *Communication, technology, and politics in the information age*. Thousand Oaks, CA: Sage.

Swartz, D. (1997). *Culture and power: The sociology of Pierre Bourdieu*. Chicago: University of Chicago Press.

Taylor, C. (1991). *The ethics of authenticity*. Cambridge, MA: Harvard University Press.

Taylor, C. (1999). Two theories of modernity. *Public Culture, 11*(1), 153–174.

Taylor, F. W. (1911). *Scientific management*. New York: Harper.

Thiboutot, C., & Martinez, A. (1999). Gaston Bachelard and phenomenology: Outline of the theory of the imagination. *Journal of Phenomenological Psychology, 30*(1), 1–17.

Torff, B. (1999). Tacit knowledge in teaching: Folk pedagogy and teacher education. In R. J. Sternberg & J. A. Horvath (Eds.), *Tacit knowledge in professional practice: Research and practitioner perspectives* (pp. 195–213). Mahwah, NJ: Lawrence Erlbaum.

Toulmin, S. E. (1990). *Cosmopolis: The hidden agenda of modernity*. Chicago: University of Chicago Press.

Toulmin, S. E. (2001). *Return to reason*. Cambridge, MA: Harvard University Press.

Turner, S. (1994). *The social theory of practices: Tradition, tacit knowledge, and presuppositions*. Chicago: University of Chicago Press.

Tuttle, G. M., & Woods, D. R. (1997). *The managed care answer book for mental health professionals*. Bristol, PA: Brunner/Mazel.

Tversky, A., & Kahneman, D. (1974). Judgment under uncertainty: Heuristics and biases. *Science, 221,* 453–458.

United States Department of Education. (2002, August 7). *News.*

Varela, F. J., Thompson, E., & Rosch, E. (1991). *The embodied mind: Cognitive science and human experience.* Cambridge, MA: MIT Press.

von Bertalanffy, L. (1968). *General systems theory.* New York: Braziller.

Vroom, V. (1964). *Work and motivation.* New York: Wiley.

Wampold, B. E. (2001). *The great psychotherapy debate: Models, methods, and findings.* Mahwah, NJ: Lawrence Erlbaum.

Wampold, B. E., Mondin, G. W., Moody, M., Stich, F., Benson, K., & Ahn, H.-n. (1997). A meta-analysis of outcome studies comparing bona fide psychotherapies: Empirically, "all must have prizes." *Psychological Bulletin, 122*(3), 203–215.

Watt, D. F. (2000). Emotion and consciousness: Part II. *Journal of Consciousness Studies, 7*(3), 72–84.

Weber, M. (1921/1958). *The Protestant ethic and the spirit of capitalism* (T. Parsons, Trans.). New York: Schribner's.

Weber, M. (1921/1968). *Max Weber on law in economy and society* (E. Shils & M. Rheinstein, Trans.). New York: Simon & Schuster.

Weber, M. (1968). *Economy and society: An outline of interpretative sociology.* Berkeley: University of California Press.

Wedding, D., & Corsini, R. J. (Eds.). (1979). *Great cases in psychotherapy* (2nd ed.). Itasca, IL: F. E. Peacock.

Wegner, D. M., & Wheatley, T. (1999). Apparent mental causation. *American Psychologist, 54*(480–492).

Wheatley, M. J. (1994). *Leadership and the new science: Learning about organization from an orderly universe.* San Francisco: Berret-Koehler.

Whitehead, A. N. (1929). *Process and reality.* New York: Macmillan.

Wiggins, D. (2001). Deliberation and practical reasoning. In E. Millgram (Ed.), *Varities of practical reasoning* (pp. 279–299). Cambridge, MA: MIT Press.

Wills, S., Swanson, L., Satchi, L., & Thompson, K. (June, 2002). *Design defects of the Ford Pinto gas tank.* Retrieved, from the World Wide Web: *http://www.fordpinto.com/blowup.htm*

Wilson, T. B. (1995). *Innovative reward systems for the changing workplace.* New York: McGraw-Hill.

Wilson, T. D. (2002). *Strangers to ourselves: Discovering the adaptive unconscious.* Cambridge, MA: Belnap Press of Harvard University Press.

Winch, P. (1958). *The idea of a social science and its relation to philosophy.* London: Routledge & Kegan Paul.

Winner, L. (1977). *Autonomous technology: Technics out-of-control as a theme in political history.* Cambridge, MA: MIT Press.

Wittgenstein, L. (1969). *On certainty* (D. Paul & G. E. M. Anscombe, Trans.). New York: J. & J. Harper.

Woolfolk, R. L. (1998). *The cure of souls: Science, values and psychotherapy.* San Francisco: Jossey-Bass.

Wundt, W. (1874/1904). *Principles of physiological psychology* (E. B. Titchener, Trans.). London: Swan Sonnenschein.

INDEX

Abbey, R., 26

Actions: actor accounts of, 58; adapting to multiple groups, 57; affectual, 37; agency in, 59; anticipation of consequences of, 83, 144; bodily, 86; boundaries for, 63; in bounds of culture, 49; calculating advantages/disadvantages of, 29; choosing, 105; competitive, 62; complexity of, 92; context of, 24; determining, 2, 19, 117; emotions as motivation for, 107; emotions as source of information for, 110; everyday, 49, 57; as expressions of habitus, 61; failed, 120, 121; as felt images, 146–147; fields of, 61–63; future, 75; habitus and, 59; human choices in, 50; in human realm, 37–39, 92, 108, 126; hypothetical solutions and, 122; of individuals, 58; inquiry and, 121; instrumental, 9, 37, 43; location in finite set of principles for governance, 103; nonconscious, 6; personal, 63; practical, 19, 59, 60, 87, 103, 104–127, 120, 121; practical choices and, 24; practitioner, 86, 87; reflective, 59; reinforcement of, 153; situation/time sensitive, 49; social, 48, 57, 58; spoken, 86; strategic, 59; technological, 43; that cause an effect, 43; thought and, 5; timing of, 24, 59; traditional, 37; unconscious, 59; value-rational, 37; variable effects of, 4; warranted assertibility and, 122

Activities: adjusting, 153; contributions to goal achievement, 7; deliberation over, 106; everyday, 63; felt meaning and, 139; meaning of, 7; meditative thinking, 43; mental, 18, 21, 154; practical, 121

Affordances, 73, 133, 143

Agency, 50; as capacity to act upon world, 51; human, 52; individual, 65

Ahearne, J., 65, 66

Analogy: demon of, 65

Appropriation, 167–168

Arendt, H., 44, 105, 169

Aristotle, 16, 44, 97, 98, 135, 150, 163, 172; conception of human being, 99; on emotions/imagination, 109–111; on human choice, 107, 108; life tasks and, 112; on living a good life, 104–127; on multiple values, 108; *phronesis* and, 45, 67, 104–127, 130–131, 139; rationality and, 23; on rules, 109; *techne* and, 99–101; theoretical syllogisms of, 19, 20; *theoria* and, 113–114; types of thought and, 132

Arnheim, R., 134